CENTRAL PARK

ALSO BY EUGENE KINKEAD

Spider, Egg and Microcosm

In Every War but One

A Concrete Look at Nature

Wildness Is All Around Us

Squirrel Book

CENTRAL PARK

1857–1995

THE BIRTH, DECLINE, AND RENEWAL OF A NATIONAL TREASURE

EUGENE KINKEAD

W·W·NORTON & COMPANY   NEW YORK LONDON

Printed in the United States of America.

*The text of this book is composed in 11/14 CRT Century Old Style,
with display type set in Baver Text Initials and Snell Roundhand.
Composition and manufacturing by The Haddon Craftsmen, Inc.
Map by Bernhard H. Wagner
Book design by Margaret M. Wagner*

First Edition

Library of Congress Cataloging-in-Publication Data

*Kinkead, Eugene, 1906–
Central Park, 1857–1995 : the birth, decline, and renewal of a
national treasure / Eugene Kinkead.
p. cm.
Includes index.
1. Central Park (New York, N.Y.)—History. 2. New York (N.Y.)—
History. 3. New York (N.Y.)—Description. I. Title.
F128.65.C3K56 1990
974.7'104—dc20   89–35449*

ISBN 0-393-02531-4

*W. W. Norton & Company, Inc.
500 Fifth Avenue, New York, N. Y. 10110*

*W. W. Norton & Company Ltd.
37 Great Russell Street, London WC1B 3NU*

1 2 3 4 5 6 7 8 9 0

With thanks
to Meryl, Donald,
and Billy B. Gummer,
without whose help
this work would never
have seen print.

CONTENTS

INTRODUCTION

*C*ENTRAL PARK, as the title of this book states, is nothing less than a national treasure. It is, in addition, a thing of beauty morning, noon, and night, and in every season. To millions of New Yorkers, it is the single most important object in the city. No rival is even close. The Statue of Liberty, the New York Stock Exchange, the World Trade Center, the Metropolitan Museum of Art, the Bronx Zoo, the United Nations, Rockefeller Center all have legitimate claims—cultural, commercial, or otherwise—to attract large segments of the public. But week in, week out, year in and year out, Central Park's drawing power far outshines the other attractions of New York. It is the only park used by residents of all five boroughs. It is the city's largest manmade object.

Scores of activities revolve around the Park; tourists flock to see it. After more than a century and a quarter of life, its name is known on every continent. It is, in my belief, of all the parks in the world, the one that offers its users the greatest opportunities for rest, healthful abstraction, and exercise. And this is not to slight the cultural enrichment Central Park provides through countless programs in art, dance, drama, and music.

A measure of the Park's value to the twenty million or more of its annual entrants is the numerous opportunities it offers for active recreation and sports—scores of them. But these far from end its allure. Performances of more than half a dozen arts—concerts, drama, folk dancing, grand opera, marionettes, musical comedy, storytelling—provide cultural uplift at various times of the year. And the Park is a welcome relaxant to the many who enter it for leisurely activity only—strolling, sitting, sunbathing, or people watching. Finally, the Park and its perimeter streets are the setting for many important annual municipal events: the finish of the New York City Marathon, the Macy's Thanksgiving Day Parade, the Fifth Avenue Mile run, to name but three that are watched by thousands.

The designers, Frederick Law Olmsted and Calvert Vaux, created a structure not only lovely but nearly indestructible. It is well they did. For over the years it has suffered gravely from long spells of mismanagement and neglect. And this not too distantly.

It was in the last period of decline, during the 1960s and 1970s that I got deeply interested as a writer in Central Park—in its scurrying squirrels, its impressive geology, its noble trees, and its bright blossoms. In all these ventures, undertaken for and published by *The New Yorker* magazine, I had the unwavering support of editor William Shawn. Much earlier I had been involved in a sketch of the place with Russell Maloney, also for that magazine but this time for Harold Ross, its founder. Perhaps my continuing attraction to the Park was inevitable, perhaps it was even osmotic, something decreed early in my life by absorbent genes. For I was born near the Park's northwest corner at No. 7 West 108th Street, in a house now gone the way of so many others in this bustling town.

In doing this book, I was fortunate in my research. When a family member left town for an extended stay, I moved into the apartment, sharing it with the resident cat. The digs were just across from the Park's stone wall, high up, with a magnificent view of all eight hundred and forty-three acres. For my on-the-spot investigations, all I had to do was cross the street. I was aided, too, by the cat. He frequently lay on my typewriter table, preventing the notes from falling off. At night, he slept on my stomach in companionable bliss. And he enhanced my spirits by ecstatic dashes through the halls and by ferociously stalking the pigeons safe outside the window.

When my serious interest in Central Park first began, I often had to trek over mud-covered paths, past graffiti-marred, vandalized structures, beside unpruned trees and patches of bare ground. Melancholy are those memories. Now, however, a brighter day has come. Central Park is undergoing a protracted period of renewal. The cost in dollars will be scores of millions. But when it is finished, Central Park will be as close to the inspired dreams of its planners and the desires of its present users as modern conditions allow.

In writing about the Park's birth, decline, and present rehabilitation, I have received much useful assistance, which came equally from the Parks

Department and the Central Park Conservancy. The staffs of both have been consistently cooperative. But I must single out especially Parks Commissioner Henry Stern and the Conservancy's Central Park Administrator Elizabeth Barlow Rogers. Of their personnel, I have leaned most heavily on Gary Zarr, the Park's press officer, and Sara Cedar Miller, the Conservancy's photographer.

However, I must not forget the two heads of the Conservancy itself, William S. Beinecke, the original chairman, and James H. Evans, his successor. Both have been as approachable as any author could ask.

Indeed, one of the most heartening features of Central Park today is the existence of the Conservancy, a relatively new development. A group of public-spirited citizens form its board and committees. They are not only raising millions of dollars annually—from individuals, corporations, and foundations—but are promising to continue this aid to the restoration of the Park into the indefinite future. Such munificent help virtually assures that the Park will not revert to its once-sorry condition. Furthermore, each year the Conservancy is persuading thousands of the Park's public users to contribute by becoming members of the Conservancy.

And this is of supreme importance.

If Central Park is to be—and to remain—the place we all want it to be, its users, and particularly the committed, must sustain and protect it.

Southbury, Connecticut   EUGENE KINKEAD

CENTRAL PARK

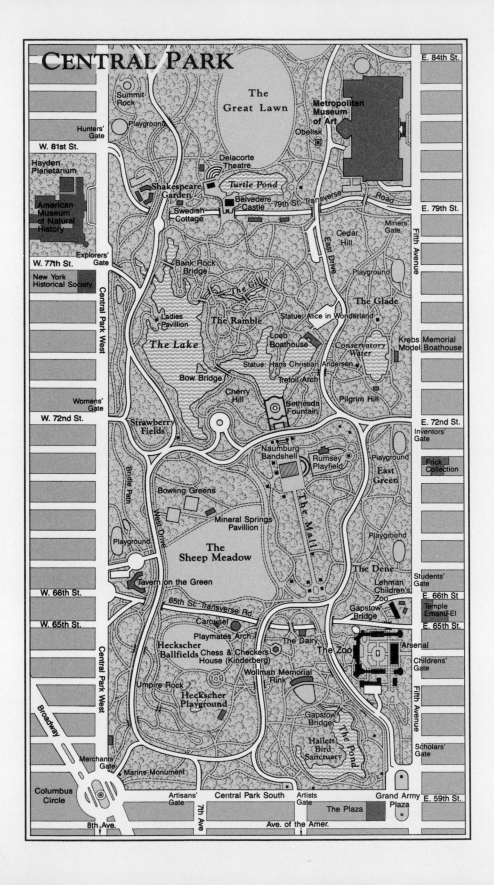

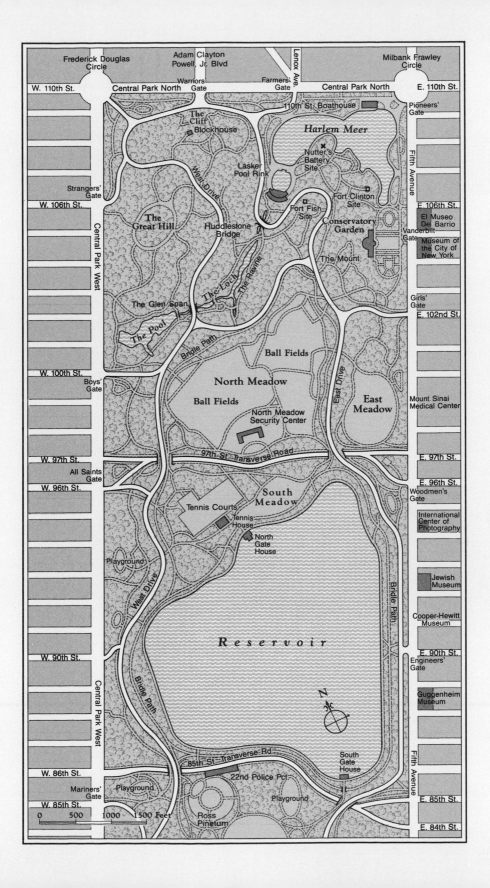

One

The Gold
and
Silver Ages

1857–1911

CENTRAL PARK, a national as well as a New York City trea- 1
sure, is the most famous park in the United States and
one of the most famous in the world. Begun more than
one hundred twenty-five years ago and completed to wide
acclaim not long after the Civil War, it has suffered periods of serious deterioration over the past century due to
combinations of custodial mismanagement and civic neglect. Since 1978, the Park has been in the midst of an
unprecedented program of renewal to correct these
lapses. As much as modern usage will allow, the program
is intended to restore the Park to the matchless urban
pleasure ground it once was. The vast undertaking is expected to cost in toto at least $150 million and, by present
calculations, to end sometime in the mid-1990s, after a
duration of more than fifteen years. It is the largest piece
of historical reconstruction ever attempted in this country.

Central Park is an extraordinary spot. Official recognition as such, wrought in bronze, is fixed to the Fifth Avenue wall of the Arsenal, the quaint, turreted building in
the Park at the level of 64th Street that houses the headquarters of the city's Parks Department, formally known
as the Parks and Recreation Department. The plaque
reads as follows:

CENTRAL PARK

Has Been Designated a
Registered National
Historic Landmark

Under the Provisions of the
Historic Sites Act of August 21, 1935,
This Site Possesses Exceptional Value
In Commemorating and Illustrating
The History of the United States

U.S. Department of the Interior
National Park Service
1965

Nine years later, the New York City Landmarks Preservation Commission named the Park a Scenic Historic Landmark, the first such designation in that body's history. Its evaluation paper noted, among other attributes, the Park's "especial esthetic interest and value." A second plaque on the Arsenal's Fifth Avenue wall records this honor. The two awards clearly express the views of officials concerned with environmental matters regarding the importance of the Park as a symbol in the country's cultural life.

New Yorkers, however, see the Park somewhat differently. To them, it is a wondrous slice of nature smuggled into the city by sleight of hand. In the verdant world of the growing season, the Park becomes a shimmering green jewel in the forehead of Manhattan. With the burst of vegetation in the spring, the resurrection of the whole vegetable race occurs almost miraculously amid the surrounding lifeless brick and stone. Fresh new leaves and small half-hidden flowers grace the trees' branches. The disparate crowns are ragged, rounded, comical, or vast clouds of green. Birds in nuptial plumage rest and sing among them. Insects buzz there, seeking the tiny sylvan blossoms. Here and there, high up the trunks, in cavities nature naturally makes, young squirrels a month or two old peer inquisitively from their aeries. On the ground, the water bodies form inlays of cerulean-bright lapis lazuli amid a matrix of enameled green. Many of the mild, clear nights find the treetops silver under moon births over the eastern skyline. Day by day, inexorably, the green umbrella steadily thickens, auguring those deep shades that in the weary heats of July and August will cool the visitor and refresh the air.

In the months of bleak, cold weather, with snow on the ground and the water surfaces now firmly solid and freshly scraped for the colorfully clad skaters, the rocks, vast presences, half-hidden during the growing season, now come into their annual prominence amid the leafless trees or show through crannies between the evergreens, enormous personalities lying there, quiescent, bulky, and overpowering, under the breath of the wintry winds whose perfume is raw ice. Now sweeps into the Park one of the happiest of its throngs, the children with their sleds, like so many brightly colored snowbirds, laughing as they coast the knolls.

This activity is only one of scores that the Park affords its users. Others are the picnic spreads in the summer on the Great Lawn before the evening performances of grand opera, or the Shakespearean productions in the Delacorte Theatre. And the jollity that surrounds the ethnic celebrations such as Puerto Rican Day that are held here. Then there are individual free-lance doings such as sketching, rowing, and biking. The Park in all likelihood offers more activities for visitors than any park in the world.

But the National Park Service's mention on its plaque of the Park's value in the history of the United States is not empty talk. The Park has had an enormous and recognizable influence on other urban parks throughout the country, evident across the still young republic from the Atlantic to the Pacific oceans almost from the Park's very inception. Similar bits of nature modeled after ours began to be constructed or planned. The 1868 annual report of the commissioners of Central Park noted, "There is scarcely a city of magnitude in this country that has not provided, or taken measures to provide, a park for the pleasure of its citizens. Brooklyn, our neighbor, has one. . . . Philadelphia has already secured grounds of great extent . . . and the subject is under discussion in Providence, Albany, Troy, Cincinnati, Pittsburgh, Chicago, St. Louis and Louisville." In the last third of the nineteenth century, parks inspired by ours sprang up too in Bridgeport, Buffalo, Knoxville, Rochester, and San Francisco, and out of this country in Montreal. Later counterparts, stemming from these, continue to appear to the present time.

But this is not all. There is a direct connection between Central Park and the national park system, that group of sites of great natural beauty set aside by the federal government for our citizens to enjoy in perpetuity. Yellowstone Park, the first of these, a Rocky Mountain area two-thirds the size of the state of Connecticut, was authorized in 1872, only fourteen years after Central Park's start and at a time when the latter's success was being hailed far and wide in this country and Europe. Congress's task in enacting the Yellowstone legislation was made abundantly easier by Central Park's example, a fact widely acknowledged then by the legislation's proponents.

In Yellowstone's train has come, with the passage of years and its wide popularity, the whole of our system of national parks, which have been extensively imitated abroad and which now in this country total almost fifty. Nor does this include the lesser offshoots of this development, the national historical parks, the national seashores, the national rivers, the national battlefields, and so on, a melange of seventeen other categories of outdoor spots, many with multiple units, which, as in the case of the parks, offer citizens a wide choice of scenic, historical, and recreational sites, all of these scores of federal units being administered by the National Park Service. The wording on the Arsenal plaque, above the service's signature, might be considered commemorative of the role of Central Park not only in the birth of the country's other urban parks but in that of the national park system itself and, indeed, in the National Park Service, as well, founded in 1916. All, yes, all are the children of Central Park.

Yet despite the importance of Central Park here and across the nation, it was by no means preordained.

*I*N THE BEGINNING, the city of New York grew slowly. In 1626, when Peter Minuit bought Manhattan Island from the Indians for trinkets worth $24, the tiny band of Europeans in the embryonic metropolis (soon to be named Nieuw Amsterdam) was a scant two hundred souls. Seventeenth-century growth was meager. The situation obtained even after 1664, when the British conquest changed the town's name to New York. A hundred years after this, only sixteen thousand people lived here. Streets were narrow in the inhabited tip of the island. Houses were built close together. The sole open spaces of any size were the Battery, where Fort Clinton stood, and a barren, dusty tract on the settlement's northern border known as the Fields, part of which is now City Hall Park. True, there was a tiny prerevolutionary forerunner of Central Park in the shape of the Bowling Green, in actuality the city's first denominated park. The little oval is still in place at the tip of Manhattan. Originally, however, it was hardly a park. Created as one by the City Council in 1733 during the reign of King George II, its half-acre was leased the following year at an annual rate of one peppercorn to a trio of gentlemen who fenced it off for use in the game of bowls.

After the Revolution, however, with the population now approaching sixty thousand, some calls for the provision of true parkland were heard. One was a 1795 letter to a newspaper pointing out the advantages of improving the Battery and the Fields for this purpose. Eventually both suggestions were carried out. But they far from fulfilled the need.

Now, to make matters worse, there was a sharp rise in the number of people living in New York. At the start of the nineteenth century the population had indeed reached the sixty thousand figure. In another two decades it had more than doubled. Further, there was every evidence that the city was soon to face a continued and much more drastic enlargement through an extensive flood of European immigrants.

The cause was the Industrial Revolution, then in full force. Cities abroad felt its impact. This dramatic alteration from the old way of life had started in the previous century, when various inventions brought into being machines, whose products, textiles among them, came out of factories. The relatively high wages paid there denuded the farms, where most Europeans had stayed put for centuries. In this new economic state of affairs, residents across the Atlantic were in a condition of flux and ready to travel. Eagerly they eyed this country's opportunities. New York City had bustling commerce. New York City had the nation's busiest port. It was a prime target for the restless overseas in search of a better life.

By 1840 these new arrivals had swelled the number of people here to three hundred and twelve thousand. New Yorkers by then had grown uneasily accustomed to being called residents of our largest city. But officials were warning of no surcease in the rise. They predicted with the continuing influx that the population would shortly reach six hundred thousand. In those days, in this country, that was a truly astounding assemblage of human beings to be living cheek by jowl.

The forecast was depressing to many still relatively youthful inhabitants. They could remember having lived in a very different place. Fifteen or twenty years before, substantial wooden houses with spacious flower gardens, trees, and turf had been common in the more northerly parts of town. A walk among them was a parklike experience. Older persons could recall an even more arcadian environment. When they were boys, the canal on Canal Street had been their swimming hole and skating rink, and an outing in the fields just a short ways north of it for picnics, berry picking, or nut gathering was always easy.

However, any idea of a bucolic, bosky future for New York City residents, based on judiciously planned green space, had been quashed long since by prosaic-minded city fathers. In 1807 the commissioners of streets and roads were appointed to lay out Manhattan Island. Four years later they submitted their plan for a gridiron of streets essentially the same as today's. On it were seven "squares" or "places" and a sizable parade ground running from 23rd to 34th streets between Third and Seventh avenues. The eight pieces, however, totaled only some four hundred and fifty acres. Omitted were such niceties as "circles, ovals, and stars" (pleasant features, for example, of London neighborhoods) because right-angled houses were cheaper and easier to build. The commissioners' argument for limiting open space within the city was that the

Hudson and East rivers, "large arms of the sea," would waft inshore all the fresh air needed—"salubrious breezes," they were called in the official records.

The notion of the parade ground was subsequently abandoned. By 1838 the land in the remaining squares had been reduced to one hundred and twenty acres. Previously established green spots—the Battery, City Hall Park, Washington Square, small downtown triangles, and enclosed residential parks—increased the area overall to one hundred and seventy acres. Since Manhattan Island in its entirety contains fourteen thousand three hundred and ten acres, the land reserved for public usage then was less than eight-tenths of a percent of the island's area. This caused one citizen to say, "What are called parks in New York are not even apologies for the thing; they are mere squares or paddocks." As a consequence of this early accent on commerce, as the city grew in size there was almost no place on the island where a person could relax in an airy, spacious, natural setting, free of the dust and din of the city, where ironbound cartwheels clanged over the cobbles all day long, and sometimes late into the night.

As a result, after 1839 New Yorkers began taking walks in Brooklyn's Greenwood Cemetery, laid out that year after the example of the widely admired Mt. Auburn Cemetery in Cambridge, Massachusetts. There, eight years earlier, had been provided the first instance in the country of furnishing the dead with a landscape of widespread grounds, trees, lawns, and winding roads in which to lie. With the dearth of anything similar in Manhattan, its living residents gave Greenwood steady play. One experienced crowd watcher estimated sixty thousand to have gone there in one season, responding understandably to a thirst for nature never truly bred away in man.

But Greenwood was not the answer for the city's mounting thousands. Crowded conditions were worsening. Housing for the new arrivals moved inexorably north, eating into the grid the commissioners of streets and roads had laid out. The structures were naturally right-angled houses and put up in a way that would hold the greatest number of occupants in the smallest space. Light, ventilation, and even the fundamentals of sanitation were sacrificed in these early tenements. Increasingly and disfiguringly, they were changing the face of the city.

As this continued, a strong voice for the establishment of green space began to be publicly heard. The year was 1844 and the voice belonged to William Cullen Bryant, an eminent man of letters. In his youth, he had been recognized here and abroad as America's leading poet, the author in his teens of "Thanatopsis," acclaimed the country's first great poem. ("No American could have written it," was the word in England.) At this time, he was the editor of a New York newspaper, the *Evening Post,* and he began to use his editorial columns to urge the city to set aside a large tract of woodsy terrain to turn into a people's park. In one such treatise he wrote, "If the public authorities, who spend so much of our money in laying out the city, would do what is in their power, they might give our vast population an extensive pleasure ground for shade and recreation." Bryant had felt so strongly on the subject that for eight years prior to his editorializing he had been having animated conversations on the matter with his friends and as many of the important people of the city as would hold still and listen. But the appearance in print of his views was much more effective.

In 1845 Bryant visited London. There he reveled in its parks. But he noted sadly in print that nothing similar had been planned for New York. Despite the omission, Bryant wrote, "However, there are yet unoccupied lands on the island which might, I suppose, be procured for the purpose, and which, because of their rocky and uneven surfaces, might be laid out into surpassingly beautiful pleasure grounds; but while we are discussing the subject the advancing population of the city is sweeping over them and covering them from our reach." Bryant's concern that Manhattan might shortly lie under a sea of brick and timber then seemed not unreasonable.

In 1848 a powerful ally joined Bryant. He was Andrew Jackson Downing, then thirty-three years of age, of Newburgh, New York. Downing owned a highly successful landscaping business in the lower Hudson River Valley, where he was kept busy improving the region's rapidly proliferating and imposing estates, the property of wealthy men in the city. But he also published and edited an influential monthly magazine, *The Horticulturist,* in whose pages he, too, began forcefully calling for a large New York City municipal park. Downing was pixilated on trees. Not a defect, really, in a park proponent. (Imagine parks without them.) Downing once compared the beauty of a tree "to the Grecian Apollo itself." As a practical landscaper, however, he employed them routinely without any recorded lyrical outbursts. Freestanding ornamental specimens were used to great effect in his work of estate beautification. But he was now also a public park zealot. His magazine hammered away at the topic.

In 1850 Downing traveled to London. This passage from *The Horticulturist* is typical of how he made his points:

We fancy, not without reason, in New-York, that we have a great city, and that the introduction of Croton water, is so marvelous a luxury in the way of health, that nothing more need to be done for the comfort of half a million of people. In crossing the Atlantic, a young New-Yorker, who was rabidly patriotic and who boasted daily of the superiority of our beloved commercial metropolis over every city on the globe, was our most amusing companion. I chanced to meet him one afternoon a few days after we landed, in one of the great Parks in London, in the midst of all the sylvan beauty and human enjoyment I have attempted to describe to you. He threw up his arms as he recognized me and exclaimed—"good heavens! what a scene, and I took some Londoners to the steps of City Hall last summer, to show them *the Park* of New-York!" I consoled him with the advice to be less conceited thereafter in his cockney-ism, and to show foreigners the Hudson and Niagara, instead of the City Hall and Bowling Green. But the question may well be asked, is New-York really not rich enough, or is there really not land enough in America, to give our citizens public parks of more than ten acres?

Later in the year, Downing's efforts and those of Bryant bore fruit. Furthermore, what the two had contended was strengthened by the growing number of American travelers abroad. These, like the patriotic braggart just mentioned, saw in Great Britain, and in France and Germany as well, the beauty of public parks and the pleasures they gave their visitors. Thus they became park advocates, too. Before the local election due to take place in the fall of 1850, both candidates for mayor, Fernando Wood and Ambrose C. Kingsland, pledged backing for a large municipal park for the city. So, after more than two centuries, New York was promised a proper park, not a mere square or a paddock, but a suitable one. Still the park did not arrive overnight. And when it arrived it came by a circuitous route.

The roundabout was the result of a difference between Bryant and Downing. Bryant had traipsed all over the island looking for the park site of his dreams; he felt the best spot was Jones Woods, an unspoiled, stream-laden, tree-covered tract of one hundred and sixty acres running from the East River to Third Avenue between 66th and 75th streets. Downing, on the other hand, believed a park site should be centrally located and at least five hundred acres. Admittedly, this was a large plot but one that, Downing said, could be found without trouble somewhere in the middle of the island between 39th Street and the Harlem River.

In the spring of 1851, to decide between these opinions, the city's Common Council, at the behest of Mayor Kingsland, the victor in the previous fall's election, referred the matter to the Committee on Streets and Places. It chose Jones Woods. In July of that year, the state legislature authorized the tract's purchase.

Almost at once, a hue and cry arose. Public hearings were held; testimony taken and weighed. There were those who wanted to retain the Jones Wood shoreline for eventual business or residential purposes. In August of 1851, Downing, in an article in *The Horticulturist,* vigorously attacked the Jones Wood selection; he outlined what was, in essence, a passable facsimile of the Central Park that was to be. Bryant, not long after this, agreed with Downing's objections and came round to endorsing a large, centrally located park site. But he argued also, "There is now ample room and verge upon the island for two parks, whereas if the matter is delayed for a few years, there will hardly be space left for one."

In response to the wide turmoil, the Board of Aldermen, in the same month as the publication of Downing's article, appointed a committee of two to investigate and judge the qualifications of Jones Woods and of any other potential park site on the island. The committee before long reported favorably on a large, centrally located site.

In early 1852, the Board of Aldermen accepted the committee's recommendation. Eighteen months later, on July 21, 1853, the legislature approved land for a central park between Fifth and Eighth avenues running from 59th to 106th Street, the original piece of land in today's park. The legislature also repassed the enabling act for the acquisition of Jones Woods, the measure passed earlier having been judged faulty.

This double approval, however, only stirred up more trouble. The resistance to the idea of two parks was very strong. Jones Woods was in the weaker position. Opposition to it was led by a phalanx of eminent businessmen, frock-coated Victorian executives standing sturdily shoulder to shoulder—no proto-environmentalists they—who wished the island's shoreline completely reserved for commercial development, the city's usual policy in the past. As a consequence of this long tradition, posterity has been systematically robbed of the recreational benefits that could have come from the wholesale development of our potentially lovely waterside. But here, as on other occasions, the businessmen prevailed. In April 1854, the legislature repealed the Jones Woods Act.

Meanwhile, the previous November saw the appointment by the New York State Supreme Court of five commissioners of estimate and assessment to recommend reasonable compensation to the owners of about seventy-five hundred building lots on the city grid that lay within the park site. Also, the commissioners were to negotiate a rise in taxes with property owners along the park's perimeter. This was due to the expected boost in the value of property lying beside the park. In a little over two years, on February 5, 1856, the Supreme Court approved the report of the commissioners. The sum of $5,069,693 was paid owners of lands appropriated. Of this, $1,657,590 came from new assessments on the owners of plots alongside. The commissioners, who had been carefully selected for reputations of probity, did their job so well that only one in forty of their valuations was protested. The names of these heroes of the process of eminent domain, which can be found in no other memorial than the city records, were Luther Bradish, Warren Brady, William Kent, Jeremiah Towle, and Michael Ulshoeffer.

Shortly the northern end of the site, from 106th to 110th streets, was added to the rest. The dramatic, hilly ground in it was recognized as an integral part of the park's whole. Furthermore, its crags and steep grades made it next to impossible to develop profitably, while to the north the land fell away to the plain of Harlem, easily transformed into house lots. The extra piece cost $1,179,590, far more than the price per acre for the original piece. Landowners had noted what the idea of a park did for land values.

Altogether, the park's site, for land and expenses, cost the city of New York $7,389,727.96. Included was $250,000 for the Arsenal and its drill ground, which the city bought from the state. The total, a Parks Department historian has noted, was more than the $7.2 million used to purchase Alaska's nearly six hundred thousand square miles a few years later.

To provide monies "for the payment of the Public Place entitled 'The Central Park,'" the city by an ordinance brought out a stock issue, "The Central Park Fund," secured by the site's land. It was soon subscribed. For years after this, the place was invariably known in print and speech as *the* Central Park. In this hereafter it will be the Park.

In May 1856, just a few months after the court's approval of the land acquisition, the Common Council appointed as the commissioners of the Central Park the mayor and the street commissioner, whose job was to oversee the development of the park site. Shortly after the appointment, to enhance public confidence in the tremendous task ahead, a Consulting

Board of seven illustrious citizens was formed. Its president was the eminent author, Washington Irving, and its duty was to assist the commissioners in their planning and decisions.

What the city had acquired in Central Park was a tract of about one and a quarter square miles, nearly twice as large as the principality of Monaco. It had a surface that featured much swampy and uneven rocky ground and some barren flats. A rugged ridge ran up the west side almost like the spine of Manhattan. Some scattered dwellings, mostly along Fifth Avenue, were present as well as a few collections of trees, the largest on what is now the Ramble. But there were also some willows near today's Willowdell Bridge, over the East Drive at the level of 67th Street, and some conifers west of the present Mall.

A noxious element in the Park was several squatter camps described as city suburbs and, according to official opinion, suburbs "more filthy, squalid and disgusting can hardly be imagined." If the inhabitants were spared yellow fever, a newspaper observed, "it will be only because Death himself hesitates to enter" such a place. There Indians, blacks, and whites lived in hopelessness, as many as five thousand, occupying caves, lean-tos, and tin-can shacks. They lived by pig farming, goat keeping, bone boiling, garbage picking, and moonshining. Around their premises, one observer said, "The low ground was steeped in an overflow and mush of pigsties, slaughterhouses and bone-boiling works, and the stench was sickening." Coiners, poachers, sneak thieves, and trollops were also present. Religious denominations sent missionaries there. The largest community, Seneca Village, was in from the west 80s. Charity-minded ladies built a church, All Angels Church, on the east side of Eighth Avenue for these people. In the churchyard the squatters could bury their dead until the city in 1851, in an ordinance aimed directly at them, forbade burials below 86th Street. When the city took title, it was judged, some hundred thousand cats, chickens, cows, dogs, geese, goats, pigs, and horses, belonging to the squatters, roamed the site.

When the Central Park commissioners were named in 1856, the most pressing work was to clean up, lay out, and develop the grounds with a force of gardeners, surveyors, engineers, clerks, and laborers. But at that point very little money had been appropriated to do this. A chief engineer, however, had been appointed. He was Egbert L. Viele, a West Point graduate, a rather stiff-necked, contentious, ex-military man. Since 1853, the year the legislature approved the park site, Viele had been preparing on speculation a topographical map of the terrain and a proposed plan for

The bleak terrain of the Park's original site with its stony wastes and the huts of squatters. (Herbert Mitchell Collection.)

its improvement, in hopes that he eventually would be paid for his work. Under his direction, action that year was limited to some ground clearing and a lengthy tussle to evict the squatters. For this last, the Central Park Police was formed, consisting of a captain, three sergeants, and fifteen men. The battle was quickly joined. Falling back before the better discipline and armament of the lawmen, the squatters with their greater knowledge of the terrain waged stubborn guerrilla warfare with fusillades of bricks. Ultimately, after combat lasting weeks, they bowed to the inevitable, retreating to the open spaces of Harlem and Yorkville.

Another duty of the Central Park Police was to prevent the theft of trees and plants from the newly acquired site, such snitching having been observed. Also, to see just what was present in the way of flora, the commissioners in their first year authorized a botanical survey. Its results were published in the "First Annual Report on the Improvement of The Central Park," issued under the date of January 1, 1857. The survey taker, or takers, unnamed in the report, stated that they had met with seventy species of plants altogether, including certain ones that were either noxious or so few in number that there was no point in naming them. (Poison ivy was rampant on the grounds; it seriously hampered the land surveyors, one of whom was laid low for a fortnight after an infection.) Species named were forty-three in number. Twenty-nine were trees, ten were shrubs, and four vines. While the value of trees to the Park is obvious, shrubs and vines are also important. A shrub is a low woody plant or bush; a vine is a less imposing growth whose stem requires support. While trees, of course, are the chief item necessary to create Park greenery, shrubs and vines have their place as well. Shrubs, depending on size and shape, make different types of understories for the overarching trees. Vines, for their part, are the minor furniture of the outdoors, tracing verdant lines to clothe bare rock or earth, or twining picturesquely around trunks or rustic buildings, should such be in their vicinity. The report ended with the belief that with regard to plants useful to the development of the Park, none had been overlooked.

In less than a year, however, that claim was challenged. Another survey was done in August and September of 1857 by botanists Charles Rawolle and Ignaz Anton Pilat. Pilat, an Austrian-trained gardener and botanist, was an important figure in the early days of the Park; he will be mentioned again later.

Pilat and his associate covered the same ground as had the previous survey. They came up, however, with a total of two hundred and eighty-five species of plants. One hundred and twenty-eight of these were trees, shrubs, or vines, or roughly three times the number in the comparable categories of the first list. Forty-four new species of trees, forty-one new shrubs, and six new vines were found. The rest of the plants, one hundred and fifty-seven in number, were what botanists call herbs. In layman's language, these are seed plants such as daisies, whose stems lack woody tissue. Some of the survey's discoveries—low bush blueberry, beach plum, mountain holly, wild yam, and one-seeded star cucumber—are not normally associated with a city. The Park is much less rich in such today. But nature left alone—as it had been hitherto in Central Park—is unpredictable.

A proposition holds that seed once dropped by wind, bird, or other means, even upon alien ground, may flower and persist if unmolested. Support for this assumption comes from a report issued around the time of the Pilat-Rawolle survey. It stated that four hundred and twenty-four varieties of plants, not found anywhere else in Europe, were growing sturdily and improbably in the terrain of the Colosseum in Rome, the result, scholars thought, of seeds haphazardly mixed with the fodder from Asia and Africa that accompanied animals brought in centuries earlier for the high jinks of imperial Rome.

The survey by Pilat and Rawolle seems unquestionably the better reflection of the botany that was on the Park site in 1857.

In April of that year, the governance of the Park changed. By act of the legislature, a board of eleven commissioners was named to replace the former two-man tandem, which, even allowing for the limited funds, had not made much progress in Park work. Clearing of the site now went forward in earnest. Much needed doing. Among the chores were the carting away of stones, the removal of the vacated squatters' shacks, the cleanup of the mush, mire, and rubbish that lay around them, and the corralling of their abandoned animals, the goats, the most difficult, being especially nimble and numerous, not to say twig-devouring. By August of 1857, two thousand men were employed on the site.

TWO ACCIDENTS gave us the Central Park we have today. The first was Downing's untimely death by drowning in 1852. Had he lived, unquestionably he would have been the designer of Central Park. His years of fame as a landscape gardener, his original powerful and successful advocacy of a large, centrally located park, and his draft plan in *The Horticulturist* as to how that spot should be developed all would have seen to that.

The second was a chance encounter that occurred five years later. The time was mid-August of 1857 and the place was the Griswold Inn, a quaint old Connecticut seaside hostelry in the quaint old town of Essex, both of which quaint entities still function quaintly today. One of the commissioners of Central Park had come to the Griswold Inn for a holiday respite and there in the lounge one teatime met an acquaintance, a literary man, Frederick Law Olmsted, who had been availing himself of the inn's quiet to polish his latest manuscript. In the conversation that ensued, both praised the idea of the Park. Olmsted's remarks were so positive and comprehensive that the commissioner said he wished Olmsted were on the board. The commissioner then said the Park's development was really going forward and a search was in progress for a superintendent. The commissioner paused briefly and then said, "Why don't *you* apply for the job?" This struck Olmsted all of a heap. While his professional life for most of his thirty-five years had been concentrated on the written word, he was as pixilated about parks as Downing had been about trees. On his travels abroad, he constantly nosed around in them. Later he was to say of his European jaunts, "While others gravitated to pictures, architecture, Alps, libraries, high life and low life when travelling, I had gravitated to parks—spent all my spare time in them."

Olmsted was definitely tempted. "What are the superintendent's duties?" he inquired. He was told that "He would be the executive officer of the Engineer with respect to the labor force, and would have charge of the police and would see that proper regulations were enforced with regard to the public use of the Park." The commissioner added that since there were other candidates being considered, Olmsted should file his application pronto.

Some ten seconds passed, and Olmsted said, "I'll take the boat down tonight. I'll think about it en route. I'll do it if no serious objection arises."

None did. In the city, Olmsted started his campaign. This centered on amassing letters of recommendation. In the August dog days, most of his influential friends were customarily out of town. But he found a nucleus and got the process started. Before long he had a sizable array of letters, including a strongly supportive one from Washington Irving, the president of the Park's Consulting Board. In September, Olmsted got the job, the Irving letter providing the clincher. The date was September 11.

Shortly thereafter Olmsted reported for work at the Park. At this point, his superb genius as a molder of natural scenery lay unsuspected and unseen, probably not even guessed at by Olmsted himself. The man who was to design the grounds of the United States Capitol, park after park from the Atlantic to the Pacific, et cetera, et cetera, was merely a somewhat slender, medium-sized, well-mannered Victorian gentleman the day he first walked onto the wastes of Central Park, some of whose vistas then were as desolate as the outlands of the moon.

Relations with his immediate superior, Viele, the chief engineer, were cool. The men were far apart in temperament. On the first morning Viele sent Olmsted, wearing street attire, out with a lumpish, uncommunicative underling named Hawkins to meet the foremen of the gangs whose performance Olmsted was scheduled to supervise. Over bogs and rocks and through briar patches, the two slogged, Olmsted soon wishing he had worn hip boots and left his coat behind. His future charges, engaged in clearing brush, opening drains, and carting stones, sniggered at the sight of the fashionably dressed Olmsted with his clearly aristocratic mien. But these rough fellows did not know their man. Olmsted, the artist, was also Olmsted the able administrator. Of course, this combination violated all established rules of artistic temperament. But the paradox existed in Olmsted. (As will be demonstrated later, who, however, has ever said Olmsted was simple?) His administrative side firmly displayed itself when, three months after taking charge, he wrote his father that the thousand men under his management were now working as smoothly as a machine, a consequence that resulted in a raise in his salary from $2,000 to $2,500 a year.

Although, as mentioned earlier, Viele had on his own produced a design for the Park, the board in June 1857 resolved that there should be an open competition. Designs for the Park's layout were to be anonymous and to be submitted by April 1, 1858. Monetary awards for the four best designs were announced by the board in mid-October. This date was only several weeks after Olmsted had come aboard.

Here the name of Calvert Vaux enters the narrative. Vaux, a doll-like man four feet eight inches in height, was a British-born and -trained architect, a former partner of Andrew Jackson Downing, and, at the age of thirty-three, two years Olmsted's junior. On Downing's trip to Great Britain in 1850, he had met and hired Vaux to be the architect for the kind of buildings, mostly villas, that Downing wanted to erect on his bucolic landscapes. Despite Vaux's diminutive stature, he was a forceful and novel character, difficult to classify. A later observer remarked, "Mr. Vaux was indeed a somewhat strange being, endowed with many of the inspirations and accomplishments of a genius and, with equal certainty, some of the eccentricities." The friend added that Vaux "was essentially an original artist, conscientious and independent to a fault." One could spend hours arguing with him over questions of design. Yet any obstinancy was not the result of vanity but a belief in the correctness of his view.

The design competition brought Vaux to see Olmsted. Following Downing's death, Vaux had run the upstate landscape gardening business, married an American woman, and become a citizen. But after several years he had moved to the city. The two men had been acquainted before Downing's death. Olmsted had contributed to *The Horticulturist,* and Downing, for his part, had written letters of introduction for Olmsted before his 1850 trip to England. Vaux had doubtless discussed with Downing the design of the pleasure ground that Downing had fought so hard to achieve, that Downing had expected to design, and in the design of which Vaux had expected to participate. Thus when a design competition was announced, it was natural for Vaux to approach Olmsted and suggest a collaborative effort.

Olmsted initially was somewhat uncertain about this. He had several problems. One was his job. It was arduous and full-time. Another was his debts, part of his literary past. A third was a book he was trying to finish, *A Journey to Texas,* of which he said, "the labor already expended in it, being too much to let slide." The last was Viele. Olmsted knew that Viele already had a plan for the Park's design and was reputed ready to present another. For Olmsted to compete without the agreement of his somewhat testy superior would be, Olmsted felt, impolitic. But when he broached the subject, Viele said this was a matter of no moment to him.

Thus, after some thought, Olmsted agreed to Vaux's proposal. From his work, Olmsted already knew the topography and other characteristics of the Park; Vaux set about to learn them quickly. Because of Olmsted's responsibilities as superintendent, the pair's planning was done mostly outside normal working hours. But now, with the intention to mold the site into a pleasance, a harmonious work of art, Olmsted looked at its qualities and quirks with quite a different eye. Time and again he sought to imagine its topography—under all conditions—when dressed in the clothes with which, from his mental closet, he hoped to provide it. Olmsted was nothing if not meticulous. Little was left to chance. He even took it upon himself to observe the tract by moonlight. Standing and turning this way and that below the silver shine, he conjured up in his mind, from south to north, the outcrops, hillocks, bogs, and flats and then fitted them into the vistas he trusted were to be. These nocturnal sessions were a boon to Olmsted. He detested noise. The nights were quiet, free from interruptions and unwanted audiences. Such tranquil strolls with the sun behind the earth were creatively rewarding.

Vaux usually was with him, there and at other places the two worked, including Vaux's house on 18th Street. The collaboration was marked then, as it was later, by argument. Each was strong-headed. Each was artistically sure of himself. And each had to be convinced before yielding to the other. It was a spirited partnership, occasionally stormy. In part, perhaps, because of the frequent debate, the joint effort, entitled "Greensward," was turned in on the very last day before the deadline.

Greensward won over thirty-odd competitors and took the first-prize money of $2,000. Like its rivals, it met the prescribed requirements for a twenty- to forty-acre parade ground, a principal fountain and prospect tower, and six additional demands. But unlike the others, it fulfilled the obligation to provide four or more crossings from east to west by sinking four roads below the level of the park surface, thus, for all practical purposes, making the traffic invisible from above. Without transit facilities, a barrier two and a half miles long and half a mile wide strung down the middle of Manhattan would have presented an insuperable obstacle to the city's trade. The facilities of the other designs would have cut rudely across the park, roiling its tranquility, whereas those of Greensward kept the two visually separated, each meanwhile performing its function. This is a heavenly blessing. It was yesterday. And it is today. From a practical

*RIGHT. Calvert Vaux,
Olmsted's British-born
co-designer of the Park. The
two men remained close
associates even after their
business partnership was
dissolved in 1872.* (National
Park Service.)

*LEFT. Frederick Law
Olmsted, the Park's
architect-in-chief, taken not
long after his appointment
in 1858.* (National Park
Service.)

point of view, it was also the most important feature of the Greensward plan. It is doubtless the detail that won the first prize.

Olmsted was appointed architect-in-chief of Central Park, and Vaux assistant to the architect-in-chief, nomenclature that is instructive.

In connection with the Greensward plan and thereafter, the men purposely kept what each contributed to the collaboration a secret. From time to time since, questions have arisen as to whose work was the more important in shaping the Park. Olmsted's, it would appear. It is true that structures in the Park—bridges, arches, and the charming original buildings—are known from the record to be almost entirely the work of Vaux, the trained architect, with some input from Olmsted and others, particularly Jacob Wrey Mould, another British-trained architect whose contributions will be mentioned later. But the rolling sweep of the Park, its hills, dales, water bodies, paths, and roads—its innate self, in other words— seem predominantly Olmsted's. Since this is essentially the Park as we know it, Olmsted can be considered its principal designer. Contemporary opinion—evidenced by the superior title given Olmsted—apparently confirms this. In addition, Olmsted's extensive later work, all as a landscape architect, would seem to consolidate the supposition.

Under the new arrangement, Viele, the chief engineer, lost his job, a circumstance that did nothing to endear Olmsted to him, as several decades later Viele would have the opportunity to demonstrate.

*T*HE ARCHITECT-IN-CHIEF of Central Park was born in Hartford, Connecticut, in 1822, the son of a well-to-do-merchant, a father highly supportive of his family and, to judge by later events, an influential role model for his son. Variety is the word for Olmsted's early life. Weak eyesight soon displayed itself. But a number of schools, some public, some private, were successfully attended. At twenty he was at Yale for a spell, but left before long. Eye problems. At the age of twenty-one, in theory to improve his health, he shipped before the mast on the bark *Ronaldson* out of New York for China, a trip that lasted twelve months.

Olmsted's physiology, his bodily functioning, that is, is a matter that should be addressed. Like much else about him, it was not simple. He did have weak eyes. And he did have a rickety nervous system, too finely tuned, you might say, a facet doubtless of his artistic temperament. But his will was unswerving, so much so that it often caused him to ask too much of his body. Even so, his constitution generally seems to have been surprisingly sturdy. Otherwise he could never have survived his year's voyage on the *Ronaldson.* He suffered weeks of seasickness, malnutrition, frequent abuse from the captain, fainting spells, and at one point, a seizure of paralysis. (The captain was, in fact, later tried for brutal treatment of the crew.) As the crew debarked, Olmsted's father was waiting for him. The elder Olmsted did not recognize his son, emaciated, yellow, and ridden with scurvy, as he walked down the gangplank of the *Ronaldson.*

Next, for a period of seven years, Olmsted took up agriculture and orchardry on farms, first in Connecticut and then Staten Island, both purchased by his father, who was ever helpful in matters financial. On these holdings, Olmsted seems to have got his first taste, although a minor one, of planting trees and setting them out to take advantage of contours in the landscape, as well as envisaging stretches of ground whose personality and features could be changed. At the end of the seven years, he began to travel and put down his impressions on paper. By 1860 he had authored four books, the best-received all dealing with conditions in the Southern states, in what Olmsted called the Cotton Kingdom. This, of course, was before the Civil War. These eyewitness accounts are still regarded as prime sources for that phase of our history when slavery, though soon to end, was still in full bloom. Olmsted also had enough talent as an artist to illustrate at least one of his books with a dozen sketches, a skill bound to have been useful later to a landscape designer who could sketch and take in from the field memorable impressions of the look of terrain before and after treatment.

In 1850 he made a six-month trip to Europe that was highly important to his future career. On it he toured Belgium, France, and Germany. But most of the time was spent in Great Britain. Olmsted walked over much of the rustic reaches of what then was certainly the world's most important island. Its gentle scenery bewitched him. Thereafter he was never free of its spell. And he visited many of the innovative public parks that were just beginning to be built in the kingdom, constructions that brought rurality into the cities to offset the growing manmade wildernesses of timber and masonry. Soon thereafter, for this or other reasons, Olmsted became a wholehearted Anglophile. It probably could be said that he was the American counterpart of those privileged Oxbridge types of the Victorian era who, with such cool efficiency, ruled the wide-ranging empire, dispensing justice evenhandedly to all their charges.

Olmsted's bonding with our cousins overseas could well account for some of the nomenclature of Central Park—arrant Briticisms such as Dalehead, Dene, Gill, Hernshead, Loch, and Willowdell, terminology that seems also to have met with Vaux's approval.

In 1856, Olmsted visited England again, this time for another six months. He stayed in London, attempting to bring British authors to the New York publishing house in which his father had bought him a share. There he met socially, and broke bread with, William Makepeace Thackeray and other English writers. On our side of the water, because of his new post as literary recruiter and as editor of *Putnam's* magazine, Washington Irving and other homegrown men of letters were prominent in his life. (Alas, the publishing house bubble was soon to burst, leaving Olmsted with the considerable debt that later caused him qualms about joining Vaux in the design competition.)

While in London Olmsted visited one or more of its public parks virtually every day, regarding their various features and what they provided for their users, with the by now keen eye of the afficionado. He little realized then that these strolls would have recompense beyond transient pleasure. Later, though, after his Central Park appointment, he said, "So that it happened when the Central Park was to be laid out and managed it was quite possible that I was more intimate with public parks, and had a better understanding of what they should be, than any other man of American birth and breeding."

What the American man of birth and breeding and his British-born associate were obligated to lay out, and to manage, was a discouragingly narrow strip of barren, unpromising land five times as long as its half-mile width. The cramped perimeters east and west were one of the problems facing the designers. Throughout their work, they concentrated on overcoming it through every strategem they could devise. For example, in meeting one of the original design demands that the Park contain a prospect tower, the pair picked lofty Vista Rock for the site, replacing the wooden bell tower that for years had served the city as a fire observation post with the present Belvedere Castle, a miniaturized stone Gothic fortress set astride the eminence. Seen from anywhere in the Park, the building's lilliputian dimensions impart to the viewer an undeniable sense of distance, giving, as the designers wished, a feeling of spaciousness to a very cramped parcel of ground.

Again, with this objective in view, trees were planted along the streets that form the perimeters of the Park. Originally they were elms, as they are today along Fifth Avenue. But elsewhere they eventually had to be replaced by the present gingkoes on Central Park South and North, and the pin oaks on Central Park West, species that better resist the hardships of city life. Olmsted's rationale was that the lofty, full-grown trees would shut from view the nearby city buildings, thereby giving the Park— with its own interior plantings—a sense of rural remoteness that would minimize the feeling that the Park was narrow.

Olmsted at this time assumed that the Park would finally be surrounded by a wall of buildings twice as high as the Great Wall of China, which ranges from twenty to fifty feet tall. He figured that the trees at maturity would block the view, putting, in his words, "an umbrageous horizon line around the perimeter." What he did not anticipate was the impetuous rush of man's technology. Only a year before his appointment as Park architect, Elisha Graves Otis, the inventor of the elevator, had installed the first truly safe specimen of his handiwork in a department store downtown. With that achievement, the race to verticality was on. Apartment and office buildings destined for the Park's edges would eventually rise hundreds of feet tall. Obscuring them would be beyond the prowess of even the most ambitious pin oak or upward-striving elm.

But Olmsted did have firm control over another feature that would seemingly much enlarge the meager width of the Park. This was the pedestrian paths, more than fifty miles of which came to be laid out. Olmsted arranged them cunningly with many curves. A stroller arriving at a turn would leave a certain type of terrain to come upon one quite different—from a meadow, say, or from a lawn to a purling stream or shimmering sheet of water, from a woods to a bare area of towering rock pinnacles. This variety managed to give the visitor the feeling that the Park rambled on forever.

Work on the site proceeded apace. Olmsted was appointed in May 1858. During the half dozen months before winter set in, part of the carriage drive in the southern part of the Park was graded, drainage of the area was complete below 79th Street, and several miles of pedestrian paths were in a condition for use; the Mall was nearly complete, flanked by a double row of trees; the bridle path was coming along, and trees and shrubs were being planted, the first of the former in October of that year, probably in the Ramble, the wooded knoll across from the American Museum of Natural History. This was the first part of the Park to be opened to the public, around the time that the first tree was planted.

A glimpse of how the Park looked in that early period has been recorded in the diary of George Templeton Strong, the aristocratic chronicler of much that went on around town in the nineteenth century. A few months after the Park officially opened, he left his Wall Street office early one afternoon with a couple of friends to get a feel of the place. Later he wrote of his trip that he had gone

to explore Central Park, which will be a feature of the city within five years and a lovely place in A.D. 1900, when its trees will have acquired dignity and appreciable diameters. . . . Reached the Park a little before four just as the red flag was hoisted—the signal for the blasts of the day. They were all around us for some twenty minutes, now booming far off to the north, now quite near, now distant again, like a desultery "affair" between advanced posts of great armies. We entered the Park at Seventy-first Street on its east side and made for "The Ramble," a patch just below the upper reservoir [the old Croton reservoir]. Its footpaths and plantations are finished, more or less, and it is the first section of the ground that has been polished off and made presentable. It promises very well. So does all the lower Park, though now in most ragged condition long lines of incomplete macadamization, mounds of compost, piles of blasted stone, acres of what may be greensward hereafter but is now mere brown earth; groves of slender, young transplanted maples and locusts, undecided between life and death, and here and there an arboricultural experiment that has failed utterly, and is a mere broomstick with ramifications. Celts, caravans of dirt carts, derricks, steam engines, these are the elements out of which our future Pleasaunce is rapidly developing. . . . Roads and paths twist about in curves of artistic tertuosity. A broad avenue, exceptionally straight . . . [the Mall] with a quadruple row of elms, will look Versailles-y by A.D. 1950.

Olmsted maneuvered through this hectic scene as nonchalantly and efficiently as though he were promenading the paths of his own garden. The look of the future was clearly in his head, and he knew that the raucous, disorderly formlessness of the moment was merely a transient phenomenon. More than two thousand laborers, directed by him, turned out the considerable achievements summed up above, progress that was noted with obvious satisfaction in the commissioners' second annual report. The report also told of the filling of the Lake, the largest body of water in the Greensward plan. The Lake met the requirement, mandated by the competition, for a winter skating ground. In late December of that 1858, a few skaters, to whom Olmsted gave his blessing, appeared on the frozen surface. Ice skating, although long popular in Holland, had been little practiced here despite the fact that the city's origin was Dutch. But the new Park activity was contagious. Soon the sport spread headlong through the town. Skate manufacturers hurriedly set up business, stores sold skates, and thousands of people took to this outdoor exercise, some of it at night by artificial illumination from calcium reflectors on the shore of the Lake. The vogue so held the fancy of New York that it moved a park commissioner, in one of the board's annual reports, to this lyrical and untypical piece of official prose:

The movements of a throng of skaters, on a clear day, chasing each other in gleeful mood over the crystal ceiling of the imprisoned lake, the fur-clad inmates of a thousand gay vehicles coursing along the silver snow to the music of bells, the dusky foliage of the fir and pine on the adjacent heights, wrapped with wreaths of fleecy white; leafless branches strung with a network of icy pearls, frail but gorgeous as it glistens and flashes with a thousand hues in every glance of the sunlight, form in our midst a winter scene unmatched by that of any capital or country of modern times, because it is obtainable only in a climate, amid an extent of population of wealth and liberality, such as peculiarly characterizes this Queen City of the Western Hemisphere.

Some in that throng of gleeful skaters in the Queen City of the Western Hemisphere were doubtless the grandparents of today's soccer, tennis, baseball, and handball players patronizing the Park. The skating, starting so early, was just one of many ways in which the Park was destined to affect the lives of New Yorkers.

Olmsted had a very clear idea of what he wanted to paint on the raw canvas of the Park. He saw an alluring medley of meadows and groves, bubbling streams and glimmering pools, rocky heights and winding valleys, areas tree-crowned and bare, trimmed with rustic, Theocritan structures—parklike things—for Olmsted believed a rural scene is never complete without such simple edifices, smacking of dales in Arcady. The whole sweep of hundreds of acres would be interlaced with a system of carriage roads, bridle paths, and footways, totaling more than seventy miles, none of which intersected but, where they met, would be carried over one another by bridges or arches, thereby preserving a sensible safety for the Park's patrons. Pedestrians, constituting, of course, the vast majority of users, would need never to fear the onrush of a rapidly moving carriage or a riding horse gone out of control.

One of the surprising things about Olmsted is that on this, his very first and very large venture of park building, he should have been, with Olympian assurance, so positive about what he wanted both in its design and its management. On both counts, the experience of years has proven him utterly right. Still, the unblemished certainty is surprising. Even a little eerie.

His design plan was simple. By 1859, by act of the legislature, the city had gotten the second piece of the Park, the rocky plot from 106th to 110th Street. This was tacked onto the flatter piece below, giving Olmsted two contrasting units to work on. The smaller northern and more rugged one, with its bold, precipitous contours, Olmsted decided to leave pretty much as it was. It represented the primitively picturesque portion—nature uncorseted. The larger southern section was softer, smoother. It required, in Olmsted's mind, considerable work to give it the gentle, pastoral, almost English countryside touch that he felt, would attract and soothe every visitor.

Threading through the whole ran the beautifully contrived system of
roads, not a grade crossing in it—the carriage drives, the bridle paths, and
the footways—the carriage drives, curving gently with long straightaways avoided, so designed to thwart racing matches; the bridle paths wide
enough to accommodate four riders, sometimes bordering the carriage
roads, sometimes diverging; and the meandering footpaths moving
smoothly from one bucolic prospect to another. Lastly, cutting across the
ensemble from east to west, moving under the Park's surface through
tunnels or under bridges, were the four sunken transverse roads, carrying the city's busy commercial traffic, all but invisible to the people above.

Following the northern acquisition, the designers' plan called for three
principal water bodies—the Lake, the largest, in the Park's center; the
Meer, next in size in the northeast corner, abutting the plain of Harlem;

and the Pond in the southeast one, under the shadow of the Plaza Hotel.

About half a dozen streams of varying volume were originally on the site, running more or less from west to east toward the East River, not all of them making it there. Their flow turned some of the site into bogs. These were drained. The southernmost principal water course, DeVoor's Mill Stream, was used to form the five-acre Pond by the southeast entrance at Fifth Avenue and Central Park South, in the early days always the most popular way in. Its entry was named the Scholars Gate, one of the eighteen, all likewise named, that the designers eventually placed in the perimeter wall.

Because of the importance of this section, Olmsted wished to make the Pond area more than ordinarily inviting. The edge was planted with trees and reached by a bench-furnished path from the entrance at the corner.

Skating on the Lake, begun shortly after the Park opened, soon took the town by storm. At night, calcium flares illuminated the area. (Museum of the City of New York.)

Rendition of traffic in a transverse. These sunken transverse roads
were the first of their kind in the country.
(Herbert Mitchell Collection.)

Olmsted hoped that this poolside nook, near the busy streets of the city, would attract passersby if only for a brief spell of quiet and repose. The Pond was, and is, considerably below the level of Central Park South. To complete the setting, Olmsted directed that a slope of from thirty to sixty degrees be made from the foot of the perimeter wall along Central Park South to the edge of the path by the Pool, ordering that enough topsoil be provided to allow the growth of small trees and shrubs on the slope. The expense of a bottom retaining wall along the Pool's path would thus be avoided.

The large twenty-two-and-a-half–acre Lake was fashioned from the south branch of the Sawkill Creek, which entered the Park at about where the American Museum of Natural History now stands. Great pipes were placed underground to take care of the inflow and outflow because its surface was, and still is, raised and lowered somewhat from winter to summer. In the all-important, crowded, and highly developed central section of the lower Park, the Lake was a crucial element in the designers' plan. It lay at the end of the wide, roughly quarter-of-a-mile–long Mall, bordered by a double row of elms. Such a promenade, Olmsted thought, should be present in every large public park to give people a place to congregate and saunter. At the Mall's upper end the visitor's gaze was directed across the Lake's impressive sweep to the long, rocky, and wooded hill of the Ramble. Peeping out atop it was the turret of the small, gray-stone Belvedere Castle. Contemplation of this extensive interconnecting vista once again distracted visitor attention from the Park's overly intimate east and west borders. Taken together, these features were the backbone of the lower Park's design.

But they were embellished by others, many of which were inventive or imposing. At the end of the Mall, before reaching the Lake, the visitor crossed a carriage road to arrive at the Terrace, a generous, stone-paved landing. From the carriage road a double flight of stairs descended, wide and ornately balustraded. The massive balustrades bore beautiful carvings of birds and fruits worked into the sandstone. The stairs led to the Esplanade, a wide, clear level space, colorfully tiled underfoot, that fronted the Lake. (Terrace and Esplanade are the original names for these features. Today Terrace is commonly used for the Esplanade. This text, however, will retain the original names.) At the Esplanade's center was the large, double-basined Bethesda Fountain, surmounted by the winged bronze statue of The Angel of the Waters, who, in the Gospel of John, troubled the Bethesda Pool in Jerusalem, giving it healing powers. Under the figure of the Angel, four cherubs—Purity, Health, Peace, and Temperance—further echoed the churchly ambiance of the Victorian era. The fountain played its streams amid an arrangement of lofty gonfalons that, on fair days from their tall staffs at the Esplanade's corners, snapped and flew in the breezes from off the Lake. Olmsted realized how water alters and tempers the light it reflects, the effects changing constantly as the hours and seasons move along.

Around the Lake's rim were rustic bench-equipped shelters and boat landings for boarding and discharging passengers from the public steam launches that in those days plied the swells. To give the water bodies variety, Olmsted created in them artificial islands. Each of his three principal water bodies had an island, as did the Pool, part of the Park's northern water system. That in the Lake, for contrast with native flora, he had planted with shrubs and trees bearing tropical-like foliage. He also added a number of swan rests for the stately birds that were originally part of the Park's wildlife, gifts at different times from Germany and England.

At the northwest corner of the Lake, Olmsted ordered construction of the Cave, an intentionally primitive architectural touch, for use by those who might wish to overlook the water from an arm of the Lake called Bankrock Bay, so named from the cliffs rising high along the eastern incline. The Cave's purpose was to add a bit of the archaic to the pastoral scene. Near it stood a similar detail, the Rustic Arch, a ponderous, narrow-portaled stone structure emanating crudity. It looked as if it might have been flung hastily together by a group of hairy-pelted Neanderthals. At the upper end of the Mall, where it broadened into what, in Olmsted's day, was known as the Concert Ground, stood a wooden, brightly painted, octagonal bandstand adorned with the charming fretwork characteristic of that time. On afternoons and evenings bands gave concerts there, beginning in the year 1859.

The Children's District, as Olmsted called it, lay south of the Lake, just below the 65th Street transverse road. It was a section that in the hot summer months, even when the air elsewhere was still, was cooled by a southerly breeze drawn off the Pond, the water body lying in that direction. Keeping children and their mothers cool in that season was the kind of service Olmsted wanted the Park to render. Infant/child mortality in the city increased sharply in the dog days, and families that couldn't leave town suffered most. For them, Olmsted said, "the best that can be done is to spend an occasional day or part of a day in the Park. It has been for some years a growing practice with physicians to advise this course." The recommendation gratified him. For Olmsted was a patrician humanist. He felt a strong need to serve others.

The aforementioned southerly breeze struck three structures in the designer's Land of the Young. The first was the Dairy, a substantial stone cottage with a portico and tables at which fresh milk and light refreshments were served. At times the countrified tone was enhanced by purely decorative cows, sheep, and chickens. Just to the west was the Kinderberg, or Children's Mountain, a knoll topped by the largest rustic shelter ever built in Central Park. The diameter of the circular structure was one hundred and ten feet. Vines twined over it. It was for fair weather use. Unlike many Park shelters, it lacked a roof.

Still farther to the west was the Carousel in its original frame version. Throughout the seasons, its piping music and arching, brightly painted, wooden steeds drew swarms of young riders. And some older ones, as well.

Southwest of the Carousel lay the Ball Ground near the entrance at Eighth Avenue. On it the designers established several frame structures, including the Ballplayers House. There was, however, no indiscriminate ballplaying then; and incidentally, compared to today's activity, the pre–Civil War game was a somewhat tepid sport. It was played on the lawn by schoolboys, but only those who had satisfactorily completed their lessons. The contests were intermittent. The reason: they were hard on the turf.

Olmsted's policies for use of the Park put an effective limit on such specialized activities. He justified his stand by explaining that the Park was for *everyone,* not for any particular group such as ballplayers. In his attitude toward sports, he was a man of his time. His lack of interest was understandable. In fact, although it may seem peculiar now, it was generally shared by those of his vintage. In 1860 there was scant time for sports. Long hours at arduous farm and factory labor left little time for leisure or the strength to engage in the kind of vigorous games and activities we enjoy today.

Recreation for Olmsted had a special meaning. For him, it was re-*creating* the body and mind through juxaposition with, and tranquil observation of, nature, the placing of persons in a setting of trees, water, rocks, and herbage, wherein rest and relaxation, emanating from the world spirit, would come easily. Stress would quietly disappear in such a *re-*creation of healthy humanity. To further this, Olmsted had set out in the Park a wide variety of flora—trees, shrubs, and plants—green, leafy cushions on which the weary refugee could, metaphorically speaking, rest his head. The chief responsibility for these verdant palliatives rested with Anton Ignaz Pilat, Olmsted's skilled head gardener.

Of course, by establishing such things as bridle paths and facilities for ice skating, Olmsted himself unwittingly assisted a citywide move toward active outdoor pastimes. Had he known the results of what he started, the turning of much of the Park into a sports arena, he would unquestionably have labeled the development a degeneration—a perversion of his rather rigid original plan—but a plan fashioned only, as only it could be, for his time. Many, many years later, only toward the beginning of this century,

Olmsted at last realized and acknowledged the need to accommodate active sports in the Park. By that time, the nation's affluence and leisure time demanded them.

An early spectator sport that Olmsted approved was the Park's daily carriage parade. Many came to the Park every day just to see it. A favorite spot was on the side of the carriage road by the Concert Ground at the head of the Mall or on the Terrace side just across from it. The procession started around four in the afternoon. The vehicles—barouches, broughams, carriages, landaus, phaetons, and victorias, meaningful nomenclature to every informed adult in those days of the long ago—arrived at the Park through its traditionally important entry at Fifth Avenue and Central Park South. They proceeded north up the East Drive for nearly a mile to

The Pool in the Park's northern water system. The designers' goal of creating a restful atmosphere is made very clear in this photograph.
(Sara Cedar Miller, Central Park Conservancy.)

the stretch that ran by the top of the Mall and exited at 72nd Street and Central Park West. The wealthy, the aristocratic, and the notorious were represented, all splendidly, or less splendidly, awheel. The socially assured, the Jays, Livingstons, Van Rensselaers, Stuyvesants, and such, affected the stodgy brougham, pulled by fat old horses under the reins of elderly coachmen. Glass paneling concealed those within. Carriages were most common. Those of the wealthy, such as that of Jim Fisk, the financier, were resplendent and gleaming. So were the teams. People riding in them were clearly visible, as were those in the barouches and victorias. Young things, the Beautiful People of that time, dashed along in phaetons, light rigs with a groom perched on back.

Among the notorious regularly in the cavalcade was the impressively

The ornate wooden Victorian bandstand, designed by Jacob Wrey Mould of Olmsted's staff, was vividly painted in bright contrasting colors. Park concerts were a popular pastime.
(Herbert Mitchell Collection.)

Daily carriage parade. This colorful event was much enjoyed by participants and spectators alike. The drawing, done in the mid-1880s, shows the procession at four in the afternoon, when the display was at its height. (New York Historical Society.)

beautiful Josie Woods, her glinting ebony tresses bordering a finely chiseled face. She was mistress of the town's most exclusive bordello on Clinton Place. She rode richly attired in silks and expensive jewelry, her equipage a dignified black. Black, too, was the carriage of Madame Restell, the English-born woman who was the city's leading abortionist, full of money and scandalous secrets. Her dress was always expensively demure but her horses spirited. The common folk gawked. And returned next day.

The parade had an effect on the local economy. Carriage makers throve. Before the Park, there had been almost no pleasure driving here, Olmsted said. But within twelve years after its inception, at least ten thousand horses were being kept for that purpose. And, of course, vehicles had to be made for them to pull.

The Park created another rise in industry, also connected with horseflesh. This was the business of saddlers. When the Park began, Olmsted noted again, there were not half a dozen New Yorkers who kept horses for riding. Nor among all the many suggestions made in advance for Park features was there one for space to be devoted to horseback riding. However, with the six miles of bridle paths that were turned out under the Greensward plan, hundreds of equestrians soon were trotting over them daily. Olmsted was proud of this. He wrote that the space "given to bridle roads was larger than that of all the bridle roads in all of the parks of London, and in three years after the plan had been settled upon more had been done at the Central Park for the encouragement of pleasure riding than had been done in ten times as many years in all the other cities of the world." Despite this leap in early activity atop a horse, the most colorful and flamboyant part of this Park pastime was still half a century off.

Just north of the Ball Ground was a large flat area. On the Greensward plan, this was the Parade Ground that had been mandated by terms of the competition. Olmsted had no real desire to see a military use of the Park. His reaction is shown in his testy note of 1864: "Two regiments of the National Guard paraded illegally in the Park." And again in his attitude toward the military display that accompanied the 1877 visit of President Rutherford B. Hayes to the Park for a statue unveiling. Firing off a letter to the head of the Parks Department, Olmsted said that with its whoopla and ability to attract hordes of spectators, the visit by the military had created chaos and much damage: "the crowd was essentially a mob, *lawless and uncontrollable.*" Italics Olmsted's. He was happy, then, when the Parade Ground became the Sheep Meadow. With some satisfaction, he realized that soldierly drills would never turn the turf there into a dustbowl.

*W*HILE THE PARK as it developed was soon acclaimed a *5*
success, success was not assured at the start of its construction. Olmsted was aware of this. He realized that it
constituted a hitherto untried sociopolitical experiment,
one that might very well fail. He wished the Park to be for
all the city's people. Many of these, of course, were
newly arrived immigrants, burdened by little knowledge of
politesse and by its opposite, brash behavior. How would
these newcomers get along in the freedom of the Park
with our more genteel, established residents? No one really knew. European parks with which Olmsted was familiar, and which he felt worked very well, were in countries
where populations had long been homogeneous.

Had Olmsted lacked doubts about the potential social
hazard in the plan for a cosmopolitan park, there was no
lack of others to remind him. The year he took over his
post as architect-in-chief, an editorial in *The New York
Herald* had this to say on the subject:

> It is folly to expect in this country to have parks like those in
> old aristocratic countries. When we open a public park, Sam
> will air himself in it. He will take his friends, whether from
> Church Street, or elsewhere. He will knock down any bet-
> ter-dressed man who remonstrated with him. He will talk
> and sing, and fill his share of the bench, and flirt with the
> nursery maids in his own coarse way. Now we have to ask
> what chance have William B. Astor and Edward Everett
> against this fellow citizen of theirs? Can they and he enjoy
> the same place? Is it not obvious that he will turn them out,
> and that the great Central Park will be nothing but a great
> bear-garden for the lowest denizens of the city, of which we
> shall yet pray litanies to be delivered?

In a few years, however, the *Herald* had reversed its
stand, saying, "When one is inclined to despair of the
country, let him go to the Central Park of a Saturday, and
spend a few hours there in looking at people, not those
who come in gorgeous carriages, but those who arrive on

foot, or in those exceedingly democratic conveyances, the street-cars; and if, when the sun begins to sink behind the trees, he does not arise and go homeward with a happy, swelling heart."

Attendance also increased. In 1867, visitors came to a grand total of 2,998,770 pedestrians, 84,994 equestrians, and 1,381,697 vehicles. These were recorded by the Park's uniformed policemen, a body created and directed by Olmsted and stationed at its various gates. There was little disorder. For the year mentioned above, the ratio of arrests to that of visitors was 1 in 60,000. For the four-year period ending in 1866, those arrested for fast driving, the major violation, numbered 232. All other infractions during the four years amounted to 209. In 1868, the commissioners' annual report declared: "Nothing has occurred during the year to disturb good order." In general, the commissioners felt, "Of the great numbers that visit the Park, but a very small portion require the hand of authority to check mischievous practices. The quietude of the grounds, the natural beauties, and the order that prevails, are invitations to enjoyment, and are all, by the mere eloquence of their silent teachings, effectual appeals to sustain, rather than transgress, the necessary regulations for their preservation," thus confirming with facts and figures the *Herald*'s later attitude.

The orderly folk in the Park's early days had much to enjoy. Portents of tree-shaded floors and sunlit clearings steadily appeared. The genesis of shadowy woods and wide-skirted meads showed themselves in and around the Ramble. Paths passed under embryonic hangings of greenery. Meanwhile, construction of the Park continued throughout the Civil War. It was wisely decided that interruption of the program would be too costly in terms of the deterioration of work already done.

By 1870 there was something in the Park for every city resident. The rich had their bridle paths and carriage roads. But the privileged folk, who rode, were free, of course, to join—and many did—with the less well-to-do and the poorest in the ice skating on the frozen water surfaces, where games of curling also took place. All of the city's families, as well, could bring their infants and children, with or without nursemaids, to the quiet recesses that lay behind the Park's cut-stone walls, treat the older ones to rides on the Carousel or in goat wagons or on saddle donkeys, sail their craft on the toy-boat pool, buy snacks for them at the Dairy, or picnic on the greensward. Or, on a torrid day, sip ice water from drinking fountains, cooled by blocks of ice in a pit below them, perhaps a surprising touch to a reader today.

All adults, too, could hire rowboats for a turn upon the Lake, or ride for a modest sum in one of the multiseated, motor-powered Swanboats that toured its confines, stopping at the Lake's six landings to receive and discharge passengers. Concerts in the Bandstand on the Mall were so popular that the street railway companies had to put on extra cars to accommodate the throngs coming from downtown. At other times a brass band played from a barge upon the Lake. These musicales were highly gregarious occasions as everyone mingled around the Bandstand and along the shore.

Simpler, wholesome activities were available to everyone. Among the most popular were strolling or sitting contemplatively in the Park on one of the seats or benches provided in the many shelters, or under the open sky. According to a contemporary text, "a man may sit for hours and hear no sound but the chirp and twitter of the birds, the rustle of the light breeze overhead, or the far-off murmur of the town."

Transient but nonetheless enjoyable features of the Park in the early

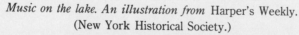

Music on the lake. An illustration from Harper's Weekly.
(New York Historical Society.)

years were a herd of deer; gilded birdcages set atop carved stone mounts peopled with singing inhabitants; gay ensigns flying from lofty ornamental staffs around the Esplanade; rustic bee hives with their murmurous swarms, resplendent peacocks and their less colorful hens could be seen traipsing the lawns, as could swans gliding over the various waters beneath which in those days muskrats swam. In the coverts, quail, both Eastern and California, prospered and produced progeny. To the delight of the young, a camel from the menagerie often pulled the lawnmower, a new contraption. Previously the grass had been cut by scythe, producing in the hands of an expert wielder a sweet whistle; the newfangled mower, however, gave a smoother greensward, whether pulled by the camel or not.

Elsewhere across the Park, in nooks and moist hollows heavy with mosses and ferns, there were spots that bore "the delicate flavor of wildness where civilization has been put to rout," where each spring there blossomed fragile and lovely wildflowers: adders' tongues, anemones, bloodroots, cardinal flowers, columbines, and hepaticas. The Park in those early days could never be said to stagnate under monotony. It enjoyed a gentle, bucolic life of its own. Those early years, in all probability, have never been equaled in sylvan serenity and visitor affability.

The last important aquatic element created by Olmsted in the Park was in the rugged, picturesque north. There the flow of a stream known as Montayne's Rivulet was led by design northeastward across the site's entire width aboveground, the only case with the Park water sources in which this was done. The others were confined in pipes underground. Montayne's Rivulet emerged from a high ridge along the western border at about 101st Street and Central Park West and crossed a deep valley that on a glowering, cloudy day still evokes in a visitor's mind a dark Highland glen. First it formed the Pool, then the Loch, and finally the Meer, named for the Dutch word for lake, the second largest of Olmsted's water bodies, then a sizable sheet of some fourteen acres. It lay in the northeast corner of the Park and was its lowest point, only five feet above sea level.

The Pool, a charming pond, tree-bordered and planted with water lilies, held a small rocky island. Water descended from it in a brook to the Loch, narrow and long, whose outflow was carried downhill by another stream to the Meer, which also had an island. The downhill flow from the Pool to the Meer tumbled over a series of cascades, colorful and splashing, forming a plentiful rivulet. At that time, water still flowed into the Park along

*In the early days a camel from the menagerie behind the Arsenal
often supplied motive power for the Park's lawnmower.*
(Herbert Mitchell Collection.)

the historical courses and, with precipitation caught in drains provided by
Olmsted, gave enough inflow to maintain desired levels. However, as
residential and commercial construction around the Park increased, these
sources were disrupted or cut off. Now water comes from the wide system of Olmsted's run-off drains and from city water pipe led into the Park.
Mostly from city water.

This uptown section had a high bluff at its northern end overlooking the
level plain of Harlem. Near the top of its southern face a natural spring,
according to a post–Civil War writer, ran "with a musical tinkle down the

slopes, falling from one rocky or reedy basin to another, until, at length, in a series of pretty miniature cascades, it reached a circular pool on the level ground at the foot of the hill." On the other side, at the bottom of the north face of the bluff, was the Lily Pond, so named for its floral planting. Atop the cliff stood remnants of military works dating from the War of 1812, namely the site of Nutter's Battery, those of Forts Fish and Clinton, and the Blockhouse, the most distinctive of all, the oldest of the structures then in the Park, a ruined, square, stone fortification with open gun ports, whose roof had fallen in. Olmsted left them alone, seeing them as primitive embellishments for a primitive part of the Park. They posed him no problem.

What did pose a problem, however, were the reservoirs some half a mile to the south. The smaller, an old rectangular sink of thirty-seven acres, whose site is now the Great Lawn, lay just below the larger, the then-new reservoir of more than a hundred acres, the one present in the Park today. The larger reservoir practically cut the Park in two, coming close, especially on the east, to the actual border. This notably complicated the designing job. Siting developments around the new reservoir was difficult. In one respect, however, the new reservoir was helpful. Instead of following the original intention of having it cover the land in a square from Fifth to Seventh avenues and from 86th to 96th streets, members of the Croton Aquaduct Board and the Central Park commissioners got together. They traded territory so that the reservoir could, with the same capacity, follow natural depressions in the Park and have a winding shoreline, thus avoiding the unsightly, artificial, boxy look of the older storage body.

In treating the terrain around the two, Olmsted screened the old reservoir as much as possible with trees. The banks of the new reservoir were so high that for visitors to appreciate its expanse, a path, now heavily used by joggers, was built around it. Outside this, Olmsted encircled the reservoir with a bridle path. Riders along it had a view not only across the wide stretch of water but, because of its elevation, over much of the rest of the young, low-treed Park as well. To the east, the new reservoir's shoreline left little space for a carriage road between it and the Park's Fifth Avenue border. To counteract this as best he could, Olmsted contrived a high bank to be planted with trees leading up to the reservoir level. Thus persons on the carriage road below could not see the reservoir. Instead they felt they were traveling through a very narrow section of the Park.

For the carriage road and the pedestrian walkway, there was no choice but to lay these out south to north as straightaways, the only such in the Park. The carriage road with its nearly half-mile of beeline was the Park's racetrack. Carriage racing, a major nuisance of the day, had been thwarted elsewhere by intentionally curving the roads. On this stretch, though, the scorchers had their contests. Most of the two hundred and thirty-four mentioned earlier as having been arrested for fast driving were apprehended here and quickly fined.

To the west, the larger body of water allowed somewhat more room. There, lining the western carriage road, Olmsted placed conifers to form the Winter Drive. Scores of evergreens to color the barren months of the year were set out along a mile and a half of the roadway. For contrast, some groves of deciduous trees and turfy glades were also included, the whole to give the impression of driving through a richly forested district.

During the Park's creation, Olmsted's chief assistants were Vaux; another English architect, Jacob Wrey Mound; and Ignaz Anton Pilat, the accomplished Austrian horticulturist who earlier had surveyed the Park flora.

Vaux furnished most of the architectural grace notes. Among the more important were the bridges, all of a different design. Some were prettily constructed of cast iron, a favored material of the day; others were masonry or timber, each with an individual twist. Also by Vaux were the arched passageways under the roads, including the lovely white Marble Arch below the East Drive near the south end of the Mall, only a remembered grace note now due to road rerouting. Other arches, often richly designed and decorative, were of various types of stone or brick. Frequently there were drinking fountains within them as well as seats.

Vaux did most of the Park buildings as well. Olmsted firmly believed a rural scene was not a rural scene without an appropriate building or two. But of equal, if not greater, importance, they served the needs of the public. The Dairy, the Kinderberg Arbor, the Belvedere Castle with its elevated terraces commanding wide views, the Carousel, and the Ballplayers House were some of these. Smaller and ancillary structures were also largely attributable to Vaux. All tended to be unpretentious and often were made of unstripped cedar. Among them were the rustic shelters, the covered boat landings, the large Dove Cote roofed over with wire, the pillared bird cages, and bee hives and pergolas, many of which under the ravages of time eventually disappeared. In addition, and most crucial, Vaux was privy to Olmsted's thinking, offering advice on landscaping as well as architectural details. On more than one occasion, Vaux acted to stabilize the moods of his mercurial partner, who could be mercurial in wholesale fashion, a frequent characteristic, of course, of genius.

Mould often collaborated with Vaux, but he alone was responsible for the design of the Esplanade, by the Lake, one of the principal architectural components of the Park. A feature was the lovely stone carvings of flora and fauna on the sides of the balustrades flanking the imposing double set of stairs leading down from the Terrace to the brightly tiled paving of the Esplanade below. Mould had had experience with stately staircases. One he had put into Holford House, a London mansion, at a time when currency was in an uninflated state, cost £56,000. That, with the pound's worth then at nearly $5, equaled better than a $250,000, a formidable sum at a time when $10,000 was a fortune. The passage under the 72nd Street road at the top of the Mall led out through a corridor between the two staircases to the Esplanade. A contemporary observer described it as a "large and delightfully cool hall." Its ceiling was covered with colorful Minton tiles set in gilded ironwork, perhaps the first instance when tiles were used on a ceiling in this country. Their complicated attachment has required some tricky innovation during the Park's current rehabilitation. Mould's Esplanade with its various details was judged by architects of the period as the equal of any constructional unit in the world, not excluding the recently completed Houses of Parliament in London.

Mould designed the Sheepfold as well, now the Tavern on the Green restaurant. It too is considered one of the finest examples extant of its kind of Victorian architecture, the cottage type.

Pilat, well trained in his homeland, had been, before coming to this country, a gardener to Prince von Metternich, the European statesman and aristocrat. As chief landscape architect, Pilat had charge, under Olmsted's direction, of planning the Park's groves, shrubs, herbs, and gardens. In these chores, however, both he and Olmsted were guided by a powerful but absent confederate, a deceased English parson, born a century before Olmsted, by name the Reverend William Gilpin, perhaps the world's greatest proponent of trees. His two-volume work, *Forest Scenery,* had come into Olmsted's hands as a child at the Hartford Public Library. Its ideas strongly influenced Olmsted then and throughout his life.

OPPOSITE. A nineteenth-century view of the Ramble, the knoll of some thirty-odd acres that lies across from the American Museum of Natural History. Having enjoyed the early care of Pilat, it still retains its feeling of wooded remoteness. (Parks Department Annual Report.)

Gilpin lived and traveled widely in the New Forest in the south of England. He was a keen and poetic observer of trees, singly and en masse. He regarded trees as the foundation of all scenery, writing, "It is no exaggerated praise to call a tree the grandest and most beautiful of all the productions of the earth." Not only did he consider, and consider in detail, the qualities of most English trees seen in all conditions of health, but even those in conditions of debility. Examples herewith of both: "To the adventitious beauties of trees, we may add their susceptibility of motion, which is capable at least of being a considerable source of beauty. The waving heads of some, and the undulations of others, give a continual variety to their forms. In Nature the motion of trees is certainly a circumstance of great beauty. Shakespeare formerly made the observation:

—Things in motion sooner catch the eye
Than what stirs not—"

And for the second: "The use and beauty of the withered top and curtailed trunk. . . . These splendid remnants of decaying grandeur speak to the imagination in a style of eloquence, which the stripling cannot reach; they record the history of some storm, some blast of lightning, or other great event, that transfer its grand idea to the landscape; and in the representation of elevated subjects assists the sublime."

But the reverend also turned his microscopic eye and voluble pen onto arboreal associates—the ivies, lichens, liverworts, mosses, and woodbine—saying of these that they were the ornaments and jewelry of a tree, the foliage being the dress.

Olmsted accepted Gilpin's feeling about the importance of trees. Often he followed his advice, such as in placing elms on the Mall. Gilpin wrote that "in leaf no tree is better adapted to receive large masses of light" and also that it "leafs early, a light and cheerful green." Luminosity and early greenery were attributes Olmsted wanted for the Mall. In went elms, *à la* Gilpin. Another instance: In his later career, Olmsted told young men coming into his landscape firm to read Gilpin as carefully as a law student would Blackstone.

Gilpin's influence is most profoundly indicated when one considers a remark Olmsted made more than once in his life: "What artist so noble as he who, with the far reaching conception of beauty and designing power, sketches the outlines, arranges the colors, and directs the shadows of a picture upon which nature shall be employed for generations before the work he has prepared for her hand shall realize his intentions."

In a landscape such as the Park, Olmsted could be referring only to trees and their little sisters, the shrubs. The other scenic components, the rocks, the lawns, and the expanses of water, once set into the design, would stay forever the same. Thus Gilpin had set his seal on Olmsted. And it was a happy imposition. For although possessed of craggy out-crops, smooth lawns, and glinting sheets of water, what would Central Park be without trees?

Pilat was mindful of this, too, completing a happy Olmstedian family of those who sought to bring design linked to nature into our city of stone.

With a top echelon of helpers—three living European experts, two of them British-born, and one additional Britisher, although a distinctly dead one—the devoutly Anglophilic architect-in-chief must have felt marvel-ously content, warmly parental, and extremely well served within his official family during the years he was developing the site.

Besides using botany to beautify the Park and assuage the visitor, Olmsted wished to make it an international arboretum of such distinction as to startle the world. Thus he sought specimens of every tree that might thrive there regardless of origin. By 1868, three hundred and thirty-four species, most of them exotics (that is, nonnatives), had been introduced. Eighty-nine were conifers, the rest deciduous. They included the Abnor-mal Norway Spruce, the Bhotan Pine, the Mt. Atlas Cedar, the Siberian Crab, the European Nettle, and the Chinese Elm. Native trees numbered one hundred and fourteen species and foreign one hundred and fifty-three. Sixty-three were of hybrid or cultivated origin. In addition, the Park then contained species of three hundred and ninety-two shrubs, seventy-four vines, and fifty-one herbaceous plants. Nineteen were unclassified forms.

Most of the credit for this diversity goes, of course, to Pilat, who was extremely adept at locating and obtaining uncommon botanical species from afar. Once in hand, he placed and nurtured them with exceptional skill.

But for economy's sake, there were other sources. Two nurseries were established in the Park to propagate seed and nurture very small and inexpensive purchases from local nurseries until planting time. One was near the area back of the Arsenal. The other stood on the site of the present Conservatory Gardens at Fifth Avenue and 105th Street. This site had a heated greenhouse ninety-four feet long by twenty-five feet wide wherein occasional gifts of rare tropical plants were cared for— although where or how these plants were later used is not made clear in the commissioners' annual reports. Nearby was a propagating house thirty feet long by twelve feet wide. Official accounts credit the nurseries, under Pilat's management, with contributing to the Park, aided by thinnings from overgrown Park plantations, more than eighty-nine thousand specimens, including hundreds of good-sized trees.

An interesting planting, not from the nurseries, went onto Cherry Hill, a knoll overlooking the Terrace to the west. It consisted of two members of the largest species of tree, the giant sequoia *(Sequoia gigantea)*. An example standing today in Sequoia National Park in south central California dwarfs the records of all other living things. Based on that tree's height of two hundred fifty-odd feet and an estimated weight of more than a thousand tons, perhaps it's well for the self-confidence of other Park flora that the pair of potentially dendroidal monsters didn't survive— although in the late 1860s they were thriving.

*C*ONSTRUCTION was a huge job. Swamps and marshes were drained. Extensive blasting took place. Much unwanted rock, the hard metamorphic stuff that underlies Manhattan, in evidence in many areas of the site or just below the surface, had to be removed. A crowbar punched downward a few inches usually struck it. Twenty thousand eight hundred pounds of gunpowder were used to oust it. The rubble went into foundations for the perimeter walls, as bog fill, as edging for paths, or shorelines; it was used to form gutters or was hauled away.

Olmsted was grateful for several flat spots. The two largest were each about ten acres. The first lay along Fifth Avenue between 67th and 72nd streets. It had been a pasture and market garden; now it is the Dene and the East Green. The other lay to the west and, although part swamp, is presently the Sheep Meadow. The only other appreciably level area was one of three acres south of today's Mall.

To finish the job, nearly five million cubic yards of stone, earth, and topsoil were moved into, or out of, the Park, a total calculated to equal ten million one-horse cartloads. Much top soil was needed to get things to grow. Over half a million cubic yards were brought in, mostly from Long Island and New Jersey. Muck, with its organic matter, dredged from the bogs, was added to it.

Fertilization, besides, was required, and several methods were tried. Horse manure, some of it from the carriage roads, was composted with grass cuttings once a few lawns were established. Topsoil, Peruvian and native guano, and poudrette, a manure made of dried nightsoil mixed with charcoal and gypsum, were other agents of enrichment. The ground, freed of undulations and contours, was stirred with a plow to a depth of fourteen to eighteen inches. Where plowing was difficult, spading was done. The fertilizer of one mix or another was then added, the ground roughly releveled, and the planting done. After this came the smoothing of the final surface.

Occasionally, before this process, buckwheat was sown and, when in full bloom, turned under as green manure, after which raw horse manure was spread, compost added, and the whole turned under again.

All told, the construction and the horticultural preparation, which came under Pilat, was equivalent to turning over the entire surface of the Park to a depth of almost four feet. The number of men to do this peaked in July 1859, with thirty-eight hundred employed. But hundreds of others worked there consistently for years.

Park administration (as well as design) was Olmsted's piece of cake, something of which he correctly felt himself the master. An important aspect of this was policing. The first force, the special police, formed to eject the squatters, was disbanded in early 1858. Shortly thereafter a contingent of twenty-four men was appointed. Called park keepers, they operated under Olmsted's direction. Almost immediately they were increased to thirty-two. By 1860 Olmsted had at his bidding fifty uniformed and well-disciplined officers. He saw to that. The gates were each guarded by an officer. Others patrolled the Park. Some were on horseback. Now, more than one hundred and twenty-five years later, this is recognized as probably the most effective way of policing a place, such as Central Park, where observation, pursuit, and apprehension of criminals is impeded by vegetation.

In addition, an officer on a horse in the Park is a commanding figure. He is a yard or so higher off the ground then he otherwise would be and visible from afar by would-be miscreants. His mere presence thus tends to curb criminal activity. For his part, he has an elevated, wide-ranging view of the surroundings. More significantly, he has the means under him to follow a suspect off the roads and paths and through the shrubbery at a pace faster than a man can run.

Olmsted supplied explicit and admirable instructions to his men. Copies of these were posted at various points in the Park for information of both police and users. They focused on public service. For instance, "A keeper finding a visitor sick, swooning, sun-stricken, deranged, paralyzed, in stupor, or apparently drugged or intoxicated, may suspend all other duties either to help him find relief or leave the park," and "He is not to try to surprise visitors, or to play the detective; is not to move furtively, or use slyness, in any way, for any purpose." Visitors, on the other hand, were told that in case of a crisis they must expect to be moved immediately out of the affected area to another, there to remain till the crisis was past.

One of Olmsted's mounted police officers, part of a force that operated
with great efficiency in the 1860s and 1870s.
(Herbert Mitchell Collection.)

To be as helpful as possible to the public, Olmsted also placed the following notice in the Keepers Room:

> I propose soon to make an examination of the keepers to ascertain how each is informed in regard to his duty, especially as to his ability to direct strangers to different parts of the Park, to instruct them as to distances, size, purposes, cost, etc. of different objects in the Park, as to his knowledge of the proper method of proceeding under certain circumstances, etc.
>
> On all points where information, likely to be inquired for by visitors, is lacking, I propose to supply it, and shall be glad to answer any inquiries with regard to Park matters, which may be proper subjects of public interest.

Commendations for Olmsted's police piled up in the early years. They were accepted and highly respected by the public. In 1860, the Senate Investigating Committee praised "the well-organized force of fifty men . . . styled Park Keepers. . . . The Keepers are in the prime of life and have been taken mainly from among the foremen and mechanics employed in the construction of the Park. They are neatly uniformed, subject to military drills and discipline, and their well-established efficiency and popularity evince the discrimination with which they are trained for their duty."

Later annual reports of the Park board confirmed the success with which Olmsted's keepers functioned. The document in 1864 noted the trend to "conform to prescribed regulations—the larger portion of arrests are for fast driving." In 1868 the board could say that the law-abiding trend continued; arrests were less than the previous year.

All these remarks show how well the force was doing its job. For its aim was to preserve tranquility, not restore it. This desirable state of affairs was entirely the work of Olmsted. He constantly held the men to his standards. What he wanted was made easier to achieve, of course, by imparting his knowledge of how the lawmen could operate best in the woods and meadows he had created. During the tenure of his police force, Olmsted was able to say with some pride that arrests in the Park amounted to only twenty per million users. In all likelihood, this period was the most lawabiding the Park has ever seen.

The other principal leg of Park administration, as Olmsted saw it, was maintenance. In his day, that meant forestry work and gardening. No need existed, as it does today, to care for a worn infrastructure, clogged drains, or restoration of outworn paraphernalia. Everything then was spanking new. But trees and vegetation had their changing seasons. They had to be tended.

Delicate specimens particularly required experienced gardeners. But experience in horticulture did not exclude such individuals from Olmsted's strict guidelines. For example, "No gardener," he said, "should use the discretion given him to secure pretty little local effects, at the expense of general effects, and especially of broad landscape effects." Concerning capable gardeners, a tribe he valued highly, Olmsted wrote, "The loss of a man of this class can not be replaced by a new one in two year's time, as well as that of a foreman, a policeman, a clerk in any position can in two months."

Until the death in 1870 of Pilat, his prized head gardener, Olmsted had high-quality horticultural help. But even in Pilat's time, and more notably thereafter, the gardening staff was undermanned, due to insufficient appropriation. This has been true throughout much of the Park's history. To counteract it as much as possible, Olmsted instituted a plan, now being considered for retrial, in which he made a certain area, reasonable in size, the duty of one gardener. Thus a single individual, and no one else, was responsible for its appearance. It was a sound psychological tactic and produced good results.

Outside the Park, development went on apace. Houses were springing up, so elevations had to be smoothed out. The Park's original uneven surface was duplicated out there. Today on the island we have relatively level streets, but those were obtained in days past through filling in hollows by cutting off bumps. This development illustrates, in apt fashion, Manhattan's original name. It comes from the language of the indigenous Indians, the Wappinger Confederacy of the Algonquin tribe, who called our island Manah-atin, or "Island of hills."

*O*LMSTED was forced to battle a pair of antagonists in implementing his grand design. His bouts with them were in addition, of course, to all the problems that inevitably arise in the course of any large-scale construction, and Central Park was a large-scale construction, indeed. The opponents fall into two time frames. The first, from about 1858 to 1865, was in the person of Andrew Haswell Green, the most powerful member of the Board of Commissioners, Central Park's ruling body. Green was far from being an evil man. In fact, he was in many ways an exemplary one, among the most powerful and admirable figures in New York City's nineteenth-century history. But his ingrained, obsessive concern with the disbursement of public funds drove the temperamental Olmsted almost wild.

The confrontation was made the more trying for Olmsted because, while he was an artist with an artist's temperament, he was also a crack administrator. He knew this himself. So did others. A contemporary, intimate with Olmsted and his work in the Park, said, "Few Americans in our time have shown so great administrative abilities." Of course, this condition is an anomaly—an artist who is a skilled administrator. But that was the case with Olmsted—really an anomaly himself. On his administrative side, he knew how to spend money efficiently, how to get prompt results. But instead, his plans for putting the Park together were continually delayed or frustrated by what he regarded as Green's senseless interference and penury.

By the middle of 1865, Green's status in regard to Olmsted underwent a change. He became Olmsted's defender against the second antagonist, a foe that actually threatened them both. This was Tammany Hall, whose politicians wanted both Green and Olmsted out of the way so they could use Central Park's hundreds of jobs as a patronage source. Green's attitude toward money at this point had not changed. He was as penny-pinching and prying as ever. By now, however, Olmsted had become somewhat hardened to the burdens. And he appreciated being able to work behind the doughty Green. For Olmsted recognized that Tammany Hall wanted nothing less than his removal, by one means or another. This could never be accomplished so long as Green held his powerful position, which, at this time, was comptroller of the city.

As for that gentleman, let's begin at the beginning. When his path first crossed that of Olmsted in 1858, Green was thirty-eight years old, two years Olmsted's senior. He was born in Worcester, Massachusetts, of well-to-do parents and early acquired a love of nature and an appreciation of landscaping from his family's estate. He studied law and soon became a partner in the firm of Samuel Tilden, one of the most prominent of the locals, a man who eventually was to run unsuccessfully for the presidency. Green moved early into civic affairs. In 1857 he was appointed one of the original members of the Park's Board of Commissioners. Throughout his tenure, he dominated his colleagues by his strong character and his superior knowledge of nature. In successive steps, he was the board's treasurer, president, and finally its comptroller.

Green gained influence from his association with Tilden. But this was superfluous. He was awesome in his own right, a determined, unreconstructed autocrat. And he had many advantages with which to enforce his opinions. He was handsome, he was energetic, intelligent, well connected, and eminent in his profession. Despite all this, he never married. One biographer has said this was just as well. To impose his inflexible character upon a wife would have been cruel and unusual punishment, for offspring a disaster.

Considering Green's influence on Olmsted, his actions were ironic. Green loved Central Park. Furthermore, he understood the importance of Olmsted's continued association with it, echoing what another of that time has said: "The public will never know all that it owes in the possession of the Park to Mr. Olmsted's vigor; to his quiet, earnest zeal; to his integrity, and to the abundance of his resources." But Green could only be Green. The core of his nature seemed to be that his true religion was the care and conservation of public money and the exact balancing of accounts—down to the last penny. The fervor displayed by Green in this could truly be called bizarre. Continually it alienated people. Perhaps Green realized it. But he could not, or would not, change. His considerable achievements came notwithstanding this.

Comptroller is simply another word for controller. A controller is an officer appointed to check expenditures. As the Park's Board comptroller, was Green a controller?

Green was perhaps the nineteenth century's controller nonpareil, an expenditure checker beyond compare. He delegated no detail of this authority to anyone. He once even examined the cost of pencils for the Park's draftsmen hard at work on the Arsenal's upper floors. The verdict: profligacy with pencils. Accordingly, he banned all further pencil purchases. The draftsmen, to do their work, had to buy their own. This is just one example of Green's financial routine.

Having glanced briefly at Green's character, let us take a look at Olmsted's. Contrasts between the two men are sharp. Olmsted was a husband and a father. He was liberal in his trust and reasonable in his attitude toward money. But the pair had one crucial similarity. Both were autocrats. And to be fair, there may have been stress on both sides of the fence. Green knew this facet of Olmsted. "An overwhelming personality," he once called him. But unlike Green, Olmsted was a beloved autocrat.

The following passage notes this along with other salient features of Olmsted's character, as seen by a female co-worker in the 1860s:

> His face is generally very placid, with the expressive delicacy of a woman's, and would be beautiful were it not for an expression I cannot fathom—something which is perhaps a little too severe about it. I think his mouth and smile and the expression of his eyes at times very beautiful. He has a great variety of expressions: sometimes stern, thoughtful and haggard; at other times observing and slightly satirical (I believe he sees out of the back of his head occasionally): and then again, and not seldom, his face wears an inspired look, full of goodness and power. I think he is a man of the most resolute self-will, generally a very wise will, I should think: born an autocrat, however, and as such, very satisfactory to be under.

The authoritative streak in Olmsted that enabled him so often to make sweeping decisions, ones that were also often humane, generous, and wise, was evident throughout his life. But in the period 1858 to 1865, this fundamental trait in his character caused him to suffer grievously in dealings with Green, his superior.

From the first, Olmsted knew his place and he tried to be a cooperative subordinate. But he had to face, and swallow, such acts as Green's failure to approve a small sum for caulking a bridge which, closed to the public, caused serious pedestrian damage to the turf and plants around it. Or the failure to allow progress on another bridge because of a one-dollar overage on an estimate. And he had to take such scoldings as, "Although an error is not a crime, yet in money matters it is a very serious affair." The reproof was occasioned by Green's discovery of a bookkeeping blunder: a laborer had been paid $12 while serving some days in jail. Here was Olmsted trying to perfect a masterpiece through the labor of hundreds of workmen. Green meanwhile held him personally accountable for a minor bookkeeping mistake. Such actions cost the highstrung Olmsted dearly. He was sometimes literally paralyzed when he had to discuss financial estimates with Green. Insomnia, stomach trouble, and headaches were the result. Olmsted's will was rugged. His body was not.

In September of 1859, eighteen months after his appointment, the architect-in-chief was a tired, sick man. Green had not helped. Neither had Tammany. Worthies there continually sent hundreds of inexperienced, unqualified men to interview Olmsted for Park jobs. To Tammany Hall they were valuable; they had votes to give or sell. To Olmsted their value was nil. He knew, of course, that rejecting them was earning future trouble for himself. But he was nothing if not a principled man. He simply refused to hire incompetents, politically backed or not. Still they constituted a worry and a time-consuming distraction that he certainly did not need on top of Green and the unavoidable stresses of managing construction, at which, of course, he characteristically overworked.

What gave way was the Achilles' heel in his makeup, his nervous system. In turn, this affected his general health, as was to be the case in at least one more instance in his life.

Toward the end of September 1859, the board granted Olmsted a three-month leave and $500 with which to visit Europe on a working vacation and take stock of its parks. Green, of course, was behind the project, and he sent Olmsted off with an unexpected, kindly word, implying that he felt the architect-in-chief was already so qualified that he had little to learn from European parks. The architect-in-chief for his part was grateful, if somewhat surprised.

On his arrival abroad, Olmsted was a bit amazed to find that the fame of Central Park had already reached the Continent. He was cordially received wherever he went. Every door opened wide. In the midst of his triumphant progress, he received another atypical gesture from Green. A letter urged Olmsted to cultivate assiduously his physical improvement and tranquility: "Let health and repose be *the first thing.*"

Olmsted's repose, though, was not heightened by other news from home. Correspondents wrote that Green was being his old self, obstructive as usual, his quibbles and persistent scrimping undermining the production of the whole Park staff, interfering with the installation of the vital, large-scale drainage system, improperly rushing the planting, and doing likewise with roadway construction, to its detriment.

Accepting these melancholy, though unsurprising, tidings as best he could, Olmsted continued on his tour. Parks, forests, and public grounds in England, France, Belgium, and Ireland were inspected, many very thoroughly, a matter of several dozen all told. Their gardeners, managers, foresters, and security people were all interviewed. What they had to say fell on fertile ground. Olmsted tucked their words away in his mind to augment notions he already possessed, verbal seed that was later to sprout healthily in the center of Manhattan. He returned to the United States in late December immersed more than ever in the lore of parks and how best to provide for, and entertain, their users.

In the next year Olmsted nearly lost his life. That August, with his wife and infant, he was driving a buggy up the west side of the island behind a horse he was thinking of buying. On the way back at 155th Street, the animal bolted, smashing a carriage wheel on a lamp post and throwing out the three occupants. Wife and baby were not seriously injured. Olmsted, however, struck a rock, damaging his left knee and gruesomely shattering the thigh bone in three places, the fragments protruding through the trouser leg. Amputation at the groin was vetoed because of his weakness. Death would have resulted. Doctors, however, viewed him as doomed in any case. Survival time was put at a week.

But there was, as has been stated, an inner resiliency to the man, a constitution that was deceptively sturdy. Week after week, instead of dying, he slowly recovered. Within a month he had rallied sufficiently to put some thoughts down on paper. Within two, he was being driven by his wife in a light carriage around the Park, directing the workmen with as much firmness and zeal as though he were whole. In due course he was able to walk without crutches, although his left leg remained two inches shorter than the right.

During his tenure at the Park, Olmsted, often harassed, unhappy, temperamental, and belligerent, submitted his resignation five times. The third and fourth were in conjunction with Vaux, who initiated the third; the fourth was taken jointly. And the fifth was Olmsted's alone. The first three were the result of what was seen as Green's persecution; the latter two came as a consequence of political interference. Olmsted's usual reasons could be grouped under obstacles to his authority (of which the same could be said for Vaux).

Olmsted's first attempted departure came in January of 1861. The cause was Olmsted's unwillingness to face what he felt would be a humiliating public tongue lashing by Green. Olmsted had been asked to put together for the coming twelve months a faultless estimate of Park expenditures. Given the normal uncertainties of supply prices, labor costs, and material availability, it was an assignment Olmsted considered that neither he, nor anyone else, could fulfill and in which he, as the man who would spend the funds, should be given some reasonable leeway. But as he knew the leeway wouldn't be granted, he submitted his resignation rather than be skewered in open court. However, the board's president, knowing Olmsted's value, persuaded him to cancel the gesture before it became public knowledge.

A few months later, in April, the cause again being irritation with Green, the scenario was repeated, again in its entirety. Although after these near rebellions Olmsted continued to remain as the Park's architect-in-chief, the Civil War was by now a full-blown conflict. Fort Sumter had been fired upon and captured. Union troops massing in Washington were soon to go on to Bull Run. Olmsted, an ardent patriot, wanted to serve his country. Barred as a soldier because of his limp, he obtained leave from the Park in June to become secretary in the nation's capital of the newly established United States Sanitary Commission, modeled on the British Sanitary Commission, which had greatly reduced casualities from sickness and poor camp hygiene during the recently ended Crimean War. The United States Sanitary Commission was the forerunner of the American Red Cross. Back at the Park, Vaux was left in charge.

Apart from its display of public spirit, which was a satisfaction to him, Olmsted regarded the shift as one that would be beneficial to both his equanimity and health, conditions that in Olmsted were connected. He felt self-congratulatory. He had escaped the stresses of working with Green without severing his bond with the Park.

But making the move to his country's aid was also indicative of Olmsted's moral rectitude. A prior step that could be said to reflect this was his marriage. His cherished younger brother John had, in 1851, married Mary Perkins, a petite vivacious young woman of good family, the daughter of a physician. But John was sickly and consumptive, and in 1857 he died while in Europe. The closing sentence of his final letter to Olmsted, alight with fraternal devotion, was an admonition: "Don't let Mary suffer while you are alive." Olmsted didn't. Instead of becoming her guardian, he married her, in June of 1859, eighteen months after John's death. Thus he became stepfather to his niece and two nephews, all of whom at this point he was forced to leave in New York. It was an early separation from the woman with whom he was to enjoy many happy decades.

When Olmsted came back from Washington, as he occasionally did on weekends, his wife, knowing his tendency to overwork, once urged him not to exhaust himself utterly on his wartime job. He deprecated his own exertions, saying they were far less than many others', then added characteristically, "It is a time for heroes. And we must be heroes along with the rest."

And it might be that Olmsted was one. As secretary of the Commission, he was its chief executive officer, a circumstance that enabled him to show his superb administrative ability. It was needed. Washington, D.C., in the summer of 1861 was an indescribable maelstrom. Outside the city, where the newly arrived troops were being encamped, Olmsted, in his new capacity, saw a sickening latrine situation, tents so poorly ventilated as to be unsleepable, soldiers infested with lice. All during his term as secretary, he fought hard to correct such conditions, to provide suitable accommodations for casualities, to ease their pain.

At least in part, he was able to do so. His contributions to the war effort were outstanding. Among other things, he wrote a comprehensive report to the secretary of war detailing the results of several hundred inspections of military installations giving the good and bad points of such matters as ambulances, campsites, diseases, hospitals, recreation, surgeons, and other points in his purview and suggesting remedies where needed. He visited war zones to get a practical view of problems. He was at Leesburg, Virginia, after the action, on a hospital ship in Chesapeake Bay during the Peninsular campaign, with Grant at the siege of Vicksburg, on the battlefield after Gettysburg.

Because of his belief in the right of the Union cause, the need to alleviate human suffering and to bring the war as soon as possible to a victorious conclusion, Olmsted imposed on himself a schedule that was near suicidal. As a consequence, he left his post in Washington, disappointed in his achievements, his health again broken. It was a story similar to that of his first eighteen months as architect-in-chief in Central Park. Stresses—and they were ever present in Washington—were stresses that he tried to endure longer than the previous ones because of his devotion to the Union. However, it was no use. He had to yield. A little more than two years after his appointment he resigned in late August of 1863, amid the lamentations of many powerful and important national figures, including some who had opposed his policies.

Meanwhile, several months before this, Vaux had finally had his fill of Green's badgering. He quit. Olmsted in Washington, loyally supporting him, did likewise. Green was aghast. Remember, Green loved Central Park. Remember, also, that Green was an intelligent man. The Park board, firmly under his control, made no move to fill the vacancies. Instead, on Green's motion, it issued a complementary resolution, first accepting the resignations and then saying, *"Resolved,* that on this termination of official relations with Messrs. Olmsted and Vaux, the Board takes pleasure in expressing its high esteem for them personally, and in its unabated confidence in their superior professional abilities." Green, from that moment on, started planning on how to get the two men back.

It could have been an impossibility. While primarily it was Olmsted's health that caused his resignation in Washington, he was also concerned about his finances. With his departure from the Park and his contemplated leavetaking of the Sanitary Commission, there arose the question of funds. Olmsted had confidence in himself. He knew he had managerial ability as indicated when he wrote to his father in 1863, "Businessmen regard me as a man of unusual capacity in several respects, and there are some matters in which it is getting to be thought that I can handle better than anyone else in the country."

And one such group of businessmen came along in the summer of 1863. They wanted Olmsted for the superintendency of a California gold mining property, the Mariposa Estate, which they had just purchased. It was a seventy-square-mile tract lying along the western edges of the Sierra Nevadas, a few miles from lovely Yosemite Valley. Gold mines and unworked quartz veins bearing gold extended in considerable number across it. But it had had an up-and-down history, of which Olmsted was aware. However, a salary of $10,000 a year, four times what he made with the Commission, caused Olmsted finally, although with some misgivings, to accept. A further disenchanting glimpse of his domain's past was revealed to him when, shortly after arrival, he scanned the account books. Mismanagement stared at him from every page. Under Olmsted's two-year rule, its inconstant life, alas, continued, this despite strong and often intelligent countermeasures on his part.

A source of pleasure, though, was the proximity of Yosemite, which he often visited, a steep, rivered gorge with startling yet tranquil scenery— towering cliffs, majestic rock formations, the country's highest waterfall, and groves of noble sequoias. It was so unusual that Congress, even in the midst of the Civil War, passed a law establishing that the valley and trees belonged to the state of California on the stipulation that "the premises shall be held for public use, resort and recreation . . . inalienable for all time." It was a law in whose passage Olmsted had a hand. People today who use the Yosemite National Park are indebted in part to Olmsted.

Thoughts of Central Park persisted even during Olmsted's California period. To get there, Olmsted sailed from New York alone in September of 1863, his family to follow later. His route lay across the Isthmus of Panama and from there up the continent's west coast to San Francisco. On the train trip from the east to the west of Panama, he was excited by the strange, beautiful botany whirling past his coach window. From California, he wrote Pilat that a tropical-type verdure like that which he had seen might, if planted on the islands in the Park's water bodies, make an interesting contrast with the temperate-zone greenery rising around them. He suggested the ailanthus, a species of tree growing in Manhattan, whose feathery leaf sprays and red fall foliage have an equatorial look, as perhaps the appropriate plant.

ꙟ Vaux meanwhile was fidgety and concerned. In friendly letters, he tried to point out that Olmsted's place was not out West with all those grizzly bears, Digger Indians, and God knows what all, but back in the East practicing landscape architecture, at which he was a consummate artist. Vaux's letters were artful. They could not have failed to impress. For one thing, they carried truth. When Vaux wrote that Olmsted was far less of a businessman than a creative adept in recasting and improving unlikely tracts of Mother Earth, Olmsted knew he was hearing gospel. The growing problems at Mariposa opened his ears a bit wider.

In addition, in early 1865, the city fathers in Brooklyn (that faraway land!) had approached Vaux to design another large park for them, the park that today we call Prospect. Understandably, Vaux wanted Olmsted in on it, and told him so. Furthermore, Vaux did not, to the same degree, share his colleague's view of Green. An annoyance, an enduring pebble in the shoe, yes, but not the exasperating monster Olmsted saw. Green sensed this. From May through July of 1865, he made concerted efforts to entice Vaux to return and, somewhat reluctantly, since Vaux would not have it otherwise, Olmsted as well.

Late in July, the two were reappointed architects to Central Park. With the telegraph out of order, Olmsted didn't get his partner's news until the end of August. Winding up his affairs in California, he reached New York in November, ready to go back to work at the profession for which he was so peculiarly suited.

OVERLEAF. Bird's-eye view. An artist looking south from the Lake drawing the Park as he saw it in 1865, late in the Tweed era.
(New York Historical Society.)

FTER Olmsted and Vaux's return, the Park development for several years could hardly have gone more smoothly. Dissension between Green's board and the architects was muffled. The Loch and the Meer were completed. The Kinderberg, the huge rustic shelter in the Children's District, was built. The perimeter wall was coming along. Belvedere Castle was started, as was the Ballplayers House on the Ball Ground, the sizable, largely flat area that is now the Heckscher Playground. The Dairy, just east of the Kinderberg, was begun. So was the Merchants Gate at the southwest corner, where 59th Street and Eighth Avenue meet; it matched the Scholars Gate, three blocks to the east. The movable Skating House on the Lake and the Curling House on Conservatory Water were constructed. Also, the two partners were working on Brooklyn's Prospect Park, which shortly gave the language a now much-used expression, parkway—that is, a conduit to a park, *vide,* Eastern Parkway.

But in the background something ominous was taking place. It came from the politicians, a body sufficiently ignoble to cause a citizen in the 1860s to write, "Disgraceful beyond all power of words adequately to express it has been of late years the administration of the Government of the City of New York." Or again, a deserved repetition, ". . . we are brought to shame by the dishonest government of the City of New York." The targets of these words were largely the barons of Tammany Hall, Olmsted's implacable enemies, who were intent on incorporating the hundreds of Park jobs into their own patronage system.

Olmsted's attitude toward politicians is clearly demonstrated in a letter to a friend written in 1860, the year after his European park inspection trip:

> My office was for several days regularly surrounded by an organized mob carrying a banner inscribed "Bread and Blood." This mob sent into me a list of 10,000 names of men

The Kinderberg Arbor, the Park's largest. Circular in shape, it was 110 feet across and stood atop the Kinderberg, or Children's Mountain, now the site of the Chess and Checkers House.
(Herbert Mitchell Collection.)

alleged to have starving families demanding that they should be immediately put to work. I had almost no assistance, but within a week I had a thousand men economically employed and rigidly discharged any man who failed to work industriously and to behave in a quiet orderly manner. Since the plan was adopted, from two to four thousand men have been generally at work besides those employed by contractors, but with a single exception, when a thousand men on an adjoining work struck for higher wages and two gangs on the park joined them and were immediately discharged, there has been the most perfect order, peace and good feeling preserved, not withstanding the fact that the laborers are mainly from the poorest, and what is generally considered the most dangerous, class of the great city's population.

The struggle between Olmsted and Tammany Hall had to be to the death—at least as long as Tammany Hall held power. And Tammany Hall intended to hold it.

In 1857 when Olmsted first joined the Park as superintendent, an individual named William Marcy Tweed was first taking control of municipal government. After a brief career as alderman and congressman, Tweed was elected to what he realized was the local powerhouse, the Board of Supervisors. Thereafter he dominated it and the city for fourteen years, growing more powerful and dishonest annually. By working in 1858 to unseat Fernando Wood, a corrupt mayor, Tweed gained a reputation for respectability. This he consistently nurtured. He was a consummate deceiver. No better example of a canny and accomplished hypocrite can be found in American political annals during the third quarter of the nineteenth century.

After Wood's downfall, Tweed became the first boss of Tammany Hall. From then on he was generally known as Boss Tweed. Nevertheless he managed, for most of the ensuing years, to maintain a public pose of honesty and civic concern. Tweed was a virtuoso in orchestrating the snakepit of politics. He knew full well the value conferred on his moves by his reputation for personal rectitude. Only his remarkable cunning enabled him to maintain the pose for so long.

In the election of November 1868, Tammany and its external allies took over the state of New York. They elected the governor and the city mayor, A. Oakley Hall, one of Tweed's boys. Another already held the comptrollership and Tweed himself, who liked to keep more or less in the background (but with easy access to the till), became commissioner of the city's new Department of Public Works. It was a stupendous victory for the machine—concerning some of whose major and minor figures Olmsted has more to say later.

To clinch the opportunities offered by its success, Tammany, using bribery, in the spring of 1870 slid a new city charter through the state legislature, one deservedly called the Tweed Charter. With it, the post-election shadow that fell on Central Park became dark night; the Park's most peaceful period of development was ended—if any period can truly be called peaceful.

Among the charter's provisions was the elimination, after thirteen years of existence, of the Board of Commissioners of the Central Park. This body wound up its business in a final report, dated April 20, 1870, to which the other commissioners attached a perhaps well-deserved encomium to Andrew Haswell Green. In the old board's place, the charter authorized a Department of Public Parks, under a five-man commission whose majority consisted of four Tammany stalwarts, headed by Peter B. Sweeny. The only member from the old board was Green, whom the mayor dared not fire. However, all power was unceremoniously taken from him. Instead, power on the commission rested in a Tammany three-man executive committee, topped by Sweeny.

Scheduled meetings of the board were regularly adjourned for lack of a quorum since Green alone showed up. The executive committee, assembling at its pleasure, made all Park decisions. These, by virtue of the new charter's terms, involved not only Central Park but all city parks north of Canal Street as well as all highways and undeveloped areas on the West Side and on the largely untenanted upper island, as well. The broad jurisdiction provided virtually unlimited opportunities for pillage and patronage.

One early decision of the new board, bearing the trademark of the wily Tweed, was a resolution formally recognizing Olmsted and Vaux as "Chief Landscape Architects, as such, advisers to the Board." But it was, characteristically, a sham. Olmsted and Vaux, along with their advice, were ignored from the start. Recognizing the hopelessness of their situation, both resigned in November of 1870, at a moment when the plunder of their Park was at its height.

The spirit as well as most of the rules of Olmsted and Vaux's carefully nurtured eight hundred and forty-three acres were abrogated almost immediately by the Tammany henchmen. Under their sway, the first grade crossing appeared in the Park, passing over the West Drive at the level of 67th Street. As a slight vindication, it might be noted that it was made in order to reach most easily a building designed under Tammany as a sheepfold, which was to hold the Park's resident flock and its shepherd. The structure, since called one of the finest examples of mid-Victorian architecture, has now, with some changes and additions, become a popular restaurant, the Tavern on the Green.

Far more damaging than the grade crossing, however, was the makework produced by the board for the multitudes of Tammany faithful. Thousands of trees were dug up and transported for planting in other parks. Trees that remained, no matter what the species, were routinely pruned of their branches up to ten or fifteen feet above the ground. The lower trunks resembled broomsticks. The esthetic effects of ground planting and clumps of shrubbery were completely disregarded. Much of this vegetation was grubbed up to "improve the circulation of air." Plans for many buildings were also drawn, a number of them, including the manifold yards and sheds of a projected zoological park, were slated to occupy and completely fill the largest meadow in the northern section, the present North Meadow, the board explaining that the meadow's landscape value wasn't worth mentioning.

Fortunately, none of these buildings was actually constructed. By midsummer of 1871 there were whispers and intimations that something was amiss at the city treasury. The impeccably reputable bankers with whom Tammany dealt, lulled by Tweed's remarkable guile, had no inkling of the impending disaster. However, by this time certain members of the press, not in Tweed's pay, smelled a rat. Resolutely, they kept digging. The books of the city's Finance Department, long shielded from outside eyes, could no longer be kept secret after a bookkeeper forwarded incriminating evidence to the *New York Times,* which printed it. Inspection of the records disclosed the fraud and its extent.

In September, the formidable Green was appointed deputy comptroller of the Finance Department to bring order out of the fiscal chaos—which, in time, he did, eventually going on to a five-year appointment as comptroller of the city. Tweed fell and was tried, convicted, and put behind bars. Still resourceful, he bribed his jailers and escaped. Eventually, extradited from Spain, he died in prison seven years later in 1878. Conservative estimates place the amount stolen directly from the city by the Tweed Ring, a number of whom followed Tweed into jail, at $45 million. When other felonies are considered, such as arbitrary reduction of taxes for money or favors, or the issuance of bonds at excessive rates of interest, estimates reach $200 million—and that in dollars that equaled twenty of today's.

After Tweed's downfall the Park's Department was reorganized with the appointment of new commissioners who provided a pro-Olmsted majority. He and Vaux were called back to their old jobs as the Park's landscape architects. For a while, when the new board president was out of the country, Olmsted went onto the board and served in his place, reverting to his customary post on the other's return. The new board ordered cessation of all Tammany ventures, building and otherwise. Repair of damage to the Park was begun as quickly as possible. Work according to the designer's original plan once again went forward.

In 1872, after the Tweed scandal, Tammany Hall had fallen into total disgrace. It was down, undeniably down. But it was not, alas, out. In fact, it was, in a way, indestructible. It had contrived a durable and foolproof mechanism to garner the ballots—jobs for the politically faithful. And it knew how to use this instrument. In a few months, the machine, now the "reform" Tammany, was renascent, a formidable power once again in city politics. This time, though, it soft-pedaled its greed. It had learned a lesson from the Tweed disaster. As far, however, as Central Park was concerned, its intention remained the same—a pork barrel two and a half miles long to be plundered for its followers.

To achieve this, it was necessary to dislodge Green. As comptroller of the city, he was no longer on the Park board. But by holding the municipal purse strings, he was the most powerful local political figure by far. The public appreciated his honesty. His word carried weight that could not be rebutted. Although by the nature of his job he could not originate projects, his complete control over expenditures allowed him to block any he disliked. Furthermore, his position toward Olmsted was protective. Green realized the extent to which the Park—the undertaking to which he and Olmsted were completely devoted—was being threatened by the politicos. Now he was Olmsted's all-powerful defender.

And it was well that he was. By 1874 a whitewashed Tammany administration was back in City Hall. Under a law of that year, the Park's board was reduced to four, two Republicans and two Democrats, the latter duo under the mayor's control. The result was months of bitter political squabbling, unhappy months for Olmsted, who tried to remain neutral and get on with his work while his protector and the mayor fought their unending battles.

One of the means employed by Tammany to discredit Olmsted and his policies was yellow journalism. "The Central Park: Its Early History— The Beginning of Greensward and Grab etc." was a headline in an issue in 1877 of the *Evening Express,* a Tammany vassal publication. The heading came over a text that included the following: ". . . the Greensward Ring, whose babble in the papers and in Society Circles, about aesthetics and architecture, vistas and landscapes, the quiver of a leaf and the proper blendings of light and shade bamboozled the citizens of that day. These were the Miss Nancies of Central Park art, the foes of nature and the aids to money-making."

Nor would the resurgent Tammany allow Olmsted the supervision of the Central Park police. He was eminently qualified for this and dearly desired it. Park management was easier with his own police. As mentioned earlier, his neatly uniformed, well-disciplined force had received many commendations in the past. Because they were so respected, the public's behavior was more exemplary. And Olmsted's management problems fewer. Finally, the Park was at its safest under Olmsted's men.

Tammany Hall knew all this, but ignored it. Instead, Olmsted was labeled an impractical man, inexperienced in police work. Later, Olmsted had this to say:

Now it happened that I was then one of the few men in America who made it a business to be well-informed on the subject of police organization and management. I had made some examination of the French system; had when in London known Sir Richard Mayne, the creator of the Metropolitan Force, upon the model of which our New York Metropolitan Force is formed; had been favored by him with a long personal discourse on the principles of its management, and had been given the best opportunities for seeing them in operation, both in the park service and in all other departments. I had made a similar study of the Irish constabulary. I had originally organized, instructed and disciplined, and under infinite difficulties had secured the reputation of, this same Central Park force.

However, the machine, under cover of the falsehood concerning Olmsted's impracticality, recaptured control of the Park police, which had reverted to Olmsted after the Tweed scandal. Its dozens of jobs returned to Tammany and were filled by applicants many of whom Olmsted would have turned away on sight. As a result, Olmsted submitted his fifth resignation. This was in September of 1873. Afterward, urged by the board's president, a personal friend, he withdrew it "to resume service under the Commission upon a modified arrangement, vindicating my professional standing and securing me against another similar experience."

In 1876 the Tammany mayor, William H. Wickham, with some jubilation, thought he saw the way to get rid of Green. In November of that year he declared Green's five-year appointment as comptroller at an end, as indeed chronologically it was. Wickham then appointed another. Green fought back. He sued. He lost that battle, however, and with the defeat, was out.

That same year an attempt was made to remove Olmsted on the grounds that, in the spring, he had taken an unpaid job to assist the New York State Survey. The attempt failed and Olmsted's salary, which had been withheld, was eventually paid.

But the pressure for his dismissal was mounting. With Green's departure, it increased. The culmination came when, once again, Olmsted's health gave way, the old weakness that had troubled him all his life. His doctor ordered a three-month leave of absence, which the board granted, to begin at the end of December 1877. A few days later, as he was about to sail for Europe, the board quietly passed a resolution that, in effect, ended Olmsted's twenty-one–year association with the Park.

When news of this got out, there was immense indignation in the city's influential circles. In early 1878, more than fifty individual signatories, including August Belmont, Jonathan Edwards, Alexander Hamilton, Henry Havemeyer, Henry Holt, John Jay, Morris K. Jesup, Whitelaw Reid, "and many others," dispatched a lengthy letter to the Park commissioners "requesting reconsideration in depriving the city of Mr. Olmsted's services." But Olmsted, from abroad, refused to take part in the effort. For years he had seen and fought the approaching separation. But in the end he realized there was no hope. Tammany had finally won. So disgusted was he with municipal politics that for the four months he was away he refused even to glance at a New York newspaper.

Fortunately by that time, twenty years after Olmsted had taken over, the Park was essentially finished. His far-reaching conceptions of beauty and design were largely in place, the outlines sketched, the colors arranged, the shadows directed. He—and the city in general—only awaited nature to mature the work he had placed in her hands.

Although the years Olmsted had put into building Central Park were often tumultuous and searing and frequently personally disturbing, the Park itself under his direction enjoyed its loveliest period. It was young, it was new, it was vigorous, it was safe. It was verdant and blooming. The time of Olmsted's personal association with it can be called the Park's golden age.

 In a letter to a friend after his departure, Olmsted wrote, "You can have no idea what a drag life has been to me for three years." The letter went on to describe the pain now as largely gone, probably due in part to the catharsis afforded by the publication some weeks earlier of a pamphlet Olmsted had written, *The Spoils of the Park, With a Few Leaves from the Deep-Laiden Books of "A Wholly Impractical Man."* Embedded in its more than twenty thousand words were some thirty episodes recounting a number, but by no means all, of the experiences Olmsted had undergone at the hands of politicians in his lengthy role as the guiding genius of Central Park.

From the miscellany, several incidents might be taken. The first is an introduction to the pervasive hypocrisy Olmsted battled.

The mayor once wanted to nominate me for the office of Street Commissioner. After some persuasion, perfectly aware I was taking part in a play, though the mayor solemnly assured me otherwise, I assented, with the distinct understanding, that, if the office came to me, it should be free from political obligations; that I should be allowed to choose my own assistants, and, keeping within the law, my own method of administration. "Which," said the mayor, "is just what I want. It is because I felt sure that you would insist on that, that I sent for you." I smiled. The mayor preserved his gravity, and I took my leave. Within half an hour I received a call from a gentleman whom I held in much esteem, to whom I had reason to be grateful; who had once been a member of Congress—a man of wealth and social position, but at the time holding no public office, and not conspicuous in politics. He congratulated me warmly, hoping at last that New York would be able to enjoy the luxury of clean streets. Conversation turned upon the character of the Board of Aldermen. The gentleman thought there need be no difficulty in getting their confirmation, but suggested that it might be better for me to let him give a few confidential assurances to some who did not know me as well as he did, as to my more important appointments. He soon afterward left, regretting plaintively to have found me so "unpractical" in my ideas. It was his opinion that half a loaf of reform was better than no bread. It was mine, that a man could not rightly undertake to clean the streets of New York with his hands tied confidentially.

Soon another, also not holding an office, but president of a ward club, and as such having a certain familiarity with practical politics, called to advise me that—[name expunged] wanted an understanding that I would give him fifteen per cent of my patronage. Not having it, he feared that — would throw his weight against me. I need not go on. When one of the mayor's friends in the city-hall understood that I seriously meant to be my own master, or defeated, he exclaimed, "Why, that man must be a fool!"

The following incident occurred when Olmsted was temporarily the president of the Board of Commissioners of the Department of Public Parks:

A "delegation" from a great political organization called on me by appointment. After introductions and handshakings, a circle was formed, and a gentleman stepped before me, and said, "We know how much pressed you must be, Mr. President, and we don't want to be obtrusive, sir, nor exacting, but at your convenience our association would like to have you determine what share of your patronage we can expect, and make suitable arrangements for our using it. We will take the liberty to suggest, sir, that there could be no more convenient way than that you should send us our due quota of tickets, if you will please, sir, in this form, *leaving us to fill in the name.*" Here a packet of printed tickets was produced, from which I took one at random. It was a blank appointment and bore the signature of Mr. Tweed. "That," continued the spokesman, "was the way we arranged it last year, and we don't think there can be any thing better."

Or this: "During all my park work it was a common thing to receive newspapers, addressed by unknown hands, containing matter designed to injure me; sometimes, also, anonymous threats and filthy caricatures."

Dismissal for cause could, it turned out, in the peculiar world of Tammany, be good fortune:

There was an intrigue to remove a valuable officer by destroying his character, in order to make an opening for a subordinate strongly backed with "influence." I asked and obtained a committee of the Board to try the case. The subordinate made an oath to a statement which was proved to be false; and for the perjury he was dismissed. Shortly afterwards he met me on the Park, offered me his hand, and, with much flourish, thanked me for having brought about his removal, as it had compelled his friends to make proper exertions, and he now held a position much more to his taste than any on the Park could have been."

Another man Olmsted discharged from the Park at the next election became a candidate for the legislature.

Let the excerpts, describing a trivial fraction of the experiences Olmsted underwent, end with this: "I have had a dozen men force their way into my house before I had arisen from bed on a Sunday morning, and some break into my drawing-room in their eagerness to deliver letters of advice. I have heard a candidate for a magisterial office in the city addressing from my doorsteps a crowd of such advice-bearers, telling them that I was bound to give them employment, and suggesting plainly, that, if I was slow about it, a rope round my neck might serve to lessen my reluctance to take good counsel." (In a letter later to a friend, Olmsted said that but for wounding the feelings of certain individuals, "I could have given more effective and disgusting illustrations.") The experiences clearly show the sink of corruption that bubbled then in the city. However, the physically fragile Olmsted, the man with the artist's sensitive temperament, never, despite what must have been an almost unbearable strain, let such constant ragging affect his decisions. His probity never faltered. How these incidents may have affected his health is another matter.

◡ Despite Olmsted's pose of distancing himself from Central Park, he never truly lost the feeling of a father for his first child. On one occasion involving a major encroachment on the site, he jumped in with both feet to prevent what he viewed as a mortal danger to the Park. Hatched at the start of the 1890s, the incursion was strongly backed by important segments of the public, namely, the city's well-to-do lovers of horse flesh. The plan sought to construct a mile-and-a-half–long straightway Speeding Track on the western side of the Park where trotting horses pulling light carriages could race. The existing Park roads, with the unavoidable exception east of the reservoir, had been deliberately curved to prevent such contests.

In a letter to the editor of *The Sun,* an influential city newspaper of the day, Olmsted in a long and forceful harangue dated December 22, 1890, summarized his arguments with the following: "I think if I were in your shoes, I would be inclined to draw up a paper setting forth the great desireability of at once providing a place for athletic sports and recreations, recognizing that the constantly growing demand for such a place *cannot begin to be met in Central Park,* except by a repudiation of its present leading purpose and a costly destruction of what has been gained for it" (italics mine). Still the sporting bloc persisted. Furthermore, it gained a temporary victory. In March of 1892, the legislature authorized the Speeding Track. The reaction to this was unexpected. A tornado of public protest ensued. Nothing less than an army formed to back Olmsted's views. Twenty-eight days later the act was repealed. Olmsted felt vindicated and relieved. Whether he acknowledged it or not, the umbilical cord to his first brain child was never truly cut.

Olmsted's fear of encroachments was strong. He had realized long before the Speeding Track that the politically motivated neglect of the Park, which he strove so to prevent, would inevitably cause the Park to decline. But the decline, relatively speaking, would be slow. Encroachments, however, were a different matter, and far worse. These, he knew, would quickly destroy it. And encroachments had menaced the Park from the very beginning.

*N*O ONE CAN SAY exactly the number of encroachments that have been broached for Central Park. But scores are on record. An early request was a permanent space for adult baseball. Olmsted quashed this on the ground that special interest groups should not reserve parts of a public park for their pleasure. But this was only one incident near the Park's beginning. As early as 1863, the commissioners noted in the year's annual report that "If all the applications for the erection and maintenance of towers, houses, drinking fountains, cottages, Aeolian harps, gymnasiums, observatories, [and] weighing scales, for the sale of eatables, velocipedes, perambulators, Indian work, tobacco, [and] segars, for the privilege of using steam-engines, snowshoes, [and] ice-boats, and for the use of the ice for fancy dress carnivals, were granted, they would occupy a large portion of the Park."

By 1872, the designers could add, to the others, these newcomers: a place of burial for the city's distinguished dead; erection of various houses of worship for every religious sect; a grand cathedral for *all* religions; an exhibit hall for the city's manufactures; a miniature model of the North American continent for teaching geography to schoolchildren; a street railway through the park's middle; a course for steeplechasing; and the presentation of a full-rigged ship to ride the Park's waters. All, like the Speeding Track, were unsuccessful.

Despite the long record of encroachment defeats, suggestions for others have never lapsed. Perhaps it couldn't be otherwise. The average citizen has a wildly inventive streak. When it comes to hatching notions of his own the peculiarities can include the inane, unexpected, impractical, vulgar, and sentimental in never-ending, mind-boggling doses. For example, among the proposals to surface in this century was one by Theodore Roosevelt's uncle for turning the more level, southern part of the Park into house lots. Others were to construct trenches to illustrate graphically for the citizenry the am-

biance of trench warfare during World War I, to lay out a field for the
landing and takeoff of airplanes, to build an underground garage for thirty
thousand cars, to create a recreation complex consisting of a swimming
pool, circus ground, and running track, to dig vaults for the storage of
motion picture film, to provide permanent circus tents, to erect broadcast-
ing towers for the city's radio station, to decorate the turf with a statue of
Buddha, and to locate within the walls of the Park an El station to serve as
a monument to the vanishing glory of the Elevated Railroad System. None
of these, likewise, came to pass.

One that did succeed, however, was the Metropolitan Museum of Art,
The Greensward plan had, indeed, included a spot for a museum. But its
place was in the Arsenal building. The Metropolitan's present site was
designated as a playground. In 1858, an ideal locale for the museum,
nearby but out of the Park, would have been Hamilton Square, the fif-
teen-acre city-owned tract lying from Fifth to Fourth avenues between
66th and 68th streets; it was half again as large as Washington Square. A
contemporary writer, admired by the environmentalists of that day, called
for more squares like Hamilton, "opening upon the park, giving the
adjoining city blocks something of the air and greenery to be found in
London" and "providing admirable situations for future institutions of
literature, art and science."

An instance of what could have been accomplished is the Met's similarly extensive sister institution, the American Museum of Natural History, located out of the Park on the western side, on Central Park West
between 77th and 81st streets on the ten acres of city-owned property
that was formerly known as Manhattan Square. However, not until 1878,
more than twenty years after the Park's beginning, was the museum
initiated through an act of the legislature. By then, Hamilton Square was
on the city tax rolls, subdivided to private ownership.

The Metropolitan inherited on its site a small abandoned red brick
building, erected several years before as part of the defunct American
Academy of Music and Art. Its masonry is still embedded in today's vastly
enlarged structure. This museum has been put together piece by piece
over the last century after the designs of more than half a dozen architects. It all lies within the Park and therefore has created opposition
from single-minded Park lovers, those who follow Olmsted's dictum to
the letter: "Where building starts, the Park ends." The feelings of one of
the most virulent of these saw print in an article in the February 1914
issue of *Harper's* magazine, which said in part: "The rear of the Metropol-

itan is a harsh assault on the landscape and the eye. It is a horrible example of starting any kind of a building not necessary to a park within a park enclosure. It is a formidable intruder, vast, heavy, addicted to excessive growth and reproachful of the greeneries it pushes into."

Olmsted himself, while in the same camp, was publicly not so severe. When writing a mock colloquy in 1895 whose meaning might well have included the Met, he said:

" 'Are not fine buildings, statues, monuments, great additions to a park?'

" 'Nay, they are deductions from it.'

" 'Do they not add greatly to the value of the Central Park?'

" 'Nay, they take much from its value as a park. They would be worth more to the city if they were elsewhere.' "

Of the Metropolitan specifically, Olmsted, who had originally agreed to its erection, said after more than a decade of thought that it was "an act now generally regretted." It stood four-square against his aim to convey soothing rurality to the city-stressed citizen through a landscape of rocks, trees, turf, and sky-catching patches of water—those and practically nothing else. Nor was Olmsted alone. Robert Moses, a later Park figure, once said that if he could have his druthers he would toss the museum out of the Park.

The museum now occupies fourteen of the Park's eight hundred and forty-three acres, an area that would otherwise be replete with greenery. Presumably, by current agreement with the parks commissioner and the administrator, all future museum expansion will halt with the completion of the new wing on the western side for the display of European sculpture and art. Presumably.

The museum, of course, despite snorts of displeasure from dedicated Olmsted followers, is not likely to move. It is a cultural gem, the largest art museum in the Western Hemisphere, a repository of priceless artifacts from around the world. By those who haunt its halls, it is distinctly and dearly beloved. All this is true. But wouldn't it be nice if one could visit it next Sunday in Hamilton Square?

In addition to the museum, there have been other successful intrusions into the Park. These are principally, but not entirely, emplaced works of art. Admission of these sorely tests the diplomacy of public servants. Donors can be persistent. In the early days, one exasperated Park official said, "It's practically a year's labor to circumvent these generous fiends."

The problem started early and continues. In considering it here, there may be lessons in how to handle unwanted offerings of the future.

More than fifty artworks, most of them statues, are within the Park today. But the only statue paid for by the city is the one atop the Bethesda Fountain, and the only other city-ordered artworks are the lovely sandstone carvings of the Bethesda Terrace balustrades. When the Park was undertaken, there was no general appreciation of art in the city. Soon, however, some citizens had become wealthy enough to encourage the work of serious artists. The consequent splurge of purchases required areas where they could be erected, and Central Park became a prime target.

In considering such potential gifts, Olmsted worked through a Committee on Statues. The committee (Olmsted in disguise) said three things should be supplied in the Park: fresh air, purified by abundant foliage; the means of tranquilizing and invigorating exercise, as in quiet roads and walks; and extended landscapes to refresh and delight the eye, these last, therefore, as free as possible from the rigidity and confinement of the city and from the incessant emphasis of artificial objects.

The committee published rules for accepting art, but these were often overlooked. An influential citizen's tender of one of his acquisitions would put the committee and Olmsted in a difficult position. Solomonic sleight of hand was required to fend off a monstrosity. How to devise an excuse that will mollify a rejected donor? It's often impossible. Consequently the committee and Olmsted, and the responsible officials after them, just gave in. Numerous statues in the Park are inferior works, and many, including the noninferior, are poorly sited. Generosity, of course, is customarily welcomed. But where the Park is concerned, any gift should be examined carefully—be it the gift in the Harlem Merr of the Lasker Pool and Rink, the proposed Huntington Hartford Cafe by the Scholars Gate, or a striking lifesize bronze of Godzilla.

Including statues, the Park is the repository, willing or otherwise, of various kinds of memorials. These salute upward of a hundred individuals and one dog, Balto, who with sledgemates in 1925 brought antitoxin to Nome to avert an epidemic. Monuments, tablets, plaques, drinking fountains, trees, playgrounds, and the Andrew Haswell Green bench are among the mementoes. The Diversity of the honorees is almost unbelievable. Thothmes III, the sixteenth-century B.C. Egyptian Pharaoh, whose obelisk stands behind the museum, is one; Baron von Humboldt, the

German naturalist who early in the last century explored the wildernesses of South America, is another. Also honored are Sophie Irene Loeb, W. T. Snead, Albert Bertel Thorvalsen, and Emma Nicholson, respectively the founder of the Child Welfare Board of New York City, an English newspaperman who went down on the *Titanic,* a Danish sculptor, and a president of the Euphrosyne Club, in Grecian mythology the name of the grace representing joy. The first of a grove of forty-five trees planted off 80th Street at Central Park West honored Mrs. Thomas Slack of the New York State Federation of Women's Clubs. This is just a sprinkling. Looking too deeply into Central Park memorials can bring on vertigo.

Following Olmsted's dismissal in 1878, his codesigner, Vaux, was in charge of Central Park management for much of the ensuing seventeen years. When he died in an accidental drowning in Gravesend Bay in 1895, he had been landscape architect to the Department of Public Parks since 1888. From 1881 to the end of 1882, he had filled the post of superintending architect of the department. Just prior to this, Vaux had taken a junior partner into his landscaping firm, a young Yale graduate, Samuel Parsons, Jr. During the coming three decades, Parsons was to be a very prominent and very pro-Olmstedian figure in the administration of Central Park.

Parsons was the son and grandson of notable nurserymen, the proprietors of the eminent Parsons Company of Flushing, Long Island, founded in 1838 by the brothers Samuel and Robert Parsons and soon one of the country's most celebrated horticultural vendors. By the time Central Park was started, it was importing from the Orient showy flora new to the United States. Among over one hundred varieties, for example, that arrived in the dunnage of one Parsons plant collector were such notable items as the star magnolia, euonymus, and fifteen double-flowered cherries, one of which has blossoms as large as a rose.

Endowed with this background, young Parsons was a happy addition to the staff of the Department of Public Parks. He joined it as superintendent of planting in 1882, soon after Vaux was lured back, the latter making it a condition of his employment that Parsons be hired. Vaux's stay this time was short because soon after he arrived an archenemy of his and Olmsted's became first a park commissioner and then head of the board. This was none other than E. L. Viele, the same Viele who, in 1858, as the Park's chief engineer and Olmsted's superior, had been dismissed when Olmsted and Vaux became the Park's two architects. Thereafter, Viele never ceased to do what he could to work against their aims, an opportunity time made easy with his new post. When Vaux resigned in December 1882, in protest against an action of the board (a new suggested placement of the zoo which happily never materialized), Parsons stayed on for more than half a year trying to work within for correct Park policy.

Then, in the late summer of 1882, he, too, resigned, realizing the hopelessness of the effort. Soon, however, when a new reform mayor and board came in, he was rehired to fill a more important post, that of superintendent of parks, which he held for almost thirty years.

Parsons' value was as a horticultural administrator. He had a marvelous green thumb. And he knew how to impart its virtues to his staff, which, needless to say, was characteristically undermanned. But so adept was Parsons's leadership that the Park managed to maintain a fairly decent appearance throughout his tenure. In fact, those in charge today consider the trees in the Park under Parsons to have reached the peak of their appearance.

Much social activity in Parson's time centered at the Mineral Springs Pavilion on the west side of the Park at the level of 70th Street, designed by Vaux in 1868 for visitor refreshment. During the 1890s it was booming. Known as "Little Carlsbad," it offered thirty different mineral waters to habitués like Jacob Ruppert, the brewer, Senator Chauncey Depew, and others of the upper crust. Negligent maintenance caused the building's razing in 1960. The present Mineral Springs Pavilion stands near the old site.

Olmsted had said that the essence of the Park was the landscape and that vegetation should hold the first place of distinction. Here is a Parsons appreciation of that view. He is speaking of the North Meadow, that open sweep in the Park's center above the 96th Street transverse:

The sheets of the grass, the varied tints of the foliage sweeping the turf to the left, the low-lying hillocks crowned with large forest trees, the great boulders entirely exposed or only half-submerged, the meadows beyond running back to seemingly unknown distances—who will picture it truly? There is dignity, there is breadth, repose, restfulness, and yet a sense of isolation that is not absolute. It is genuine park scenery that the eye is tempted to linger upon and the foot to walk on, and presents, if viewed as a single feature, one of the best examples we have of good park work.

Could such a man keep Central Park close to Olmsted's ideal? Relatively speaking, Parsons did. A park superintendent just before him had

The first Mineral Springs Pavilion, designed by Calvert Vaux. Known
in its heyday as Little Carlsbad, it offered thirty different mineral
waters to its customers. (Herbert Mitchell Collection.)

ordered a number of trees felled to let visitors admire the tall buildings
that were rising along the borders of the Park. Parsons during his long
stay saw that the screen of trees was regrown. In other ways, too, he was
a staunch Olmstedite. Stubbornly he confronted the never-ending wave of
would-be encroachments. He fended off the placement of Grant's Tomb
within the Park. He prevented the towering equestrian statue of William
Tecumseh Sherman—now standing felicitously on its lofty stone pedestal

in the Grand Army Plaza at Fifth Avenue and 59th Street—from being set up at the southern end of the Mall. There it would have obliterated one of the more matchless vistas in the Park, the tree-lined footage that sweeps north from that point along the lordly promenade. Parsons said with feeling, many times, that the Park was New Yorkers' greatest treasure.

He finally resigned in the spring of 1911. The Park, despite Parsons's best efforts, had, because of financial problems, begun to look a bit seedy even before the first decade of the present century. Resoiling was deemed the remedy. Parsons, working through a commissioner, asked the city in 1910 to allot a $250,000 for resoiling, to be spread over the next five years. The following year the whole scheme foundered on the political question of whether it was necessary. In disgust, Parsons quit. With him departed the remaining remnants of the Greensward hopes for Park perfection. Central Park historians usually refer to Parsons as the last of the old incorruptibles. His widow said his lifelong ambition always was to keep the Park as Olmsted and Vaux had planned it. Admittedly, he did his best. Under Parsons, the Park could be said to have enjoyed its silver age. After severance from the Park, Olmsted moved to the Boston suburb of Brookline and thereafter worked on dozens of projects, among them the designs of the U.S. Capitol grounds in Washington, D.C., the Arboretum in Boston, the Vanderbilt estate, named Biltmore, in North Carolina, and the World's Columbian Exposition in Chicago.

As the years rolled by, Olmsted recalled Green in relatively kindly fashion, saying of him that, as a commissioner of Central Park, he was one of a "superior body of men; they gained the public confidence and, taken altogether, they deserved it more than the bodies of public servants in our cities often do."

Green, for his part, enjoyed an active law practice and continued to work diligently for the public weal. As executor of the will of his partner, Tilden, he helped form the New York Public Library; he battled to keep City Hall where it is, joining the 1857 Greensward plan's opinion that the building is "the best architectural work in the State." And he was long president of the New-York Historical Society. But he is best known as the father of Greater New York City. For years he argued for the consolidation of the five boroughs into one metropolitan unit. He met heavy xenophobia and local pride, but he persisted—the project was known as "Green's hobby." After decades, he finally won. Consolidation took place in 1898. Instead of the pre-Green scenario featuring five neighboring

cities each throbbing with sectional vanity and self-centered conniving, we have the city we know today, not perfect perhaps, but, oh, so much better than five warring neighbors. It was a tremendous achievement.

Green and Olmsted, for so long apart, were joined once again by the year 1903. Both left the world within three months of each other that year. Olmsted, for nearly eight years, had been afflicted with what today might be called Alzheimer's disease. He ended his days under hospital care. But all around the country his monuments stood shining. As is the case with Green and New York City, the beneficiaries enjoy what has been done whether or not they know the name of their benefactors.

Green, in contrast to Olmsted, was a vigorous oldster to the end. While Olmsted's end was quiet and sad, Green's was violent and tragic. He was

*Pilgrim Hill in 1898 at the Park's botanical
prime, under the tenure of Samuel Parsons.*
(Parks Department Annual Report.)

assassinated. A jealous and mentally deranged black man was obsessed by
love for a black woman. She was the mistress of an elderly, white-haired
white man who somewhat resembled Green. The distraught lover met
Green in front of his house and pumped five bullets into him. Green died
on the spot. He is memorialized in Central Park with a commemorative
bench in the northeast corner at the level of 105th Street.

Two

DECLINE, REVIVAL, AND FURTHER DECLINE

1912–1978

*W*HEN PARSONS RESIGNED, William Jay Gaynor was mayor of 10
New York, the first in a series of five Irish mayors of
varying quality. John Purroy Mitchel followed Gaynor.
The somewhat unsavory John F. (Red Mike) Hylan succeeded him. Hylan, for example, ordered no competition
for previously competitive Park posts because of their
"exceptional and sensitive nature," a nonsensical turn of
phrase designed to make patronage easier. James J.
(Beau Brummel) Walker, a supposedly "reform" Tammany mayor, eventually forced from office in disgrace,
was next. And last was John P. O'Brien. None of these
men cared deeply for the Park, although Walker liked to
host parties (on the cuff) in the Casino, originally designed in 1870 by Calvert Vaux as a charming and rustic
Ladies Pavillion. By the 1920s, after several changes, the
building had become a fashionable night club. But, except
for Walker's interest in the Casino, under the administrations of these gentry, the attention to the Park was mini-
mal. Instead, the Park was looked upon as a dumping
ground for aged Tammany retainers and their depen-
dents. Other jobs went to misfits or incompetents with
political backing. The period was a bleak one in the Park's
history.

In 1927, however, in an uncharacteristic move, Walker, the "reformer," hired landscape architect Herman
W. Merkel to put forward a plan for Central Park's improvement. Its highlights addressed the problems of vandalism, vegetation failure, and active recreation needs.
Two of its remedies echoed methods suggested by
Olmsted. These were curbing vandalism and litter with a
special force of Park police, such as once operated so well
under Olmsted, and increasing the gardening force and
breaking it into detachments responsible for certain specific areas, as Olmsted had once outlined. Although de-
ploring the wire-enclosed tennis courts below the 96th
Street transverse (which had slipped past Parsons' pro-
tests) and the seventeen acres of meadow area that had

been turned into the Heckscher Playground, Merkel nevertheless recognized the growing need for recreation. Included in his plan were eight other playgrounds to be sited at Park entrances, a number he felt was an absolute maximum for the Park.

A suggestion that was acted on immediately was an underground sprinkler system, installed at the cost of a million dollars. This replaced the old method of hosing turf and vegetation from Olmsted-installed hydrants. A Park historian, Henry Hope Reed, later noted: "One of the great sights of the Park in the early 1930s was the sea of white spray on the lawns during the summer." The ease with which the facility came into being was due in part, perhaps, to civic guilt. Merkel pointed out that much of the vegetation in the Park, through neglect after Parsons' departure, had been allowed to approach a state of ruin or to disappear entirely. Merkel said that rare weeping varieties of beech, birch, larch, and linden were gone as well as the lone example of a special strain of a large, low-spreading English

In the 1920s, swimming meets were frequently held on Central Park Lake. Such events became popular during the period of the Irish mayors. (Parks Department Annual Report.)

elm known as Camperdown. The evergreens along the lengthy Winter Drive, too, had perished. But those on the Winter Drive were not alone. Merkel went on: "All but three or four of the varieties of evergreens have to all intents and purposes disappeared from the Park, and very many of the deciduous ones."

As a contrast, Pilat in 1868 had reported three hundred thirty-four species of trees in the Park, most of them evergreens. A paramount cause of this vegetation loss was recognized to be earth trampled down around the trees, the result of human traffic deviating off paths. Merkel's solution for this was lots of fences.

But these and most of his other ideas never were authorized. The stock market crash and the Depression during the Hoover administration caused the Merkel report to be put aside and not reconsidered until, eventually, Tammany's rule of City Hall came to an end. With the rigors of the Depression, the Park descended to its worst state up to that point.

During the Depression, scores of the jobless made their home in Central Park. The shantytown pictured here, known as Hooverville, was located on the dry bed of the old Croton reservoir, now the site of the Great Lawn. (Museum of the City of New York.)

The old rectangular reservoir, drained in 1929, became an area dotted with the makeshift shanties of homeless men, recalling the sad habitations of the bone-boiling squatters three-quarters of a century earlier. Later, the vagrants spread throughout the Park. It was a difficult time there and elsewhere. The Depression is generally considered to have lasted through the decade of the 1930s. The years of the Park's slow decline ended following the administration of Mayor John F. O'Brien, the last of the Tammany mayors.

ITH THE ADVENT on January 1, 1934, of the Fusion adminis- **11**
tration, Fiorello H. LaGuardia, mayor, the affairs of
Central Park changed dramatically. The city's new chief
executive appointed as parks commissioner the redoubt-
able Robert Moses. And what a parks commissioner stood
there! For the first time since Olmsted, Central Park had
a director who could be called a director, a mover and a
shaker, a farsighted, opinionated man, a dreamer of great
dreams. His own. Not all of his dreams suited all the people they touched, to say the least. But as far as Central
Park was concerned, it awoke to a new life under a new
master. Once again it had a presiding genius.

Robert Moses, in contrast to Olmsted, was not only a
first-class administrator but a political magician, a man
who could perform feats of legerdemain involving construction, eminent domain, and other politically associated matters with or without mirrors. His impressive
techniques had been acquired through more than twenty
years of public service and strenuous combat. During
them, the early idealism of the young Yale graduate had
been tempered by his rude contact with public and private
greed and public and private ambition, both often ruth-
less. As a consequence, he became an accomplished arm
twister. He was a stunning political adept, one of the
greatest of this century, as both friend and foe could tes-
tify.

One of Moses's first actions on taking office was sum-
marily to dismiss the five borough park commissioners
and their secretaries, whose qualifications and work habits he regarded with scorn. Other Tammany appointees
infested the Arsenal, the building from which Central
Park is managed, who were, theoretically, protected in
their jobs by civil service status. But here the malingerers
and lovers of the multiple coffee break met with a man
who refused to countenance sloth in a work force. He told
his executives whom he put into the Arsenal to size up
their personnel. Those who didn't meet requirements

found no shield in civil service. Personnel in Manhattan, some of whom were in the enviable position of being able to walk to work, were suddenly transferred to the farthest regions of Staten Island and the Bronx. Others were asked to perform such obnoxious tasks that they resigned. Moses also ousted the automobiles of twenty-three employees who were gratuitously using as a garage the basement of the Arsenal, reached by a ramp from Fifth Avenue.

Two of the more ludicrous relics of Tammany mismanagement were a pair of freewheeling crones, both with powerful past political backing. Emboldened through the long Indian summer of Democratic mayorships, one, the caretaker of a ladies restroom near the Belvedere, had substituted curtained living-room space for much of the plumbing and brought in a grand piano. Commenting on the matter some years ago, a periodical noted that the unexpected sound of a Chopin nocturne used to startle women who had entered the place in good faith. Moses soon took care of this anomaly by ousting the attendant.

The other case involved an obstinate Arsenal employee, a stubborn granny who looked well past the retirement age of seventy. For years she had been accustomed to doing her knitting while ensconced in a rocking chair, pausing only to brew afternoon tea. When queried, she denied she was past retirement age. Nor, after an exhaustive search, could her birth certificate be found. At this, Moses ordered a dose of steady work for her. And he detached a supervisor to oversee the process. One task after another followed completion of the last. The routine continued after quitting time, after midnight. Around 2 A.M. the day after the experiment started, the woman agreed to receive a pension.

During the Depression's lengthy period of high unemployment, Moses made effective use of the three federal programs that had been initiated to create jobs—the Civil Works Administration (CWA), succeeded by the Public Works Administration (PWA), which, in turn, was supplemented by the Works Progress Administration (WPA). With typical arrogance, Moses bent the rules of the CWA to get the wage scale he wanted. He put hundreds of its recipients—architects, engineers, draftsmen, laborers— to good use, effecting within a matter of months an almost miraculous change in Central Park, all the more impressive considering the neglect of previous Park administrations.

He inherited a monumental mess. Macadam roadways and footpaths were broken. Furnishings and ironwork—fences, benches, and playground equipment—were rotting and rusted. Lawns were scuffed or unmown. Many trees were dead or dying; almost all were improperly pruned. Statues and monuments were dirty and vandalized. The Indian Hunter's bow was missing. The Tigress was slipping off her rock. Bayonets were gone from the rifles of the soldiers in the Seventh Regiment Memorial at Fifth Avenue and 67th Street. The gift animals that formed the zoo—including one surprising exhibit, an Airedale—were housed in cages in twenty-two flimsy, rat-ridden wooden structures behind the Arsenal, the security of whose bars was questionable. The fire hazard was recognized as great. Keepers were armed with rifles. In the event of fire, when the big carnivores, maddened by the flames, might burst from their cages, the keepers were to shoot.

All during early 1934, with its abnormally bitter winter weather, architects, engineers, and draftsmen inside the Arsenal worked fourteen-hour days, and engineers and laborers outside in the Park did the same. They were toiling to produce the result that Moses had visualized, a concept whose outlines were quite fixed in his mind. Among other things, the Merkel report was reread and some of its suggestions implemented, such as walling off the Cave. This happy invention of Olmsted's, a jocular touch of outdoor Gothic, lay in the Ramble northwest of the Lake. In the early years of this century, less mannerly than the last, it had become a toilet chamber for the untidy. So Moses doomed it. Moses also adopted Merkel's idea of the perimeter playgrounds. But the new commissioner installed nineteen instead of the "ultimate concession" of eight.

Moses believed that the Park was a place where people—the people of the twentieth century—should have a good time. A primary factor in this, Moses thought, was active outdoor recreation. Here he differed sharply from Olmsted. The vast changes that Moses was about to make couldn't truthfully be called a decline of the Park. Olmsted, a handy type with words, might have called the actions well-intentioned heretical tinkering. However, the disparity of view between the two men isn't surprising. Public habits and expectations had changed markedly during the years that separated them. And Moses saw the new leisure of the populace as crying for means of active recreation.

In less than a year, in early December 1934, Moses, the miracle worker, had opened his new zoo to concerted municipal cheers. In place of the previous moldering shacks were attractive red brick and white concrete buildings forming, with the Arsenal, a square surrounding the seal pool. This was set amid concrete walkways enlivened by patches of green turf back of low hedges. One of the buildings contained a restaurant selling good food at reasonable prices, with an attached terrace from which diners could watch the gamboling of the seals. At the four corners of the seal pool quadrangle were towering wire cages inhabited by eagles and hawks. Many large and small artistic touches typical of Moses adorned the newly opened site, including colorful striped awnings over the dining terrace and a nineteenth-century artistic animal sculpture, the Dancing Goat, rescued from obscurity elsewhere in the Park and placed where Olmsted long ago had suggested was the proper environment for animal statues. The assemblage of buildings had neatly designed arcades between the animal houses and atop of each were white stone friezes bearing likenesses of the exhibits within.

Moses's constructions and improvements in the Park included, but did not end with, reseeding lawns, repaving walks and roads, repairing comfort stations and drinking fountains, removing dead trees and planting new ones, repairing and replacing benches and waste baskets, resurfacing tennis courts and playgrounds, where new equipment consisting of jungle gyms, slides, and sand boxes were installed along with benches for the mothers, sandblasting the six miles of the exterior walls, which revealed after many years of sullen drabness their original attractive dark cream color, placing low, iron-loop fencing around the lawns, the psychological intent of which being to deter trespassers without challenging them, and cleaning and restoring the Park's neglected statues and monuments. The Maine monument, for example, at the southwest corner off Columbus Circle, the Park's largest art work, commemorates the two hundred sixty officers and men who died in the explosion of that battleship in Havana's harbor in 1898. Projecting from one side of the enormous marble pylon is the shape of the bow of a ship representing the "Anti-Bellum State of Mind." It carries four figures, the foremost of which is of that of a boy depicting Victory. Originally he held an olive branch in each hand. When Moses came to office, not only was the centopath crusty with bird droppings and civic grime, but the leafy sprays and the boy's hands, to boot, were missing. For weeks, tarpaulins hid scaffolding holding diligent Moses workers. When the cloths were removed, not only was the surface resplendently clean but the boy's hands once again held the symbols of peace.

Another Moses construction was the Wollman Rink in the Park's southern center at the level of 62nd Street, formed from the northern bay of the Pond. The artificial surface provided skatable ice throughout the

*The zoo in the Robert Moses era, circa 1934. The umbrellaed terrace
afforded a full view of the sea lions and other goings-on in the
foreground, and was a famous gathering place for European émigrés.*
(Parks Department Archives.)

season. Lewis Mumford, the architectural critic, as well as a number of
landscape pundits, with an eye to the Park's original design, called the
rink an affront. Still other opposers lamented the loss of the waters of the
Pond. Moses paid no attention. The rink was at once, and has remained
throughout the years, enormously popular.

Moses also had Central Park's buildings, including the original rustic
ones, overhauled and mended. He banished the herd of malformed sheep,
the sorry product of municipal neglect that had allowed decades of inter-
breeding. The architecturally notable Sheepfold was turned into the
Tavern on the Green, a plush restaurant-cum-terrace-cum-dance floor.

Depression drifters were chased from the Old Reservoir bed, where, instead, Moses established the thirty-acre Great Lawn, with flagstones around it and rimmed with scores of Japanese cherry trees.

South of the Lawn he placed what he called the Belvedere Lake, now renamed Turtle Pond. He revived the Shakespeare Garden, where the West Drive crosses over the 79th Street transverse. Each plant he had marked with a relevant quotation of the poet. He instituted an effective rat

extermination program in the old zoo area, where for years the rodents had been in charge. On the North Meadow he installed handball courts, wading pools, and more than a dozen baseball diamonds, all in pursuit of his ideal of giving New Yorkers the wherewithal for recreational happiness.

During more than a quarter of a century, Commissioner Moses ruled Central Park with an iron hand. Who, today, can say he ruled badly? He did

At the original Wollman Rink (1951), skating classes were held for schoolchildren. The adjoining building had a restaurant and a roof terrace. (Parks Department Archives.)

not really care to leave a park in its most natural state. When he saw a lordly grove of trees, he saw not an imposing sylvan array, an act of nature breathtaking in its dappled beauty, with leaves sparkling and trembling in sunshine, but an active baseball diamond or soccer field. Very often, and in very short order, that's just what the grove became. Moses, partly by the power of his personality and partly by his reputation as a selfless public servant, somewhat shamelessly conned the environmentalists of the day. They believed him utterly devoted to the Park ideal. Actually, for much of the time, particularly in the early years of his reign, these good people did not understand his aims. They were naive, unalloyed nature lovers. Often they were persons of some influence.

Moses took care, as much as possible, never openly to confront presumptive dissenters. He was a practiced nighttime marcher. His weapon was covert surprise. Before those who might be antagonistic knew what he was up to, the deed was done. Herewith an example. Knowing how possessively those around the Park watch its features, he ordered a forestry squad to remove a notable old gingko tree before dawn, while its guardian angels were in dreamland. Early political infighting had long ago taught Moses the value of the end run, the quiet fait accompli, of which the gingko coup was a case in point. While complaint thereafter was theoretically possible, it was largely ineffective. Was Moses sometimes underhanded? Yes. Was he successful? Almost always.

The most notable occasion when he was *not* started in April of 1956, well along in the era of his imperial rule. The episode centered on a parking lot, which was to be installed for the fashionable and wealthy patrons of the new Tavern on the Green. The spot selected was a grassy hollow shaded by maple trees, barely to the northwest at 68th Street. Neighborhood mothers, however, habitually frequented it with their children. It was a small, secluded ampitheater, ideal for rest and recreation, safe for youngsters, and soothing for adults. Learning of the plan through observation of an exposed blueprint left on the grass by Park engineers, twenty-three mothers signed a petition to Moses asking that the parking lot idea be abandoned and their children's play area left as it was.

The whole affair at that point, by the parks commissioner's standards, was a silly piece of opposition. As Robert Caro in his biography of Moses has pointed out, he had just finished dislodging hundreds of mothers in the Bronx rather than alter the course of his Cross-Bronx Expressway by one lone block. Currently he was in the act of ousting five thousand mothers for the construction of Manhattantown, a West Side urban renewal project, and four thousand more for that of Lincoln Center. When there were outcries at such Moses acts—and there had been many—most local papers paid no attention, so great was the impression that Moses could do no wrong.

In the eight days following the petition by the Central Park mothers, some trivial backing and filling between the two sides took place. Then Moses made a characteristic move. Without public notice, he dispatched a bulldozer to the site to take off the turf and topple the trees. Seeing this, a few indignant mothers quickly assembled and stood in front of the machine. Whereat the operator stopped work. Such an impasse between Moses and mothers elsewhere in the city might have been a journalistic cipher. But this was *Central Park*. Media representatives of every stripe came running. The event received wide coverage. As a *New York Times* editorial was to say, "If this were land somewhere else there would be nothing to get excited about. But Central Park is different. To New Yorkers, and especially those who live near the Park, it is sacred land. To use it for anything but park is like insulting the flag."

Sensing instinctively the feeling that lay behind the *Time*'s words, the mothers fought on, vexing the commissioner more than a little. They were joined, con brio, by newsmen whose stories uncharacteristically began carrying an anti-Moses bias. The mothers were hailed in a headline as "Fighting Park Moms" and described in another paper as "embattled mothers."

Within a week Moses struck back under cover of darkness, shortly after midnight, when the watchful eyes of the mothers were closed. An elite task force composed of gardeners, laborers, a bulldozer, its operator, and more than thirty police officers under the command of an inspector went to work. A fence was erected, ringed by the police. Inside, the bulldozer started up and axmen attacked the trees. Dawn came and the treachery was discovered. Mothers flocked to the scene. The assault continued. There were tears. These were accompanied by the steady grinding of cameras—movie and television—and the clicks of still ones, held by photographers of every ilk, bulwarked, naturally, by their note-taking colleagues, the reporters.

With this sneak attack, the roof fell in on Moses. The episode with the mothers had unmasked him as someone who, as though by divine revelation, knew both what New Yorkers needed and who was the person to provide it. Most of his arbitrary acts in Central Park, such as the introduction of soccer fields and handball courts, could be considered Park purposes, according to the broader post-Olmsted use of that term. But there was no way—absolutely none—to confuse the construction of a parking lot for a restaurant with a legitimate Park purpose. In July a Parks Department press release went out. It announced that the parking lot would not be built. The site, raped of its trees and turf, would, instead, become a playground for children. Nobody was fooled.

Four years later, at the age of seventy-two, the old lion abdicated the Park's commissionership. He had done an enormous amount for Central Park, made enormous changes in it, most of them constructive considering they were for use in the twentieth century. And he skillfully used federal money, avoiding cost to the city for much of his modification. But no longer (courtesy of the mothers) was his an unflawed image. The man who had radically altered the face of Central Park (not to mention that of the city and its environs) left a somewhat diminished figure. The halo that had rested for so long above that imposing head was a bit askew.

Except for Gordon J. Davis, who held office from 1978 to 1983, eight commissioners over a period of eighteen years followed Robert Moses and filled—or attempted to fill—the large sitzmark of their illustrious predecessor. Under these eight short-termers, the Park suffered its bleakest period yet. Also, and further confusing a confused situation, the parks commissioner title in 1968—in the middle of the Lindsay administration—became the commissioner of parks, recreation, and cultural affairs. The cloudy rationale for this was that parks in the city were no longer merely parks but also centers of recreation and cultural affairs. Furthermore, heavy thinkers in the department believed that a bureaucracy with a long name operated better than a bureaucracy with a short name. The more activities could be crammed under a departmental umbrella, the better the department would work and the faster and more generously federal money would arrive.

Eight years later, Mayor Abraham Beame, in the middle of *his* administration, disagreed. At his instance, under a new law, the commissioner headed the Department of Parks and Recreation, the recreation tag being retained because of the many sports facilities throughout the city's wide-ranging 26,410-acre departmental realm, which encompasses 572 parks, 900 playgrounds, 104 swimming pools, 535 tennis courts, 6 beaches, and various supplementary oddments. With the Beame move, the Department of Cultural Affairs became another city entity, which it remains to this day. As far as Central Park was concerned, under both departmental names its old problem persisted: it was underfunded.

Tenure among the first eight successors of Robert Moses ranged from nearly six years to only four months. The longest was that of Newbold Morris, a protégé of Moses. Old-timers in the department say that no day passed without a call from Morris for advice and encouragement. Although the eight commissioners were of highly diverse ability, none, unsurprisingly, had Moses's power or prestige, or his easy ability to get things done for Central Park with federal money. All the commissioners had to look to City Hall for money and to no other place. Often it was like taking a bucket to a dry well. Parks maintenance dollars had always been hard to come by, now they were even scarcer. In addition, increasing vandalism spread the available funds still thinner. Toward the end of the

LEFT. Several cascades in the Park's northern section flowed from the Pool to the Loch to the Meer. (Herbert Mitchell Collection.)

RIGHT. By the 1970s, this Cascade had become a pile of dry rock. (Sara Cedar Miller, Central Park Conservancy.)

Further evidence of unchecked erosion in Central Park. (Sara Cedar Miller, Central Park Conservancy.)

post-Moses period, partly because of rampant vandalism and partly because of the city's fiscal straits, some of the eight men had to be entreated to take the commissionership.

Long before the time of the eight short-termers, and around the time that Parsons was having trouble with finances, a number of public-minded citizens began to agitate for improvements in Central Park that were clearly necessary. From these groups, which first became vocal in 1904, there arose The Parks and Playground Association of the City of New York, the earliest of the effective park-defense bodies. Among other things, it helped prevent plans for cemeteries and library buildings in the Park and open-cut subway construction through the Park.

The threat of further intrusions caused all the Park guardian groups to band together. A nucleus of these invited the leaders of more than forty civic organizations to draw upon their resources in aid of all the city parks. As a result, the Parks Conservation Association was formed. During this rather benighted environmental period in our country's history, the association's prestige and accomplishments were so unusual that requests for its advice about park management came from a number of states, including Kentucky, Pennsylvania, Tennessee, and Virginia.

In 1926, the Central Park Association was formed. A *New York Times* article suggested how much this was needed: "The gradual devastation of lawns and foliage which began three decades ago was accelerated and brought to a head by the eight years of the Hylan administration. The Park, as it now stands, with its sordid litter under foot and its gaunt, starved branches overhead, does not win the love and loyalty of those who think of it as it was in its prime." The new group's purpose is given herewith: "The Association was organized to stimulate and aid the City of New York to restore Central Park to life and vigor, and then keep it as a public trust, to keep it for the benefit of those living and those to come."

Three years later the Park Association of New York City was born through the amalgamation of three of the strongest park associations, the Central Park Association, the Battery Park Association, and the Parks and Playground Association. Its objective was set as follows: "The Park Association of New York City is an association of citizens who believe that parks are a fundamental need of city life, essential to the mental, moral and physical well-being of city dwellers." Its platform was to develop and protect existing parks, to fight encroachments, and to extend the park system.

Since the late 1920s other organizations seeking to aid Central Park have arisen. Among them are the Council on Parks and Playgrounds, the Parks Council, the Friends of Central Park, the Greensward Foundation, the Central Park Community Fund, the Central Park Task Force, and the Consultative Group of Organizations Interested in Central Park, whose forty-one components number, among others, the Central Park Bird Watchers, the Central Park Medical Unit, the Central Park Police Precinct Community Council, the Citizens Committee for New York, the Frederick Law Olmsted Association, and Save Central Park. Most of these bodies are still active. All had, or have, a similar hope: Central Park's resuscitation.

That hope was succinctly expressed by the closing words of a little book setting forth the rationale of the then-new Central Park Association: "If the congestion of 1851 required the erection of Central Park, the greater congestion of 1926 requires its ample restoration and protection."

But over five restless decades—the 1930s through the 1970s—despite the valiant hopes and efforts of all these organizations, the restorer and protector never materialized.

Three

Our Prime Recreation Ground Restored

1979–1989

A NINETEENTH-CENTURY EDITORIALIST called Central Park as great a masterpiece as the Parthenon. When one considers the many forms in which art reveals itself, this is not so strange a comparison. While the creators of the Parthenon shaped its marble into the breathtaking symmetry that for so long has awed and humbled gazers, Central Park, a quite different type of architecture, is the country's oldest and perhaps still its greatest example of the *landscape* variety.

Today the Parthenon is no longer as it came fresh from the hand of Phidias. Time and history have left it a ravaged pile of stony beauty, yet a vision still unforgettable on a moon-blanched night atop the Attic hill. The Park, too, is not as its creators left it. Like the Parthenon, its large-scale design remains as it was—supple, beautiful, and largely indestructible by man. But only a few years back this was not true of much of the rest of the Park. The Moses recovery period did not last forever. Man's ineptitude thereafter was displayed in lack of general maintenance, which rendered the whole infrastructure of pipes and drains largely inoperative. Partly as a result of this and partly due to other forms of neglect, water bodies, roads, and paths were badly silted, comfort stations were closed, lawns were often incipient dustbowls, the drinking and ornamental fountains went dry, and many Park structures were heavily vandalized and graffiti-marred. The disheartening situation was similar to that which had confronted the designers a century before. Now, it was manmade disfigurement in place of the nineteenth-century squatters shacks, pig pens, and swamps that had once dotted the place.

Today, the bleak scene for Central Park is changing. The long-term outlook is, in fact, rosy. This began in 1978, when the city's lengthy fiscal crisis ended and funds became available for the Park's rescue. The person then overseeing all the city parks was the newly appointed Gordon Davis, a black graduate of Harvard Law School, the son of a Chicago clergyman and the parks commissioner. Edward L. Koch, mayor at the time, called him "one of my stars." Koch plucked Davis from the City Planning Commission, a seven-member body concerned with planning and zoning and public improvements in all aspects of the city's development, including parks.

From such a background, Davis came to his post with pronounced ideas as to what should be done. Most of his ideas were logical; all were firm. One of the best was his support for the idea of an administrator of Central Park, someone whose immediate obligation would be to oversee the Park's programs and betterment. In 1979 Davis persuaded the mayor to approve such an appointment. The person named was Elizabeth Barlow, a transplanted Texan who likes to be called Betsy. For the first time since the city's dismissal of Olmsted in 1878, a single individual had the primary responsibility for the Park's maintenance and day-to-day operation.

Then forty-three, Betsy Barlow, a Wellesley graduate with a Yale master's degree in city planning, had strong feelings about preserving and bettering the environment. She had written three books, one about Jamaica Bay and Pelham Park, *The Forests and Wetlands of New York City;* another on Frederick Law Olmsted, *Frederick Law Olmsted's New York;* and a third, *The Central Park Book,* the product of Barlow, as author and editor, and three collaborative specialists in Park art, geology, and nature.

In the half dozen years before her appointment, Barlow had been prominent in the private (and quite determined) effort to save Central Park during New York's fiscal crisis. While the movement was small, it included influential individuals and several influential organizations, among them the Central Park Community Fund, the Central Park Task Force, the Friends of Central Park, and the Parks Council. Through their combined efforts, more than one improvement or reconstruction was accomplished with the aid of federal or private money. An example of the latter was the 1972 restoration of Bow Bridge, spanning a narrow section of the Lake, the most beautiful and elaborate of the Park's original six cast iron bridges, of which five remain. All were designed differently, as was virtually every one of the arches, benches, boat landings, bridges, fountains, shelters, and spans installed in the Park. The $200,000 cost of putting Bow Bridge back in shape was borne by Lucy Moses, the widow of a New York lawyer, and Lila Acheson Wallace, cofounder of *Reader's Digest,* highly philanthropic women. Before Betsy Barlow's appointment as administrator, she was active on this scene, as executive director of the

Central Park Task Force, perhaps the busiest of the organizations in the Park rescue effort.

In 1980 Commissioner Davis dusted off another useful notion, namely, to solicit help from the private sector. Barlow was in enthusiastic accord, and Davis, his arguments at the ready, went to see the mayor once again. Success followed. In December of 1980, the mayor announced the formation of the Central Park Conservancy to raise funds from corporations, foundations, and private individuals. A thirty-four–member board of trustees was appointed, largely composed of public-spirited citizens, and William Beinecke, a recently retired lawyer, was named chairman. Since then the Conservancy has handsomely performed its task of fund raising and undertaking various jobs connected with the Park's renewal. These have included project design, repair and maintenance, horticultural chores, and visitor services. More about the Conservancy's activity will appear in Chapter 14.

Before long, the truth became apparent: a patchwork approach to the rehabilitation of the Park was worthless. A different treatment would have to be found, with an effective maintenance schedule. But before such a gigantic scenario could be fashioned, it was necessary to know what the current Park had, and lacked, in physical plant, current maintenance, and user needs.

Ten surveys were commissioned in 1981, to be undertaken by various specialists, with the Conservancy footing the bill. With one exception, the surveys, were completed at various times through 1984. They dealt with the Park's archives, circulation, hydrology, management, use, security, soil, structural inventory, trees and vegetation, and wildlife.

The archives survey aimed to find and classify the thousands upon thousands of Park documents and pictures produced during its century-plus of life; circulation was to chart the present pedestrian, equestrian, and vehicular traffic patterns and to suggest better patterns; and hydrology dealt with surface and subsurface water, erosion, watershed systems, and the like. Management, the one exception, was completed in 1985. It was to devise the best way to handle the three essentials of good park-keeping: restoration of features and structures, their day-to-day care, and the wisest policies for their continued use. The Park use survey was to learn from Park visitors how and why they used the Park, the demographics of the users, and the relative popularity of the Park at various times of day, as well as the relative popularity of areas and facilities. Security was to provide safety data, including an analysis of crime statistics and a review of the emergency callbox system. The soil survey, the first such urban investigation undertaken by the Soil Conservation Services of the U.S. Department of Agriculture, provided a description and map of all Park soil types; the structural inventory inventoried the manifold man-made objects in the Park, past and present; trees and vegetation provided that data for botany; and wildlife did the same for that category. The results of these investigations caused the administrator to say, "No tract of this size has ever been so thoroughly scrutinized."

The statement seems accurate. The Park use survey, for example, was supervised by two sociologists from the City University of New York. Its findings were based principally on the following: a one-day check of more than a thousand visitors leaving the Park during one summer and one fall month; counts and reasons for entry of all users on two other days; general crowd observations during a three-month summer span; and interviews with selected Park staff.

The survey estimated that at least thirteen million visitors have come to the Park each year since an earlier study was done in 1973. Despite a population loss of 10 percent in Manhattan and more than that in areas immediately adjoining the Park, attendance held steady, showing that actual use of the Park increased. Most of those who come are New Yorkers, but 750,000 are not. Thus the Park ranks as an important tourist draw along with the Statue of Liberty and the United Nations, the other major attractions in the city.

The survey also provided data on local population changes. The earlier study found Park entrants to be 77 percent white, 12 percent black, 9 percent Hispanic, and 2 percent other; in the one ordered by the administrator, 55 percent were white, 20 percent black, 19 percent Hispanic, and 6 percent Asian.

Sports, of course, have increased considerably in the Park. Partly because of this influx of law-abiding users, and partly because of the uniformed forces of Park Rangers and the Park Enforcement Patrol staff, commonly known as Peps, as well as greater city police protection, the survey found that people felt the Park was safer than formerly. (Our hopes that incidents such as that which occurred to the woman jogger in 1989 will remain as exceptional cases.)

Olmsted's strongly held assumption about a park's true purpose was found by this survey to be correct. An overwhelming majority of visitors, more than 57 percent, enter the Park solely for relaxation, supporting the designer's theory that men and women are tightly linked to nature by their own makeup. Exposure to turf, trees, fresh air, and the glint of light on water revives city-worn psyches like nothing else.

The next largest category of Park users is sports addicts. They comprise a mere 9.7 percent, but, being vocal, are often responsible for changes. With their impetus Olmsted saw baseball diamonds and tennis courts dot his one-time lush and sweeping meadows, developments that he philosophically accepted as unavoidable.

The user survey admittedly was not airtight. In order to be all-inclusive, it would "be necessary to schedule an ambitious gate-by-gate count of Park traffic," which had not been done in more than a century. Among the uncounted users, the survey pointed out, were concert audiences ("Today's concerts routinely draw over 300,000 persons"), also joggers, numbering by police estimates 5,000 daily, and those who attend political rallies or important athletic events, such as the New York City Marathon, that terminate in Central Park. The survey also did not count the students from thirty private schools within walking distance of the park who use it every fine day for exercise, from 2,200 to 3,100 young people, or of forty-five more distant public or private schools that schedule sports programs there, or the several thousand people, mostly from the West Side, who "commute" through the Park to work daily. The survey did note, during its summer observation period, that fifty to one hundred people slept in the Park, most of them around the rocks south of the Dairy. Overnight occupancy, while in violation of the rules, probably always has been, and probably always will be, a feature of the Park.

The survey also found that the Park's busiest time was fair, warm Sunday afternoons, and the busiest place was the Zoo, a circumstance that may recur now with the new Zoo.

The closest thing to a complete count of Park visitors took place under (who else?) Olmsted, in the years 1863 to 1873. Keepers at each of the gates daily tallied the entrants for the Park's busiest nine-hour period, enumerating those who arrived on foot, on horseback, or in vehicles. From 1871 through 1873, more than ten million Park visitors were counted annually. At this time, the city's population center was two miles to the south. It therefore seems plausible, considering the nineteenth-century numbers and the omissions by the 1982 study, that today's entrants number at least twenty million a year.

The structural inventory, similarly, is typical of the depth of the surveys. It enumerates every manmade object known to have stood on the surface of the Park, now or in the past, those vanished and those still present. Its twelve categories consist of arbors, bridges (and arches), buildings, fountains, gardens, major equipment housings, monuments, towers, playgrounds, plazas, shelters, and water bodies. It records four hundred seventy-two items, of which three hundred seventy-six survive and ninety-six do not. The longest section is that for buildings. Of its total of one hundred eleven, seventy-two can still be found, thirty-nine cannot. The largest intact subdivision therein is that for maintenance buildings, all of the sixteen erected still being in place, as is the case with the reservoir buildings. Almost in that situation is the segment on concession structures, whose total of eighteen has lost only one to time or circumstance. However, nineteen of the thirty comfort stations have disappeared.

Monuments are the second largest grouping. Of its one hundred and two total, only three have gone, all animal or allegorical representations. The other classes of monuments, in some cases admittedly arbitrary, are busts, commemorative portrait statues, equestrian portrait statues, benches, gates, plaques (with twenty-one the most numerous entry), mixed forms of art, and other, less easily classified works.

Of the remaining ten headings whose composition so far has not been broken down, the total units under these amount to thirty-one, comprising two hundred sixty-three objects, existing and vanished. To detail them would overburden the point that the surveys were comprehensive. But comprehensive they certainly were, as those for park use and structural inventory clearly show.

For over two years the staffs of the Conservancy and the administrator studied the surveys, including the by then complete management survey. They realized that a plan that would deal effectively with the operation of the Park would also have to seem reasonable—or as reasonable as possible—to the Park's diverse sets of users, some notably opinionated.

With this in mind, those responsible came up with a six-point program: to resurrect the functional and structural integrity of the original Park design when necessary; to protect and preserve these features in the future; to give special attention to the historical aspects of the Park, the prototype for so many others; to provide for public safety and enjoyment within the wide spectrum of user activity; to maintain a clean and structurally sound Park, attainments that notably decrease crime and enhance visitor gratification; and, last, to encourage the Park's horticultural beauty.

Following the study, a document that embodied these requirements was published in May of 1986. The ninety-six–page, heavily illustrated treatise with the measurements of a tabloid newspaper was entitled *Rebuilding Central Park: A Management and Restoration Plan.* At a press conference that included slides to explain the highlights of the paper, speakers emphasized that the document was a draft and thus could be amended as necessary. A September deadline was set for public comments. Of these, the most numerous came from the Park's equestrians, a group who pay an estimated fifty thousand visits a year. They objected to the proposed elimination of the bridle trail below the West 86th Street entrance and its conversion to a walkway. Originally the bridle path began in the southeast corner at the 59th Street and Fifth Avenue entrance. In the nineteenth and early twentieth centuries there were many more riders than now. Most of them owned their own horses and belonged to a stylish group called the Early Risers. Followed by liveried grooms, the men wearing derbies and the women sometimes sitting sidesaddle, they entered at the southeast corner and regularly rode mornings from six to nine. A formal dinner at Sherry's for the members one winter was also attended, naturally, by the horses. Imagination has often been unconstrained in users of Central Park.

In the middle years of this century, however, construction of the Wollman Rink, the Hecksher ballfields, and the southward extension of the Zoo eliminated the southeast entrance to the bridle trail. This meant that it started in the Park at the level of 62nd Street and Seventh Avenue and had no outside entry there. Today's riders, almost without exception, rent horses from the Claremont Stable on West 89th Street. The steeds are citywise and automatically stop at red lights. Horse and rider enter the Park at West 86th Street and concentrate on the miles of trail looping the reservoir and extending into the northern section. Under these circumstances, the proposal to turn the largely unused southern portion of the trail into a pedestrian path seems an improvement and will be carried out, despite the feelings of the equestrians.

At the end of the nineteenth century, many people owned their own horses. Note the well-maintained bridle paths. (Parks Department Annual Report.)

*F*OR SATISFACTORY PARK USE, there must be rules. Also, changes, where desirable, must be effected according to past Park traditions. Furthermore, facilities must be created to care for new needs. Some examples follow.

An important rule limits the use of automobiles. It prevents cars entering the Park on weekends year-round from 7 P.M. the day before to 6 A.M. the day after. In the Park's busiest season, from early spring through October, cars are also banned in the Park daily from 10 A.M. to 3 P.M. and from 7 P.M. to 10 P.M., the sole exception being that the lane running north from 59th Street and Sixth Avenue to 72nd Street and Fifth Avenue is closed only from 7 P.M. to 10 P.M. These regulations particularly favor joggers and cyclists. The restriction is good for the flora, too. Trees, especially, droop under automobile fumes. How these affect *us* is another matter.

The administrator has given Park lighting an improved optical system with a metal-halide bulb, affording cool, even, abundant light. The whole is contained in a new, vandal-resistant luminaire, whose attractive, basket-shaped head was designed with the aid of a grant from Consolidated Edison of New York. The lights have been sited to increase illumination in areas of heavy nighttime use, such as Bethesda Terrace, where three- and five-headed fixtures have been installed, and, on the other hand, to curtail it in sections where public use after dark should be discouraged. Through these technical advances, the former number of 1,541 lamp posts has now been reduced by a third. Almost all the posts that remain have an additional virtue. They help the visitor know his location. A metal tag affixed about four feet up on the post bears numbers. The first two give the street level; the last two, if even, mean the east half, if odd the west half, of the Park. Thus 8612 says the post is at the level of 86th Street on the Park's east side.

Signs are important, too. These publicly displayed notices provide essential information, telling visitors such things as how to get where they want to go, where they are then, and what they can and cannot do. A scheme of coordinated placement of a new batch of signs in the Park features those with clear, succinct text and newly designed graphics, displacing a much larger number of haphazard and often unsightly examples. Clear, crisp signs, well maintained, are a manifest mark of good Park management; they increase a sense of security.

Among other innovations is the Visitor Information Center in the Dairy. It is now staffed Tuesday through Sunday, 11 A.M. to 5 P.M., March 1 through October 31, except Fridays, when the opening hour is 1 P.M.; in the colder weather from November 1 through February 28, closing time is 4 P.M. Personnel at the other end of the phone line (212-397-3156) will answer all queries about current and upcoming Park activities. The center offers changing exhibits and slide shows of Park design and history, a library of Park-related books, and stocks an assortment of Park-connected gifts.

Large and highly visible locator maps are attached to stout posts at eleven Park entrances. In addition, the third floor of the Arsenal, the Parks Department headquarters in the large, turreted, 1848 building facing Fifth Avenue at 64th Street, is now an art gallery and cultural events center whose presentations change periodically throughout the year.

Also, there are passive recreation areas, where team sports are prohibited. A prominent example is the Sheep Meadow; here, activities are quiet ones—lounging, sunbathing, and picnicking. Recreation lanes for cyclists have been marked out along the drives to keep riders safe from car traffic. The once dank arches, with entries often shrouded by vegetation, have been cleared and are electrically lighted at night by small specialized bulbs.

On top of all this, ornamental benches with a light metal frame supporting a wooden seat and back have been set out in selected spots, such as along the Mall and around Belvedere Castle, to provide a touch of elegance. (The common Park bench, that sturdy creature of concrete side pieces to which are bolted heavy wood slats, is elsewhere, posing an almost insurmountable challenge to vandal-incited demolition.) Altogether, the Park has 7,674 benches, with seating for 23,022 adults.

Finally, to name just one more change, flags are flying once again in the Park, a colorful tradition throughout much of its history. Vandalized or rusted flagpole paraphernalia—lines, hardware, halyard boxes, and cleats—have been repaired or replaced thanks to the generosity of a flag

*Recreation in the Park. Lawn bowler on the Bowling Green, north of
the Sheep Meadow.* (Sara Cedar Miller, Central Park Conservancy.)

and flagpole company. The halyard boxes, which raise and lower the colors atop the poles, have been placed fifteen feet above ground, out of the reach of mischievous hands, and new flags of polyester, more durable than the old cotton, have been supplied.

Much of this rehabilitation took place after the arrival of Commissioner Davis in 1978. However, five years later, after heading an administration that had been outstandingly resolute and active, he resolutely and actively left to join a downtown law firm, feeling that his goals had been achieved, including instilling in the department a high level of esprit de corps, bestowing on the word *Parkie*—the intimate term for one of his people—a certain chest-expanding satisfaction.

Mayor Koch filled the vacancy with another superior civil servant, the present commissioner, Henry J. Stern, then forty-eight years old. At the time of his appointment, he had been a member of the City Council for nine years and before that active in city government for eleven more. In naming Stern, the mayor said, "I believe there are few people in this city who know as much as he does about the workings of government, and, in particular, the value of parks and how to expand their use by the people of this city. . . . He will bring something special to the job of parks commissioner." Under Stern, the morale of the Parks Department has remained high, and so has the priority of rehabilitating Central Park.

Were one to compare the two commissioners, Davis seems more the forthright executive type, unafraid to brandish the iron fist when necessary. Stern, on the other hand, is more a green-thumb type, carrying out his policies with the amiable quality one associates with gardners. And, indeed, some of his moves have had a distinctly botanical touch, such as pointing out unusual trees in the Park and replacing unused pavement with grass. Stern would also like to see grass once again on the nearly one-quarter of the original turfed surface that has become bare. And he has a feel for apt nomenclature, having rechristened Belvedere Lake as Turtle Pond.

Of the restorations so far accomplished in the dual Davis–Stern commissionerships, the most extensive and expensive has been that of the Esplanade containing the Bethesda Fountain, one of the designers' especial prides. It is the formal focus, fronting the Lake, of the southern, more heavily used part of the Park. From it the visitor can view the ample water body and the wooded Ramble beyond, topped by the toy castle sitting on Vista Rock, the second highest elevation in the Park. This is only a few feet lower than the high point, 137 ½-foot Summit Rock, standing just inside the perimeter wall at Central Park West and 83rd Street.

The Esplanade lies in the middle of the Park at the level of 72nd Street. Its center holds the impressive, three-tiered, twenty-six-foot–high, statue-surmounted Bethesda Fountain, the largest fountain in the city, its basin of ninety-six–foot diameter holding fifty-two thousand gallons of water. The bronze, winged figure at the top, the work of the sculptor Emma Stebbins and emplaced in 1873, represents the Angel of the Waters, who, according to the Gospel of John, descended into Jerusalem from time to time to trouble the waters of the Pool of Bethesda, imparting to them the ability to heal the sick and infirm.

Surrounding the fountain is a spacious flagstone plaza whose formal name is the Esplanade, its northern edge bordering the Lake, its eastern and western edges ending against waist-high stone walls, backed by knolls once bearing lawns and selected plantings of trees and bushes. Its edge to the south runs into two massive balustraded stone staircases, copiously ornamented with sandstone carvings of birds, flowers, and fruit, representing some of the finest Victorian art work of its kind anywhere. Between the two staircases is a long arcade running beneath the 72nd Street cross-Park drive and emerging at its other end at the foot of stairs leading to the upper limit of the Mall, the wide, stately promenade with its flanking rows of elm trees, by which many users arrive at Bethesda Fountain. The arcade is roofed with beautiful Minton tiles set in gilt ironwork, originally forming an underground jewel box, as someone in those early halcyon days remarked.

When renewal began on the Esplanade in 1983, it was in sorry shape. Weather and human hands had marred the exquisite sandstone carvings. Seepage from the driveway above the arcade had loosened the tiles and rusted the gilt ironwork. Trees injudiciously planted too near the stone walls had shaded out the turf, causing sediment to wash around the barrier ends onto the Esplanade. Roots from the trees had pushed the walls out of line. Frost had heaved many flagstones and buckled stone risers in the staircases. Sections of the fountain coping were damaged or awry.

During restoration, as many readers will recall, the Esplanade and much of the surrounding area were completely fenced off. Extensive waterproofing was undertaken where needed, and a new concrete deck laid under the driveway above the arcade. The landscape of the knolls was refitted with shade-loving grass and shrubs and fewer trees. Cranes lifted clear great sections of the ponderous stone balustrades for repointing. Deteriorated sections of the fountain coping were renewed with their identical bluestone, to obtain which the original quarry was reopened up, as was the case with the one in Nova Scotia, which supplied material to repair the carvings. Master stone cutters duplicated the figures, fastening their work to the old surface with steel pins and a polyester-resin adhesive. A larger pumphouse was obtained for the fountain, allowing a cloud-like mist from spray to surround the Angel, as was the original intention. After two years and an expenditure of $4.5 million of the city's capital funds, and several hundred thousand more from private sources and the Conservancy, the arduous and delicate task was done.

Another important restoration, completed in 1982, was the Belvedere, the castle on Vista Rock. From its terraces and upper floors the views of the Park east, west, north, and south are superb. Olmsted particularly

The Esplanade of the Bethesda Fountain, at the turn of the century.
(Herbert Mitchell Collection.)

meant the view to the Lake, Bethesda Fountain, and the Mall to be clear, not obscured by trees. The Castle, in this century, long the office of a weatherman, became a virtual wreck when the meteorologist departed in 1969 for another Park location. After that, the unoccupied building became the target of some of the most ambitious masonry demolishers the Park has ever known. And it has known experts.

Thanks to funding of design proposals by two foundations, the city

One of the more difficult and demanding Park restoration projects took place in 1983. A huge crane removes an entire section of the massive balustrade at Bethesda Fountain Esplanade for cleaning, resetting, and recarving of the sandstone birds and flowers.
(Steve Zalben.)

Belvedere Castle, before the current restoration. The work of vandals is all too clear. (Sara Cedar Miller, Central Park Conservancy.)

committed $1.2 million to restore the Belvedere, and today it is the Central Park Learning Center, managed by the Conservancy, and visited monthly by thousands who come for the many cultural and educational programs presented there. Groups of schoolchildren arrive with teachers on weekdays and children with their parents on weekends. The Castle's hours are the same as the Dairy's.

Another important restoration is the transformation of a badly eroded, two-and-a-half–acre, tear-shaped piece of ground just inside the Women's Gate at Central Park West and 72nd Street into a site known as Strawberry Fields. This now verdant, tranquil pleasance honors the memory of the singer and composer John Lennon, who lived in, and was murdered in front of, the Dakota apartment house only a stone's throw away. Strawberry Fields was the name of one of his songs. Its namesake in the Park was funded by his widow, Yoko Ono, who provided $600,000 for its construction and a $400,000 endowment for its maintenance. Lennon was a much beloved international figure for his efforts to foster understanding between nations. Gifts, mostly botanic, from over one hundred countries are on the site, along with twenty-five hundred strawberry plants.

*I*N *THE* roughly nine years of the Central Park Conservancy's existence, it has provided substantial assistance to the multimillion-dollar renewal program. It expects to do so until the job is complete, now estimated to be sometime in the mid-1990s, and into the indefinite future as well. Quite simply, rehabilitation could not have gone forward without the Conservancy's assistance. It seems to be the long-awaited restorer and protector so avidly desired by the various Park betterment groups in the discouraging decades early this century. 14

Much of the credit must go to the Conservancy's first chairman, William Sperry Beinecke, a blunt, intelligent man, wise in the ways of the world. In 1979 Beinecke retired as chairman of the board and chief executive officer of a family business, the Sperry & Hutchinson Company, well known for its green stamps. He and his wife left New Jersey, where they had long lived, and bought an apartment in the East 70s overlooking Central Park. Beinecke's grandfather had arrived from Germany in the nineteenth century, prospered, and in time become one of the owners of the Plaza Hotel.

After his move, what the later Beinecke saw he didn't approve of, either from his vantage point high above the Park or during the frequent walks that he began to take in 1979 with his wife. Beinecke is an orderly man. Disorder—unpruned trees, epidemic erosion—annoys him, and in those days there was plenty of that. However, by the spring of 1980, Beinecke noticed a few green-and-white signs indicating construction and improvements to come. As these proliferated, so did his interest, and in June of that year he entered the Arsenal to call on the Central Park administrator.

Barlow's eyes took on a luminous gleam. For months, she and Commissioner Davis had been hoping to encourage the private sector to back the Park rehabilitation as it does such cultural institutions as the American Museum of Natural History, Lincoln Center, and the Metropolitan

Museum of Art. In their view the Park was also a cultural institution, and possibly a more urgent candidate for assistance. The administrator hustled Beinecke upstairs to Commissioner Davis's office. Davis, too, saw in Beinecke the hoped-for catalyst. After some conversation, Beinecke was asked to consider heading a private group that would raise funds to help support the renewal of the park.

This was in June of 1980. Although retired, Beinecke was also civic-minded. He was on the Board of Managers of the New York Botanical Garden and trustee of the American Museum of Natural History and of his alma mater, Yale University. Furthermore, he liked challenges. He said he'd talk with his wife about it (an old male stratagem to give himself time) and get back to the administrator and Davis in the fall.

Beinecke knew the task was a big one. He realized he had to produce a board that included persons of power and influence, a necessity for a fund-raising organization. But because of what the Park *is,* the board could not be seen as blatantly patrician. Democratic insight was needed, as well as sensitivity to the diverse constituencies of the Park.

In September, Beinecke returned to Davis and said he'd give the job his best shot. After Beinecke had had various meetings at Parks Department headquarters in the Arsenal and at City Hall, Mayor Koch and Commissioner Davis announced in December the formation of the Central Park Conservancy with Beinecke chairing a distinguished thirty-four–member board of trustees. Three of these—Administrator Betsy Barlow, Parks Commissioner Gordon Davis, and Manhattan Borough President Andrew Stein—were ex officio members.

But first a little background on a pair of predecessors.

Among the Park savior organizations mentioned earlier, two of the more recent were prototypes of the Conservancy. They sprang up in the 1970s with the city in fiscal crisis, when all Park betterment by that body ceased. The Central Park Task Force was formed in 1975 and the Central Park Community Fund a year earlier, but the aims of both were more or less the same—to mobilize private citizens and private money to take care of such elementary matters as Park cleanup and the most urgent Park repairs.

Beinecke very sensibly wanted to have on the board the experience of some of those connected with the earlier efforts. From the Central Park Community Fund he picked Richard Gilder, Jr., the president; Arthur Ross, a director; and Joan C. Schwartz, the vice president. Gilder was president of Gilder, Gagnon & Co., real estate; Ross was vice chairman of

Central National Corporation, a paper firm, and a frequent Park benefactor; and Joan C. Schwartz was an editorial associate of *Partisan Review.*

From the Central Park Task Force, Beinecke selected Adele Auchincloss, a director; Jason Epstein, the president; and Grace Hechinger, a director. Adele Auchincloss was also an industrial designer, an environmentalist, a former deputy administrator of the Parks Department and twice the president of the Parks Council, the organization concerned generally with city parks. Epstein was editorial director of Random House, book publishers. Grace Hechinger was an author and educator and consultant to the Aspen Institute for Humanistic Studies. The remaining trustees were equally important in diverse ways.

Beinecke's selection of trustees gave him the broad spectrum he sought. While board membership has increased and changed somewhat down the years, it has remained potent, with many of the original members still in office.

To increase public awareness of past and present citizen participation by others, Beinecke also named a forty-four–person Founders Committee, those who had supported with their enthusiasm, time, and money the creation of the Conservancy. This list, too, was impressive, with such names as Mrs. Vincent Astor, George T. Delacourt, Lucy Moses, Paul Newman, and Jacqueline Kennedy Onassis.

To function effectively month by month, Beinecke created four Conservancy working committees.

The Program and Planning Committee, headed by Victor Marrero, consulted with the administrator on such matters as concessions, design, horticulture, maintenance, and permits for events. The Development Committee, under J. Paul Lyet, solicited contributions from major corporations, foundations, and individuals. The Nominating Committee, directed by Howard L. Clark, offered to the board new trustee candidates. The Audit Committee, chaired by Reginald F. Lewis, handled Conservancy funds and kept the books.

Following its foundation, the Conservancy spent the next half dozen months working itself into shape. At first its duty was to fund the design of structures and areas to be restored. Eventually its role broadened to provide teams of craftsmen and specialized workers who perform many maintenance and construction jobs in the Park. In addition, it pays certain field and office workers. As a consequence, the payrolls of the Conservancy and Parks Department in Central Park are almost extricably intertwined. The Conservancy, for example, footed Betsy Barlow's $60,000 annual starting salary and currently underwrites one hundred of those on her staff of two hundred thirty.

An early move in January 1981 was hiring Pamela Tice as executive director, or chief executive officer, in business parlance. For a year and a half before that, Tice, then thirty-seven years old and a graduate of Boston University, had been assistant director of the city's Bureau of Management Services, so she was familiar with the local scene and the ins and outs of organizational activity. Her job at the Conservancy was to pull things together, a task that required close liaison with the Parks commissioner and the administrator, the heads of the various Conservancy committees, and the chairman as well.

In offices outside the Park at 315 West 57th Street, she headed a staff of about ten whose duties included public relations, internal accounting, photography and maintenance of picture files, and community consultation. She oversaw the details of these operations and was in touch with Barlow to get the Parks Department's wishes (or hopes) for coming aid. She kept an eye on the schedule of day-to-day moves of fund-raising activity with the general public, done by direct mail. She also monitored the approach of corporations and foundations by the Development Committee's subcommittees, each of which had its special field—advertising agencies, banking, and so on.

All these activities were connected with finding funds, and both Tice and the administrator were involved not only with rustling up money but finding new ways to rustle up money. Occasionally they did so directly themselves. Both women have gracious personalities, a characteristic that in no way inhibits this. In fact, both are flat-out formidable fund-raisers; they have the skins on the wall. In 1984, Betsy Barlow became Betsy Barlow Rogers.

Beinecke, for his part, was a very active member of the organization. A man well seasoned in the quirks of humankind, he wanted the mayor's assurance that Conservancy money for the Park's renewal coming in the front door wouldn't see an equal amount of city money for the renewal going out the back. He taxed the mayor with this and got a detailed and categorical denial on paper of any such possibility. Beinecke carried the letter around with him, and it was often useful. A prospective donor would frequently raise Beinecke's very question, whereupon Beinecke would say, "I just happen to have that answer here," whip out the letter, and have the prospect read it. A pledge or contribution frequently followed.

Beinecke did various things to keep the troops happy and animated.

One was a luncheon with the mayor at Gracie Mansion for the nearly twenty subcommittee chairmen. At it Beinecke asked for, and the mayor vividly reiterated, the pledge he had made in his letter to Beinecke, thus disseminating the promise very publicly into very necessary quarters. But at one point or another Beinecke occasionally had to put out fires. His colleagues came from an upper economic segment of our society. Furthermore, as corporate viscounts or the equivalent, they were used to making judgments, which judgments they were used to having followed without question. And, sporadically, they judged some of the Parks Department's suggestions, arrangements, and policies, geared to the proclivities of *all* the Park's users, to be, for one reason or another, silly or wrong. Being powerful personalities, they would powerfully object. Beinecke thereupon would mount the figurative dais and calm the objectors with part tact, part soothing syrup and part a clarification of roles. "Of course, each of us can have his own ideas, his own standards," Beinecke would say. "Of course. But the Conservancy has *no* responsibility whatsoever for Park policies. None at all. That is the parks commissioner's province. We are not the parks commissioner. We are the Conservancy, whose sole function and purpose is to aid the Park by our fund-raising efforts, which, through your dedication, are going well." The tactic worked.

As plans and progress fell into shape for the Conservancy, Beinecke issued the first annual report. It covered eighteen months and was for the fiscal years ending June 30, 1981, and June 30, 1982, the first year, that of the Conservancy's founding, being an abbreviated one. In it, Beinecke said that his organization had been able to provide $400,000 to the Park for the ten studies on which the projected Master Restoration Plan would be based; to expand the intern program by hiring from horticultural schools eight interns able to revive Park gardening; to form a repair and graffiti-removal crew to tackle the huge mass of defacing scrawls all over the area's eight hundred and forty-three acres; and to purchase nine horses to supply the needs of the Park's Mounted Ranger Corps.

Soon the Conservancy grew more and more effective. Help to the Park increased materially.

In the first annual report for the combined fiscal years, a total of $2 million was listed as raised. As has been usual each year with Conservancy operations, most of it came from major contributors of $1,000 or more. Seventy-one of these were corporations, fifty-three were foundations, and sixty-two were individuals, many of these entries being husband and wife. There was one bequest and one federal government grant. The total was one hundred eighty-eight major monetary contributors. Fourteen companies also donated services amounting to $1,000 or more. In addition, the response to two mail appeals addressed to the general public produced more than $165,000, or what Chairman Beinecke called a highly satisfying average of $41 a person.

Gifts of $25,000 or more came from AT&T, Bankers Trust, Bristol-Myers Fund, Chase Manhattan Bank, Exxon, Manufacturers Hanover Trust, Morgan Guaranty, New York Telephone, Rockefeller Center, the Starr Foundation, and Union Pacific Foundation, names that often appeared on later reports.

Such longstanding and generous friends of the Park as Lucy G. Moses and Iphigene Ochs Sulzberger, of the family owning the *New York Times,* and such traditional and willing philanthropists as David and Laurance Rockefeller were substantially represented.

Nineteen eighty-three was a year of fiscal improvement. The number of donors to the Conservancy increased. So did the amount of donations. A 50 percent upturn in the last category provided $3 million instead of $2 million for the report. The total of major contributors was three hundred and sixteen when twenty-nine service donors were included. New major contributors were an encouraging one hundred and ninety-three. Furthermore, $282,000 came from four thousand givers who were solicited by mail.

Fiscal year 1983 saw the introduction of two new fund-raising events. The most remunerative, which brought in $172,000 was the first Frederick Law Olmsted Awards Luncheon, organized by the newly formed Conservancy Women's Committee. Honored with awards for long and devoted service to the Park were Lucy G. Moses, Iphigene Ochs Sulzberger, and Lila Acheson Wallace. Warner LeRoy, owner of the Tavern on the Green, where the event was held, furnished the accommodations, food, and entertainment, including mimes and musicians, for the scores of guests, a not inconsiderable service donation.

"You Gotta Have Park" Weekend, on May 14–15, was the second novelty. Some months before, a jogger suddenly had a thought: why not a celebration on a fine spring weekend during which volunteers would ask visitors for a dollar or so to show appreciation for the Park. The Conservancy liked the idea and went into action. Close to fifty thousand entrants during the two days gave over $50,000.

The 1983 money went for strengthening and expanding the previous year's commitments. Horticulture was continued. Pruning, mulching, and weeding, done in part by volunteers, went on at various sites around the Park, among them the northern end, the Gill and Point in the Ramble, as well as inside the wall along Fifth Avenue between 72nd and 76th streets. Several jungles of Japanese knotweed, which spreads perniciously, were uprooted. Almost four thousand new trees and shrubs were put in, including twenty-five large American elms on Fifth Avenue between 90th and 105th streets, whose predecessors had fallen victim to Dutch elm disease.

Fifteen thousand more square feet of graffiti were removed, courtesy of Bankers Trust, which consistently has supported the project. The Master Restoration Plan progressed. Over ten thousand visitors a month—school children daily, family groups on weekends—came to enjoy the Conservancy-operated programs offered in the first two months of the newly opened Belvedere Castle. In the Dene near Fifth Avenue and 67th Street a vanished summerhouse was re-erected.

Olmsted fancied Englishisms such as Dene. His employment of the term here asks for an explanation. In modern usage, dene is a sandy tract by the sea, which this stretch of the Park is most certainly not. But going back in the language to Old English, "dene" meant vale or valley, a small example of which the restored summerhouse could be said to overlook. A hundred and twenty-five years ago it was this sense of the word that Olmsted must have had in mind.

Fiscal year 1984 turned up a bit static. Although something more than $3 million was raised, there was not the notable increase the previous year enjoyed. Nevertheless, contributors continued in good numbers. To boot, there was a new section, the sponsors of goods and services for the "You Gotta Have Park" Weekend. Twenty-five were in this subdivision, or which seventeen had not appeared heretofore on a Conservancy list. Furthermore, twenty-five hundred new donors made gifts of under $100, bringing the total in that category to nearly $300,000.

A large capital construction work was helping restore the ornate Bethesda Fountain and Esplanade, the Park's sumptuous centerpiece. Of the total $7.8 million cost, the Conservancy furnished $1.2 million.

Conservancy crews were busy throughout the year improving the Park grounds. Among the efforts was rebuilding the heavily used East Green near Fifth Avenue from 69th to 72nd Street, a turfy mead with lovely possibilities for visitor enjoyment, but then in a decrepit state. Drainage pipe was relaid there and an irrigation system installed, as was a porous-type soil and new sod. The Gill, the woodsy stream in the Ramble, had its two rock spillways rebuilt and three hundred feet of its length relined with stone.

The year's new endeavor was helping staff a modernized security center, operating twenty-four hours a day, which was installed in the North Meadow Fieldhouse in the center of the Park at the level of 97th Street. It acted as headquarters for the Urban Park Rangers, the Park Enforcement Patrol, and the Mobil Security, the last being nighttime Park protection forces. A versatile communications system in the center enables it to provide greater safety throughout the Park at all hours.

Fiscal year 1985 regained momentum. More than $4 million was raised, nearly a third more than in the preceding year and over 40 percent more than in 1983.

The increased number and high level of the contributions in 1985 showed the diligence of the chairmen of the various subcommittees. Three new donors of $25,000 or more joined others who had made such gifts in the past. The Cop Cot, the first and largest rustic shelter erected in the Park, was rebuilt on a knoll in the southern part of the Park, where Sixth Avenue and 61st Street would meet. Its replica stands there, too, and is heavily used. The soil laboratory analyzed soil productivity. Lawns of the bowling greens, Heckscher ballfields, Sheep Meadow, East Meadow, and Conservatory Gardens were dethatched, top dressed, seeded, and fertilized. At Conservatory Gardens a wildflower bed was put in at the back and new perennials planted in the borders. At various sites around the Park fourteen hundred understory trees and shrubs and thirty-five hundred groundcover plants were set out. Volunteers, as usual, aided, painting benches, cleaning water bodies, planting bulbs, pruning, and weeding all over the Park.

Visitor services broadened noticeably in 1985, centering around Belvedere Castle, the Conservatory Gardens, and the Dairy. Belvedere Castle's programs burgeoned—concerts tied to Shakespeare texts, joking jesters, magic shows, traditional dances of Norway, to name only a few. Conservatory Gardens offered occasional concerts and tours once a month during warm weather. Also wedding receptions and wedding photo sessions were held against the backdrop of floral brilliance. Concerts and slide and stereopticon shows were given at the Dairy, the last with many views of the nineteenth-century Park; also from here the Rangers led walks through the Park. At the Chess and Checkers House atop the Kinderberg ten inside tables for games and twenty-four outside were particularly popular with the elderly. In the summer, the other end of the spectrum is served with a chess day camp for six to sixteen year olds, overseen by the Manhattan Chess Club, which became involved at the instance of Marie Ruby, the Conservancy's innovative director of visitor services. In all, hundreds of thousands of people each year are entertained, helped, or informed by the Conservancy-funded Visitor Services.

Nineteen eighty-five's largest gift came from Mrs. Janice H. Levin, to restore a perimeter playground with wading pool and drinking fountain near Fifth Avenue at 76th Street. Also more than $75,000 was allotted by the Conservancy for a design to rehabilitate the Pulitzer Fountain–Grand Army Plaza area at Fifth Avenue and 59th Street beside the Park's important southeastern entrance.

Fiscal year 1986 saw only a modest increase, 3 percent, over donations

The refurbished Dairy of Civil War vintage, where children sipped
milk on the loggia. The Dairy is now the Park's Information
Center, with space for exhibitions and meetings.
(Sara Cedar Miller, Central Park Conservancy.)

of the year before. But the total exceeded $3.5 million, nearly a third of which were gifts from individuals. Projects for which the funds were spent included a major one, redoing the East 67th Street playground. Also six acres of new greensward, an addition dear to the heart of Commissioner Stern, went in at, among other places, the Loeb Boathouse and Bethesda Terrace. The Belvedere Learning Center gave science training to school-teachers from Districts 2 and 4. Families around the north end were more and more resorting to the Park, and the desolate top of Great Hill at the level of 105th Street with its abandoned games courts was turned into a picnicking meadow for them. A gondola reappeared on the Lake after an absence of many years, the gift of Conservancy member Lucy Moses. Two gondoliers were brought from Venice to instruct local boatmen in the figure-eight motion used to work the oar. Quiet zones, free of radio playing, were created in the Sheep Meadow and Conservatory Garden, to the applause of many. Five thousand chrysanthemums and twenty thousand tulip bulbs went into Conservatory Garden. And Bow Bridge was repainted by a Conservancy conservation crew.

Money increased in fiscal year 1987. Income rose nearly $1.5 million, some 33 percent more than the prior twelve months. A pledge of $1.5 million was received from the Weiler-Arnow family for the Conservatory Garden. Also eleven gifts of $100,000 or more came in. Other large bequests or commitments were received, as well. Mrs. Levin again gave for playground restoration, this time $636,000 for completing the work on the East 76th Street playground, which is for younger children. More than $300,000 was donated in memory of Roberta Rubin by her family to upgrade Shakespeare Garden. Diana Ross, the singer, furnished $300,000 for sophisticated equipment for older children who use the playground at West 81st Street. Laurance S. Rockefeller, whose wide philanthropic interests include monument conservation, provided more than $250,000 for Park monuments following the highly successful restoration of the equestrian statue of King Jagiello, Poland's great medieval ruler, standing east of Belvedere Castle at the level of 80th Street. The Grand Army Plaza–Pulitzer Fountain Partnership was formed by a pro bono trio—Leonard A. Lauder, Ira M. Millstein, and Ira Neimark. Monetary contributions were to be solicited from surrounding neighbors to implement improvement of the area from the design previously funded by the Conservancy, an effort the partnership has reported as successful.

Fiscal year 1988 saw a 13 percent gain over 1987. Contributions came to more than $6 million. Four gifts were of $500,000 or more. Yet the

*Workmen repainting the Vanderbilt Gate at 105th Street and
Fifth Avenue, at the entrance to Conservatory Garden. The
striking iron portal, manufactured in France, once graced the
Vanderbilt mansion at Fifth Avenue and 58th Street.*
(Sara Cedar Miller, Central Park Conservancy.)

small giver was represented, too; more than twelve thousand of them, not counting those who donated during "You Gotta Have Park" weekend, are in the total.

The Conservancy, prudently considering the future (which is ever uncertain), formed the Greensward Trust to guard against lack of funds for Park upkeep in the years ahead. The name memorializes the Greensward plan, the winning design by Frederick Law Olmsted and Calvert Vaux for the layout of Central Park, finished a hundred and thirty years ago. By the end of fiscal year 1988, thirty-seven contributors had supplied over $2 million in cash and pledges to the trust.

The 1988 report also noted the creation of the Campaign for the Central Park Conservancy. Henry R. Kravis, of Kohlberg, Kravis, Roberts & Company, investment bankers, was chairman. Lawrence A. Wein and Laurance S. Rockefeller were honorary cochairmen. The campaign seeks to raise $50 million to add to the receipts of the Greensward Trust for maintenance and to endow Park objects and activities and further to secure the Park against the possibility that the city might again run into a budget problem and decrease, or halt, Park maintenance.

The campaign issued an abundantly illustrated pamphlet, *Where We Live,* showing the public enjoying Central Park. An insert accompanied it, giving ways in which wealthy donors could aid in meeting the campaign's goal. Nearly seventy possibilities were presented. The top opportunity is for restoring the Mall, whose improvement would include paving stones for the present quarter-mile asphalt walk and six islands of elm trees rimmed with benches, as in Olmsted's day. In the middle range is one of $400,000 to fix the last of the five original cast iron bridges, which needs, among other things, a new wood floor, a balustrade, and repointing of the stone abutments. At the end of the line is sponsorship of a walking tour guide, $1,500.

In fiscal year 1988, contributions were almost three times as much as those of 1982, the first full operating year, when a little over $2 million came in. Seeing this progress, Commissioner Stern was emboldened to say, "Central Park's regreening, advancing so well, makes us all happy and proud. And our bodies healthier, too."

The commissioner had reason to be cheerful, in part because of the Conservancy. It had flowered surprisingly, growing far beyond its original scope. Its expansion included not only the trust, campaign, and partnership mentioned above, but the "You Gotta Have Park" function and the

Conservancy Women's Committee, sponsor of the Frederick Law Olmsted Award Luncheons. Dozens of the most energetic and influential people in town now were working for it happily and productively. And all this in a few short years.

*O*NE OF THE STRENGTHS of the Conservancy is its ability to find, train, and finance workers. Crews of specialized craftsmen who can build, maintain, repair, restore, or nourish objects—animate or inanimate, above or below ground in the Park—have greatly augmented the Parks Department forces. A while back the Conservancy's masonry crew set out to repair the Girl's Gate at Fifth Avenue and 102nd Street and to correct deterioration problems in the adjacent territory. Because the drainage system there functioned poorly, erosion from a steep slope behind the gate had brought down enough earth to push the perimeter wall out of line. Runoff had undermined the walkway itself and broken up the bluestone steps at the end. The crew reduced the width of the walkway by two feet, installed a new drainage system with fifteen hundred feet of pipe, put in two hundred and fifty feet of bluestone steps, fifteen hundred square feet of hexagonal pavers, resodded the slope, and planted it anew with earth-retaining shrubs.

But all this, sad to say, was achieved the second time around. On the first, the crew, relying on a 1918 map, laid pipes to the nearest catch basin. What they didn't know was that this particular line had been capped. The day after the job was finished, it rained. Gaily floating away toward Fifth Avenue went the newly laid pavers.

The incident vividly illustrates one of the most difficult aspects of the Park's rejuvenation—the unknown condition of the drainage system. Olmsted put in one that was adequate to the Park of his day. This was apart from an arrangement of enormous mains to raise and lower the level of the Lake with city waters. Olmsted, that ever surprising individual, had more than a little knowledge of drainage systems (in his youth, he had studied engineering for two years). Olmsted's system had two units. The first consisted of lines of earthenware pipe, or tiles, one and a quarter inches to six inches in diameter, with perforated or open tops, laid about forty feet apart to get rid of water falling on the turf. The result was fed into catch basins connected with the system that supplied the Park's water bodies. The second, also of tiles, paralleled the transverse roads, drives, bridle trail, and paths. All but the paths were crowned at the top and all were bordered with gutters feeding into catch basins. These also joined the first systems emptying into the water bodies.

Beneath the paths and sections of the drives and bridle trail, whose

Huge pipes such as these lie underground in the Park. Installed in the early 1860s, they are used in raising and lowering the level of the Lake. (Victor Prevost Collection, New York Public Library.)

material was porous, were tiles similar to those on the lawns, whose return again fed into the water bodies. Olmsted's drainage system contained one hundred and fourteen miles of pipe. The maps of this system unfortunately have been lost.

But hold: there is more underground pipe. In 1905, city sewer lines came in and connected with the Park's comfort stations. In 1910 the last map of *all* subsurface water pipes, those for drainage, irrigation, drinking water and sewage, was made. Included were the Park's over seven hundred catch basins. In 1915 water from the newly completed Catskill aqueduct became available through newly laid lines to keep water in the Park's water bodies at the desired level. About a decade later fourteen more miles of pipe were laid down for Merkel's lawn irrigation.

Today nobody knows the exact amount of pipe, including electrical conduits and unused gas lines, that lies under the Park. Or the condition of the pipes and catch basins. Repairing or replacing these, mapping them (including the electrical ducts), deciding what to do about the gas lines, and maintaining the pipes and their attendant catch basins are vital chores facing the administrator and Marianne Cramer, chief of design and planning. It is far from an easy, quick, or inexpensive task.

One remedial step has been taken, that of preventing flooding on the four transverse roads after heavy rain. Mud, leaves, fallen branches, and refuse wash over the walls, stopping up the catch basins. More than once, water several feet deep has stopped traffic completely.

This has been corrected through a combined operation by the city's Department of Environmental Protection, the Parks Department's Maintenance and Operations unit, its Forestry Division, and the Conservancy's horticultural and graffiti crew. DEP personnel cleaned and flushed the catch basins and sewer lines, M&O cleared the roadway of sediment and debris, Forestry and Conservancy pruners lopped dead branches from trees and shrubs overhanging the transverse walls, thus eliminating future litter problems, and the Conservancy team removed graffiti from the walls. The 97th Street transverse, the worst offender, has had chain-link fence sunk along the top of the walls to catch and hold blown leaves, and the surface behind the walls has been lowered so the water will sink into the ground, not flow over the walls.

Also, behind the walls, the Conservancy horticultural force has planted shrubs and groundcover to produce an erosion-resistant landscape and conceal the chain-link fencing. Each fall, Parks Department M&O people and city Department of Sanitation sweepers travel the transverses to get

Heavy flooding on one of the transverse roads a few years back.
Because of clogged, unmaintained drains, the waters often were
several feet deep. (Mary Bloom.)

rid of fallen leaves, which otherwise would repeat the process of plugging the drains.

Once there were fifteen summerhouses, open and airy, in the Park. All but one, in the Ramble, fell victims to time and poor maintenance. The very first summerhouse, named Cop Cot, went up in the early 1860s on the highest point of the lower Park, the hill back of Central Park South and Sixth Avenue at the level of 61st Street. A Hungarian carpenter, Anton Gerster, designed and constructed it. He was responsible, too, for many of the other summerhouses and introduced to this country their style of construction—rough, unmilled cedar timbers with the bark left on. This type of construction, now generally known as American rustic, became very popular in the large Adirondack lodges of somewhat later date. Also, it was used in the Park's boat landings, and in the rustic railings and bridges, arbors, benches, beehives, dovecotes, and birdhouses.

The rebuilding of the Cop Cot took place in 1985. Its cedar timbers were carefully selected from Vermont woodlands by a Conservancy construction team who had to be sure to cut limbs not only of the right diameter but also with the right shape and bends. They put the structure together from photographs of the original and, following restoration by their masons of the bluestone base, erected the quite substantial building on its old site. They intend to do the same for all missing summerhouses. Well before the new Cop Cot was completed, they had repaired the surviving summerhouse in the Ramble.

The Cop Cot is now very popular with New Yorkers at lunch time. Olmsted wanted those entering the Park to be completely free of city cares. In the roomy interior of the Cop Cot, whose benches seat dozens, a person can munch a sandwich within a design of the horse-and-buggy days and, with comparative serenity, regard the nearby skyscrapers of Manhattan, filled with their frantic goings-on.

The name *Cop Cot* is a curious one. But it is simply further evidence of Olmsted's fondness for Britishisms. Webster's Unabridged indicates that cop, meaning top or summit, comes to English through the Anglo-Saxon; cot, from the same source, means cottage—thus Cop Cot is a hilltop cottage in Olmsted's lingo, a fair enough description if a shade exotic.

The cast iron Ladies Pavilion on the west shore of the Lake, with its lacy, fantastic ironwork, received a new look in 1983. Soft tones of blue, gold, green, and red were applied by a Conservancy conservation crew. The next year a Conservancy horticultural team reworked the surrounding terrain, enriching it with topsoil and leaf mold, setting out shrubs,

*Central Park Conservancy carpenters in the 79th Street compound
assembling the replica of the Cop Cot, the Park's first rustic shelter.*
(Sara Cedar Miller, Central Park Conservancy.)

ferns, and wildflowers, and narrowing and rerouting an existing asphalt
path so that it pointed at the building.

The Ladies Pavilion was built in 1871 after a design by Jacob Wrey
Mould and originally was called "Ombra for Passengers in Waiting." It
stood at the Eighth Avenue and 59th Street entrance to the Park to shelter people waiting for horsecars. After more than fifty years of that use, it
was replaced by the Maine Monument and brought to its present location
beside that part of the Lake called the Ladies Pond, originally a section
reserved during the ice-skating season for women and children. In the
Pavilion, they could put on their skates, using its benches. Hence its
present name. The Ladies Pavilion enjoyed substantial neglect in the first
seven decades of this century, as did so many other things in the Park. In
1971, to thwart vandals, the rickety Pavilion was taken down. New life for

it began in 1979 with a $7,000 grant from Arthur Ross, whose frequent gifts have also included the Pinetum, a grove of select foreign and native conifers, northwest of the Great Lawn. Joseph Bresnan, then the Parks Department's monuments officer and a respected architectural historian, supervised reassembling the Pavilion prior to its present colorful reincarnation.

Ombra, in the Pavilion's original name, is a puzzler. No dictionaries,

including Latin ones, carry it. What is an ombra? The Classics Department at New York University said the correct spelling probably should have been umbra, the Latin for shade. Manuscript copiers over the years, this source noted, often changed letters, and *u* into *o* was frequent. Somehow the original namer of the Ladies Pavilion got hold of an ombra instead of an umbra, the department thought. Oh, well . . .

The Ramble, just east of the Ladies Pavilion, is a secluded, thirty-eight–

The original Boathouse, opposite Ladies Pond, on a winter day. (Parks Department Annual Report.)

acre section bordering much of the lake, consisting of woods, meadows, and many winding paths. It was the first part of the Park to be opened to the public, several years before the start of the Civil War. A minor bit of reconstruction here precipitated what has been the rehabilitation's most traumatic upheaval so far. Late in 1981 a Conservancy crew set to work to redo the Point, a finger of Ramble land projecting into the Lake opposite the Esplanade. From below the water, the men hauled up large boulders that once had edged the shoreline, protecting it from waves. These they reset, digging them in securely. Then they brought in fresh earth to augment the Point's worn surface, planted it with hundreds of shrubs and trees, and the job was done.

The attention of the rehabilitators next turned elsewhere in the Ramble. This time the whole area was involved. Olmsted had desired to keep a clear line of sight between the Bethesda Fountain and the Belvedere Castle atop Vista Rock, to be achieved through proper botanical maintenance of the intervening turf, shrubbery, and trees. The view was intended to be—and was—captivating from either terminus. The purpose was to impart an illusion of sweeping distance to the Park, whose actual boundaries are so narrow and constrained, and, as a final touch, to embroider that illusion with botanical riches. Well before the start of the decade, however, the view and much of the Olmstedian botany had disappeared, a casualty of that old Park bugaboo, poor maintenance.

The Administrator's Office earlier had completed a thorough study of needed Ramble improvements, including reopening the Esplanade–Belvedere view. As soon as the weather seemed right, which was the early spring of 1982, implementation of the plan began.

Among the most devoted users of the Ramble are birdwatchers, scores of them, young and old, who wander the woods in their peaceful, often solitary fashion, binoculars in hand. Birdwatchers, or "birders," as they call themselves, are, with reason, seen as admirable and well-behaved folks, among our most praiseworthy citizens. So much for their deserved reputation.

The massive Ramble rehabilitation plan was initiated, as luck would have it, in early spring, which is, of course, the start of bird migration, the birdwatchers' busiest season. Following the plan, shrubbery was thinned. Vines, particularly the noxious and overabundant Japanese knotwood (where small birds—skulkers, in birder parlance—liked to hide) were uprooted. Trees, twenty to sixty, according to different counts, were cut down. Seeing the lessened shrubbery, the vineless patches, the tree stumps, the well-mannered birdwatchers turned tiger. In no time at all, a petition with three thousand signatures arrived at the Arsenal protesting the destruction in the Ramble of "mature and irreplaceable trees." But this was only the beginning. A blizzard of letters flew to newspapers, politicians, and nature organizations decrying the tree felling and similar desecration of birdwatcher turf.

Such a reaction is understandable. It was also, in this case, a bit short-sighted. It was almost as if the birders were suggesting that a feathered migrant aloft, one of a flock over the Ramble, would turn and say to its fellows, "Hey, chaps, let's go on to Canada. Some trees cut down below us." The Ramble would still have been the Ramble as far as birds were concerned, with or without sixty more trees.

Olmsted, an advocate of the sensible use of the ax, had realized much earlier that the health of the Park depended on the proper thinning of trees. But even in Olmsted's day there was opposition to tree cutting, and even among his Board of Commissioners. Here are some of Olmsted's words on aspects of the subject:

"The Park suffered great injury, which it is even now impossible wholly to retrieve, through the neglect of timely thinning of the planta-tions. . . ."

"Men seen cutting trees under my direction have been interrupted and indignantly rebuked by individual commissioners, and even by the 'friends' of commissioners, having no more right to do so than they would, for like action, on a man-of-war. I have had men beg me, for fear of dismissal, to excuse them from cutting trees and, to relieve them, have taken the axe from them and felled the trees myself."

But as in Olmsted's day, our modern birdwatchers were aroused by the tree loss. They kept the pot boiling. Community councils took the matter up. Each police precinct in the city has a community council, an organiza-tion of civic-minded citizens interested in neighborhood affairs. Central Park has a police precinct but not legal residents, that is, people cannot legally live in Central Park, although people do, and always have, without permission. Nevertheless, it has a community council, called the Central Park Precinct Community Council, which ordinarily meets six or eight times a year, at the Jewish Guild for the Blind on 65th Street, just off Central Park West. Membership is open to any Manhattan resident inter-ested in Central Park doings, particularly its safety. Naturally a good deal of wordage on tree cutting flowed from concerned community councils, including this one.

On May 5, 1982, the *New York Times* published a three hundred and fifty–word editorial siding with the birders. Ten days later on its editorial page appeared a letter about twice as long from Commissioner Davis and the administrator justifying the Ramble rehabilitation plan. The authors went to considerable pains to point out that the intent was to improve, not mar, the Ramble for the bird population. They presented a list of migrants seen already, and of bird-attractive plantings that were in the Ramble or planned.

But a spokesman for the New York City Audubon Society (seven thousand members) said Olmsted would regard the work as destroying, not restoring, the Park, the evidence presented earlier in the Parks Department letter having received the usual layman's indifference. And an official of the Linnaean Society, with a membership seriously interested in nature, protested that previous talks with the administrator had given him a quite different impression of what was to be done in the Ramble. The administrator took extended walks with many of her critics, pointing out the benefits to wildlife of the plan. And there was much reason on her side. However, the score on converts is not known. The pot kept boiling. And the Parks Department was badly shaken.

At last, in late June, a public hearing, not only on the tree cutting but the Park rehabilitation plan in general, was held under the auspices of the New York City Landmarks Preservation Commission. In 1974, nearly ten years after having been named a National Historical Landmark, the Park was designated a New York City Landmark. Ordinarily city landmarks are buildings. But the Park was dubbed a *scenic* landmark, thereby coming under the protective wing of the commission. It was, of course, a unique classification. But, as such, perhaps deserved by an entity that could also be called unique. By law, any changes in a landmark involving noncity staff, as was the case with the Conservancy people in the Ramble, must be reviewed at a public hearing before the commission. Normally commission approval for such changes is worked out quietly behind the scenes between the commission and the Parks people. But this was not a normal situation. The parks commissioner and the administrator were only too glad to air the matter before the Preservation Commission.

The hearing was raucous. It lasted over five hours, ending at one-thirty in the morning. Almost fifty speakers were heard, pro, con, and in between. Much steam was vented. In the interval that followed, the Parks Department essentially maintained its position. Birds continued to be seen in the Ramble. Things gradually simmered down. On July 28th, the

Times published another editorial, now approving and somewhat longer than the disapproving original. It concluded that "in an authentic wilderness, a laissez-faire policy might be justified. Like a private garden, however, this unique public space requires careful but constant intervention if it is to remain hospitable to birds and people alike."

So ended an uproarious episode, one that virtually paralyzed the department for weeks. For the Central Park staff members who had faced the birders in the trenches, it was an experience not likely to be forgotten. "Hell hath few furies such as one of these," a member of the walking wounded cautiously observed, looking behind as the words came out.

Nevertheless, it was a profitable lesson, perhaps a deserved one; the depth of New Yorkers' feelings about Central Park was clearly indicated. And the birders' incident may have prevented another ugly confrontation. The roots of twenty-four pin oak trees, planted after World War II to commemorate the dead, were among those dislocating the stone walls of the Bethesda Fountain Esplanade. In addition, the trees' foliage prevented sunlight from reaching the underlying turf, causing erosion. The administrator had originally marked all the trees for removal. But after the birders' to-do, it was decided to eliminate only the most threatening nine. The intent of the grove would be honored by relocating and rededicating nine new trees in situations that caused no harm to the Esplanade. Thus a confrontation was avoided.

Besides the Landmarks Preservation Commission, the Central Park Precinct Community Council, and other precinct community councils bordering the Park, there are two other principal organizations that offer counsel, criticism, and praise to the Administrator's Office: the Parks Council, with citywide interest in the utilization of parks and open spaces; and the Friends of Central Park, which suggests ways to better the Park's functions. In essence, these are all advisory bodies whose work with the Administrator's Office is not on a public but a consultative basis. The commissioner and the administrator have the authority to make the requisite decisions. An organization whose wishes receive especial consideration is, of course, the Conservancy; what its board and staff desire to do for the Park often becomes Park policy.

A cogent but unjustified criticism of the Administrator's Office at the landmarks public hearing in 1982 was lack of a master plan for the Park's rebuilding. At the very time work was proceeding on the as yet unfinished management surveys. In May of 1985 the plan was published, a thorough and comprehensive report, the product of efforts by architects, engineers, financial and personnel management specialists, historians, sociologists, horticultural and wildlife experts, and photographers. The next month the American Institute of Architects conferred on the Parks Department and the Conservancy an award for the plan. The institute's nominating committee wrote that "Central Park's design ranks as one of the finest works of art in American history" and also that the plan is a success because "it respects the ingenuity and beauty of the Park's original design."

*U*NDER THE GUIDANCE of Tim Marshall, the Conservancy *16* gives substantial assistance to the city treasury in various areas of the Park renewal. Marshall, director of construction and preservation, directs a staff of twenty-eight persons, some city, some Conservancy paid, as is the case with much of the Park's renewal work force. Two of Marshall's staff are subdirectors, who supervise all restoration and maintenance work on objects above and below ground in the Park, with the exception of the horticultural tasks. This work force is composed of carpenters, ditch diggers, graffiti removers, masons, metal artisans, and plumbers. Two salient points of Marshall's task is to see that what's been renewed is properly maintained and to keep his body of in-house craftsmen at required strength, enlisting new ones when funds allow and added assignments arise. Marshall also keeps an eye on Park maintenance work done by Parks Department personnel and by outside contractors as well.

Marshall's people, in partnership with consulting conservators, have been involved in conservation, using a blasting technique of tiny glass beads to clean and repatinate the Lehman Gates to the entrance of the Children's Zoo and, near Turtle Pond in the center of the Park at the level of 80th Street, the equestrian statue of King Wladyslaw Jagiello of Poland. In restoration, Playmates Arch under the Center Drive at 65th Street has been repointed and its missing stones replaced, and Bridge No. 24, one of the five remaining cast iron bridges, has had its missing ironwork copied, recast, and reinserted, as well as its wooden decking restored and the whole structure repainted a soft tan. In construction, Marshall's crews have rebuilt a rustic shelter at 67th Street off Fifth Avenue where one once stood, rebuilt the Wisteria Pergola at the Mall, and have done the same for a rustic bridge in the Ramble at the mouth of the Gill, the little stream that flows through that woodland and descends down a cliff into the Lake.

Another notable area of Conservancy help is horticultural—the improvement, replacement, and care of lawns, flowers, shrubs, and trees. What is a park without thriving botany? Particularly Central Park, sunk in the lowering stonework of the city. All during the year's lengthy growing and fruiting seasons, it should be an animate panorama of living emerald. It strives to be. And usually is these days. Botanical care thus is vital.

The horticultural people, under director Neil Calvanesie, are divided into groups: tree care, two landscape maintenance teams, a turf-care crew, and a soils conservation laboratory force, each with a supervisor.

The tree-care group, five or six in number, prune, cable, fertilize, water, mulch, and plant. They remove dead trees and fight Dutch elm disease.

The landscape maintenance crews, each of seven persons, care for the understory vegetation—the small and medium-sized trees and the shrubs, which create an esthetic link between the broad lawns and the tall trees in the woods. As part of the restoration plan, in the fall of 1983 alone, the workers set out fifty-six hundred understory trees and shrubs.

Planting is restricted to the seven-month period between last and first frost. Between plantings the crew mulches, weeds, prunes, fertilizes, works the soil to provide the proper environment for the plants selected, monitors insect and disease damage, transplants, installs and maintains site fixtures such as snow fences, and—using anything from buckets to six hundred–gallon water trucks—waters, waters, waters.

The turf-care team, a trio, does all the mowing, aerating, dethatching (removing the decaying organic material between the grass and the soil), overseeding, fertilizing, and restoring the Park's four hundred twenty-five acres of lawn, some two hundred acres of which are mowable.

The soil management duo work in a laboratory, testing and analyzing soil and plant tissue. The information is used to evaluate various management practices such as fertilizing and composting. Approximately a thousand soil samples are examined each year.

Control of Dutch elm disease is one of the horticulture director's major tasks. The Park has one of the country's largest remaining stands of American elms, nearly two thousand. Many line the Mall and the east boundary of the Park along Fifth Avenue. Since the disease came here from the Netherlands by way of the Bronx in 1930, more than half the nation's American elms, the most susceptible species among the elms, have perished, the toll being especially heavy in the East. The loss in the Park has been reduced to around 1 percent a year, eighteen, for example, in 1988. All American and English elms in the Park are inspected weekly for signs of trouble, the Fifth Avenue trees fortnightly. If analysis of a suspect tree shows the disease is not in the trunk or in more than 30 percent of the crown, the affected branches are merely lopped, the cutbacks including six feet of sound wood. Then a fungicide is injected. Terminally sick trees, including the roots, are removed and burned.

By the time rehabilitation had started, many of the beautiful and exotic species of the Pilat era had vanished through poor care. The vulnerability of the conifers in particular increased with the arrival of the automobile. Conifers have needles for leaves. Unlike leaves of deciduous trees, the needles stay on year-round. Thus they are continually exposed to exhaust fumes. When the conifers disappeared, so did much of the winter colors the designers had directed Pilat to provide. By 1868 he had set out no less than eighty-nine kinds of conifers, many rare, among them the Abnormal Norway Spruce, the Bhutan Pine, and the Mt. Atlas Cedar. A century later, these, along with most of the rest, were gone. To compensate somewhat, the Conservancy since 1981 has purchased and emplaced Nordmann firs, smoke trees, eastern red buds, sawtooth oaks, katsura trees, Japanese white pines, Himalayan pines, kousa dogwoods, sourwood trees, and Siberian crab apples.

An early survey of all Park trees showed the percentage of dead wood on nearly half of all the Park's trees to be between 11 and 44 percent. Many trees, forty to eighty feet tall, had, in fact, never been pruned; some of their dead branches loomed dangerously over paths and playgrounds. Several springs ago the largest pruning operation yet undertaken was completed. Of its $200,000 cost, $175,000 was met by the Conservancy, the balance coming from a yearly state grant. Outside contractors in the four-month undertaking pruned over three thousand of the largest trees; the in-house crew, supplemented by seasonal help, added another one thousand, these being small or medium-size trees.

Besides seasonal workers, the Park has other temporary help, interns and volunteers, who are used almost exclusively by the conservation and horticultural staffs. The number varies depending on the annual work schedule and the funds available, most of them coming from the Conservancy, which pays the seasonals $6.50–$8 an hour, depending upon skills and length of service. Interns, usually high-schoolers who work on summer vacations, receive $3.75–$4.75 an hour. Volunteers, who range in age from elementary school children to retirees, are recruited by the Park's LIVE (Learning and Involvement for Volunteers in the Environment)

A large conifer near Conservatory Water. The planting of trees and
shrubs is an important segment of Central Park renewal.
(Brian Rose.)

program. In spring, summer, and fall, the volunteers work for eight weeks
either on a Wednesday, Saturday, or Sunday; in winter, the tour is
Wednesday or Saturday fortnightly for eight sessions. Volunteers who
complete the stint get perks—a certificate of program completion, a volunteer button, and a T-shirt or sweatshirt with the LIVE logo.

Interns normally arrive in the summer, when horticultural chores are
heaviest. The fifty who come annually to Central Park through the agency
of the Parks Council are part of the citywide Summer Youth Employment
Program. They are paid by the city and federal government and work
daily from July 1 through August 23 under their own technical director,
who consults with the director of horticulture. Tools and materials are
supplied by the council. Interns brought in by the Conservancy are principally from high schools in the Park area. They do such horticultural jobs
as weeding and mulching and such conservation ones as cleaning stream
beds and lake edges.

Volunteers, for their part, perform a wide range of tasks, including picking up litter, planting bulbs, retrieving submerged rowboats, uprooting duckweed in the Lake, spreading wood chips for mulch, clearing areas of brush, removing graffiti, cleaning debris from the Pool in the north end, and painting benches. Normally the Park's temporary help—seasonals, interns, and volunteers—totals more than a thousand persons.

The administrator has said that trees, their number and appearance, are one of the principal factors that give the look of "parkness" to a park. Happily, New York City, and thus the Park, is blessed with a benign climate, whether residents realize this or not. The environment is thus good for growing things. Moderate precipitation is distributed more or less evenly throughout the year. And in the twelve months the city receives 59 percent of the sunshine possible at this latitude—a value comparing favorably with any other east of the Mississippi River except Florida and its purlieus. While the Park's original astonishing variety of sylva no longer exists, including two young giant sequoias standing on a knoll by the Lake and exotic evergreens from all over the world such as the Bhutan pine and cedar of Lebanon, the Park still does have many trees, some of them rather unusual.

In order to find out just what was present, the administrator commissioned the 1982 exhaustive tree survey, which disclosed 147 known, and 1 unknown, species. The number of trees with a breast-high trunk diameter of six inches or more was 24,595. Of these, the most frequent by far, comprising more than 4,000, and one-seventh of all the Park's such-sized trees, was the black cherry, whose prevalence is bird-effected, the fruit being eaten and the seed widely dispersed. Furthermore, the number of that species is far greater than the total above since a whopping slew of saplings are in the Park. It is a less desirable tree than many from an arborist's point of view, and plans are afoot to thin it. After the black cherry, the Park's next two most numerous species are the American elm and the pin oak. Trees of more than usual interest include the Kentucky coffee tree; bald cypress; *Hupeh evodia,* an Asiatic species; cucumber and saucer magnolias; persimmon; and black walnut, the increasingly rare wood of which is so prized for gunstocks that walnut rustling has occurred in the Midwestern states.

But perhaps the most interesting species is the metasequoia, or dawn redwood. Three of these stand near each other west of the Seventh Avenue entrance at the level of 61st Street. They are a kind of conifer thought to have become extinct sixty million years ago, when the mild

*Volunteers cleaning the Harlem Meer. These men and women aid the
Park in many ways—through such work as painting, planting, debris
collecting, and auxiliary police duty. (Brian Rose.)*

climate of the northern hemisphere turned cold. Their fossilized forms are frequent in the strata of the Eocene. However, in 1944 Chinese scientists brought out specimens of the supposedly extinct species that had survived in the narrow valley of a mountainous tableland in south central China. The species was then cultivated, and, through the Arnold Arboretum of Harvard University, examples were brought into this country. In the 1960s, these particular trees were planted. Although relatively young, the trio with their slim triangular shapes, dark orange bark, and deciduous needles, turning a lovely russet in the fall, are fast-growing and could, by early in the next century, reach one hundred feet in height.

Another notable native of China is the giant Chinese elm barely inside Fifth Avenue just south of the level of 72nd Street. It stands back of a square iron fence, the only tree in the Park thus honored. With a trunk girth of thirteen feet, it is perhaps the largest and oldest Chinese elm in the country. Its leaves emerge late, causing concerned friends of the tree to phone the Parks Department each spring with the erroneous impression that the tree is sick.

This elm is one of the botanical prizes brought here in the 1840s and 1850s, when plant hunters from the Western world were allowed access to the luxuriant flora of China and Japan. Another such example is the huge wisteria wine entwining the pergola above the northern end of the Mall on the Fifth Avenue side. Wisteria originally was rare enough in its Chinese homeland to be considered a novelty by the Chinese themselves. The species was first noted by Westerners in the gardens of Consequa, one of the greatest of the Cantonese Hong merchants. How the species made its exit from China is not clear, but in May of 1816 it arrived in England, where it grew well and was speedily propagated by nurserymen. Before long it reached this country.

The most memorable Central Park event associated with a tree occurred one hundred and twenty-some years ago. Baron Renfrew was one of the titles of the then Prince of Wales, who was later to rule as Edward VII, and this was the name under which the future monarch in October of 1860 arrived in New York City. It was the first visit to these shores, once part of the Crown, by an heir to the British throne. Noting his arrival, a local paper reported that the city "gave His Royal Highness such a welcome as never before had been known in history." Whether or not this is a fact, his presence certainly initiated a rash of functions. Among them were inspections of New York University, the Women's Library, the Astor Library, the Cooper Institute, the Free Academy, and, topping all others, a huge ball in the visitor's honor on the evening of October 11th, the day of his landing here. The Academy of Music was the site, the ball being preceded by a fete, in actuality a gargantuan feast at Delmonico's.

Despite the rigors of that night, the baron, two days before leaving the city, proceeded the next day under escort to Central Park. There, west of the Mall, alongside what is now the disused center driveway at the level of 68th Street, he supervised the planting of an English oak and, near it, an American elm. He also nodded from a distance to Frederick Law Olmsted, still limping from his recent injury, perhaps a sign of royal pleasure at what His Highness considered a royal job well done.

For years after their planting the twin trees prospered. Then the elm, its passing unnoted in official records, died. But at the start of this century the oak was alive. Louis Harman Peet, the respected recorder of Central Park botany at the time, in his 1903 volume, *Trees and Shrubs of Central Park,* said of the baron's oak: "The tree has since been known as 'The Prince of Wales Oak.' It has had every care but, for some reason, it does not seem to be doing very well—indeed, it is just about holding its own." The malaise, whatever it may have been, eventually brought its demise, again at an unrecorded date. Despite frequent statements to the contrary, it has vanished—along with the city's memories of the doughty baron.

The tree with the largest trunk in the Park stands just a piece south of the onetime site of the Prince of Wales Oak. It is an English elm with a trunk whose circumference breast-high is a couple of inches over seventeen feet. However, the bole is padded with excrescences, lumps that protrude below the bark. "It's the champion," the horticultural director told me, "but it's sort of a cheater." A tree with a straight, smooth and majestic bole is the London plane south of the 96th Street transverse near the center of the Park. In circumference, the trunk breast-high is only a shade short of sixteen feet, and its impressive height, now eighty feet, caused Peet to say it was doubtless part of the original planting, as was the English elm just noted.

Although one might suppose trees to be safe in Central Park, this is not the case. In the last few years, more than twenty trees, among them birch, catalpa, pin oak, and turkey oak, have been felled, mostly in the northern section. The perpetrator seems an inexperienced axman whom an outraged Commissioner Stern has dubbed The Mad Chopper. A $1,000 reward has been offered for his arrest.

᠍ Botanical business, more normal than offering rewards, includes the planting each spring and fall of hundreds of wildflowers in the Park's meadows and copses. But Central Park has always had wildflowers. In the early days such cherished species as arbutus, bloodroot, columbine, hepatica, and trillium were to be found. By the 1920s, the showier native blooms had dwindled to dogtooth violet, jack-in-the-pulpit, rueanemone, and wild geranium. A decade later, only the dogtooth violet was found. But even by the 1970s, when Park maintenance was lowest and its abuse highest, inconspicuous wildflowers, hardly to be noticed by the average visitor, still dotted the Park. Often visually insignificant, they are nevertheless true wildflowers.

In 1978 an amateur naturalist recorded more than fifty of these modest posies, their blooms sometimes tiny, sometimes not, their colors blue, green, pink, violet, white, and yellow. One was the curled dock. *The United States Pharmacopoeia* has long named its root as a gentle tonic, astringent, laxative, and alternative (a medicine that gradually changes morbidity into a state of health). Another was the Star-of-Bethlehem, an immigrant with a curious history. It is mentioned in the Bible. In ancient Palestine, where it was abundant, the translation of its common name was "dove's dung," doubtless because the white flowers made the landscape resemble building walls that had been blanched with bird excrement. The plant's roots, when properly treated, can be dried, ground up, and mixed with flour to make bread. The passage of 2 Kings 6:25 tells that during a famine in Samaria a measure of the plant sold for five pieces of silver.

Today plants in the Park, as well as in Samaria, can be, and have been, used for food. Technically, of course, their removal is illegal. Olmsted wanted his flora protected. Because of this a law, perhaps never invoked, subjects to arrest a visitor wearing a flower in a buttonhole, or carrying a bouquet. The plant removal rule, however, has generally been honored in the breach. Specialists who know the edibility of wild plants have long taken groups through the Park, pointing out things good to eat and gathering them. These include black walnuts and hazelnuts, crab apples, grains of millet, berries, fungi, and herbs. One of the specialists, Gary Lincoff, has published a calendar of recipes from plants available each month in the Park. One is called Japanese Knotweed Jam:

2 quarts cubed knotweed (about 2 pounds)   1 quart sugar
1 cup water   2 lemons, juiced

Simmer Japanese knotweed in 1 cup of water about 10 minutes, or until soft. It
should now be reduced by half, or about 1 quart.
Add lemon juice and sugar.
Bring to boil and stir about 12 minutes (until candy thermometer approaches
222° F.).
Pour into sterilized jars and seal.
Makes about 3 quarts.

Another specialist, Steve Brill, was arrested a while back after leading a
paid tour whose members extracted some edible plants. "You don't want
people eating up your Park," explained Commissioner Stern. However,
with his conciliatory policy, Stern has asked Brill to lead free Park-spon-
sored tours from March to December. Members, as participants, can pick
foodstuffs; the casual visitor still legally may not. And Brill can be kept
busy in other ways. For instance, Michel Bras, an entrant in a recent New
York City Marathon and chef of a two-star restaurant in France, sought
out Brill, as the official department expert, to show him the edibles of the
Park.

A second example of the Stern administration's accommodative policy
toward transgressors concerns the famous, elusive treehouse builder.
Now in his twenties, Bob Redman was mysteriously drawn to trees in
early childhood. Beginning as a teen-ager, for an eight-year period, he
constructed and lived in thirteen houses, no less, high in the branches of
Central Park's trees, each dwelling larger than the last. The final one, a
split-level unit of five rooms near the top of a towering beech on the west
side near 79th Street, not far from where his mother lived, provided a
sweeping view of the Park and its environs. From it, "the view at night of
the city lights and the stars was beyond description," Redman recalls.
This house and all the others were destroyed by Park officials as being
bad for the trees. Cleverly placed and camouflaged, they usually remained
inhabited and undetected for months. Only in the last one was the builder
apprehended. But then and there he so impressed officials with his tree
savvy that all was forgiven. Today he is a climber and pruner on the
Conservancy's payroll.

Each fall a number of Chinese come into the Park for the ripened nuts
of the many female gingko trees. The numerous tan, olive-sized fruit
come from the oldest tree species extant. Today it is the only example of

its once large family, the rest of whose members are to be found only in the fossil record. The gingko is another instance of survival in nooks in China, in this case, the yards of temples. Its nuts are brought down by weighted ropes thrown over the teeming branches. The fruit's slimy pulp hides a crisp, bright green kernel, which when raw tastes like a green pea. The grilled nuts are used in Oriental cookery, including some fairly complicated dishes, but the simplest way to eat them is hot, after roasting.

REES, whether food producers or not, harbor some of the Park's wildlife, and that is no mere trifle, by the way. A visitor living on the ninth floor of a well-heated, air-conditioned apartment overlooking Fifth Avenue could well be excused for not realizing the number of wild things below him, dozens of which could be quietly watching him during his next stroll.

Birds are the chief category. Central Park, you will remember, is only slightly more than one square mile, yet in this relatively small confine, or in the air above it, two hundred and eighty-three species of birds, more than a third of those known to inhabit North America, have been observed over the years. The first list was put together in 1860, only two years after the Park was opened to the public. So Park birders are an ancient breed, as devoted then as now.

The Park's great total of birds is easily explained. The Park is a stretch of countryside lying directly under the Atlantic flyway amid an extensive metropolis of brick and stone. The Atlantic flyway is the most easterly in North America of the four great avian migration routes between the tropics and the Arctic. Birds are most frequent in the Park, of course, in spring and fall. Over the city, the travelers, seeing a space to rest and feed, drop down from the sky in great number, and sometimes in great diversity. But birds of some kind are present in the Park year-round. During a year, there are thousands.

Among the rare birds that have been recorded was a snowy owl, a powerful, swift, and strangely beautiful creature, two-thirds the size of an eagle, an example of which is now present in the new zoo. Woe betide the harassing crow, a noted owl hater, that comes too close to the snowy, assuming that like most owls it is blind in the sunlight. The American eagle, too, has been seen more than once overhead, an imposing raptor with a strong yellow beak nearly the length of its head; it has a wing-spread of up to seven and a half feet and is, after the great

174

blue heron, the largest bird that has been seen in or from the Park. For two months in the fall of 1866, a representative of our national symbol hung around the Deer Park, a transient feature in which the Park's herd of deer were then quartered. No eagle has been so intimate since.

The smallest of the Park avifauna is the ruby-throated hummingbird, an iridescent pygmy whose newborn hatchlings are the size of honeybees.

A historical note concerns the arrival of the starling to this country. The introducer was Eugene Schieffelin, prominent member of an old New York family, who was head of the American Acclimatization Society. Acclimatization societies were common after the Civil War, formed to import the bird species that new immigrants from Europe were accustomed to seeing. Schieffelin's goal was to acquaint New Yorkers with the birds that appeared in the works of Shakespeare. Accordingly, he imported from Europe the starling, the skylark, and various others mentioned by the Bard; all were released in Central Park, but only the starling survived. Eighty birds were set free in the Park in 1890, forty more the following year. From that beginning, the species, considered noxious by many, grew until today its countrywide roosts contain billions.

The English sparrow, also sometimes considered a nuisance, is often mistakenly said to have been liberated originally in the Park. In fact, the sparrow imports were purchased in Europe in 1852 by a Brooklyn resident to attack that community's numerous inchworms. The birds arrived in the Narrows on the steamship *Europa,* and fifty were released in the Narrows. The rest went to an aviary in Greenwood Cemetery, on whose grounds they were set free. An attempt two years earlier to establish the birds elsewhere in Brooklyn and in Madison Square in Manhattan had been unsuccessful. The Central Park sparrows were introduced there in 1864 and did very nicely, thank you.

Numbers of Park nesters and year-round residents vary considerably according to ecological factors. Nesters include the black-capped chickadee, blue jay, brown thrasher, cardinal, catbird, downy woodpecker, eastern kingbird, flicker, grackle, hairy woodpecker, house finch, house sparrow, mallard duck, mockingbird, pigeon, robin, starling, and tufted titmouse. Among customary year-round residents are the blue jay, cardinal, chickadee, downy woodpecker, hairy woodpecker, house finch, house sparrow, mocking bird, mourning dove, pigeon, robin, starling, and titmouse.

If one rules out *Homo sapiens* as a form of wildlife, always an uncertain supposition, the number of mammal types found in the Park (outside the

Zoo) is fourteen, nine resident and five transient. The latter are the five species of bats native to the state of New York—the big brown, little brown, hoary, red, and silver-haired—which for varying periods of time are in and out of the Park on migration. The best chance to see them is in spring and fall at dusk, when their aerial activity begins. By day they may be found sleeping upside down, the big brown and the little brown in cavelike places such as under bridges and in building crevices, the other three dangling from limbs of trees.

The commonest Park mammal is, alas, the Norway, or brown, rat, an alien species, and the most aggressive of its tribe. It is present in burrows and crannies in ineradicable legions. Extermination campaigns that have killed tens of thousands only open the way for others. Last year the Parks Department tried a new technique. Three boxes for barn owls, immensely skillful rodent predators, were set out in hope of denting the population. If it diminishes, more boxes will appear.

The frolicsome and lovely gray squirrel is the commonest native mammal, an endless gratification to children, to connoisseurs of animal grace, and to the scores of its feeders. The estimate of squirrel numbers, including a few black, or melanistic, ones, in the administrator-commissioned wildlife survey is more than six thousand nine hundred. This estimate may well be way, way too high, although there is no paucity of squirrels in the Park.

An unsurprising resident is the house mouse, which, along with the dog and the cat, is a form even the most unenlightened towny is familiar with. Both dogs and cats are of the feral sort, the name for domesticated animals gone wild. Cats are in the large, fenced, tranquil Bird Sanctuary above the Pond, its barrier and bird life providing feline-appreciated privacy and provender—although it's fair to say that some of the latter is passed through the fence by kindly old ladies. The official name of the Bird Sanctuary is the Hallett Nature Sanctuary, in honor of the late George Hervey Hallett, Jr., a prominent nature-loving New Yorker. But generally this wooded tract is still known as the Bird Sanctuary.

Dogs on the loose keep to the less frequented parts of the Park and have been known to do so with considerable success. Some years back, Brownie, a small Schipperke-like dog, easily evading the police, well-wishers, Parkies, and the ASPCA, was, for more than five years, fed in the Park by Frieda Hempel, the opera singer.

Creatures people usually consider wildlife also occur in the Park—cottontail rabbits, muskrats, raccoons, and woodchucks. Rabbits and muskrats, the sole aquatic mammal, have been resident from the beginning. Rabbits frequent the Bird Sanctuary, the Ramble, and the heavily wooded northwest section. Muskrats are in the Pond and the Lake.

The origin of the raccoons and woodchucks is somewhat mysterious. Neither was known in the early days of the Park. The assumption is that they are descended from summer holiday pets children brought back to the city and then were forced to release in the Park, following God only knows what family scenes. Raccoons, as their increasing numbers in suburbs show, are critters that are successful living near man. They have been sighted in the southern end of the Park near Heckscher playground, the Bird Sanctuary, and the Ramble. They're happy wintering in tree cavities, or under overturned rowboats, dozing off during winter's harshest weather and emerging only on mild days.

Woodchucks, on the other hand, are true hibernators and sleep away the winter in their burrows, most of which are in the Bird Sanctuary. But they have also been seen by the Dairy, Wollman Rink, Belvedere Castle, and the shores of the Lake. A while back one moved to a corner of the Children's Zoo. Another is Gregory. On Groundhog Day, Gregory is routed out of residency by the Conservatory Boathouse to predict the arrival of spring.

A completely unexpected wild animal seen some years ago was a gray wolf. The owner the day before had left it at the ASPCA shelter on the East Side, but the wolf escaped, made its way to Central Park, and was enjoying its new-found freedom until the ASPCA folks bore down on it and, with the aid of patrolmen from a couple of squad cars, recaptured the runaway.

Five species of amphibians and reptiles have been confirmed by herpetologists as being in the Park. Two of them, bullfrogs and snapping turtles, are successful breeders. Bullfrogs occur in every permanent water body except Conservatory Water, the sailboat pond. Snapping turtles inhabit the Lake, the Pond, Turtle Pond, and the northern waters; they are the first species of turtle known to reproduce in the Park. Other confirmed reptiles in various Park waters are the musk turtle, a little fellow under six inches in length; the painted turtle, also small, whose name comes from bright yellow or red markings, a familiar pond dweller in the Northeast; and the red-eared slider, the commonest turtle of the pet trade, whose owners, bored with their charges, must have created the Park population since the species is not of this region.

The wildlife survey lists five more amphibians and reptiles as observed by Rangers and others: the American toad, brown snake, De Kay's snake, garter snake, and green frog. The toad, a squat ground dweller, protects itself with a very caustic secretion of the skin; the green frog, a land and water denizen, is in most water bodies, its habitat, from which it seldom ventures far. The three varieties of snake, all relatively small, were once prevalent, particularly in the north end of the Park. But increased Park use and rat predation has meant that the one or two specimens occasionally seen are probably introductions.

Animal drop-offs of many kinds are frequent in the Park. One, a turtle more than a foot long, was found near Belvedere Castle by a boy who brought it inside. The staff summoned Michael Klemens, a herpetologist from the American Museum of Natural History nearby, who identified it as a Suwanne cooter, native to the Deep South. It was marked and placed in Turtle Pond, just under the Belvedere, into whose depths it disappeared with alacrity.

The survey discovered eleven fish species in Park waters. The most interesting to anglers is the largemouth black bass, a desirable game fish; specimens over a foot long are in the Lake, Meer, and Pool. Bluegills and pumpkinseeds, two varieties of sunfish beloved by young sportsmen, are present, as are banded killifish, a minnow; the black bullhead and brown bullhead, small catfish; the European carp, a food fish; the well-known goldfish, doubtless aquarium escapees; golden shiners, small members of the carp family; guppies, little aquarium fish; and yellow perch, another food fish. Crayfish also live in Park waters.

The survey did not include fish found in the reservoir, which is not under Parks Department supervision. But a count taken some years back showed that it contained bass, carp, eels, sunfish, trout, white perch, and yellow perch. One of the more intriguing, not to say mysterious, facts is that, in some fashion, they have been known to escape into the Manhattan public water system. In a letter published in the *New York Times* in 1978, Jack Gasnick, owner of a plumbing supply shop on the East Side, wrote, "I have caught eels in a Sixth Avenue main and a pickerel in a flooded basement on East 52nd Street. I am proud to boast of the horned dace, suckers, catfish, brook trout, yellow perch, and carp I have found trapped in broken water pipe sections."

The fish, Gasnick believes, enter the system from the reservoir when small enough to pass through the screens. They seem to thrive in the large pipes, living, in Gasnick's opinion, on the minute plant and animal life—aquatic lice, beetles, and vegetation, among other biota—that he has found there, a theory that seems the explanation for specimens eighteen inches long he has recovered from the mains.

Perhaps the most surprising wildlife discovered in the survey was a large population of jellyfish *(Crasoedacusta sowerbyi)* in the sailboat pond, an organism not previously known in the Park. *Sowerbyi* was discovered in 1880 in Regents Park, London. It likes artificial environments such as aquaria. It was first found in natural surroundings in 1907 in a creek near Frankfort, Kentucky. Another surprise, not in the survey but surprising nonetheless, was brought to light by a marine biologist from the American Museum of Natural History. The finding occurred on submerged beer cans in the Lake. Colonies of bryozoa, or moss animals, delicate, often beautiful, glasslike creatures, were found on them. Reportedly they showed no preference between Coors and Bud Light.

The survey also mentions butterflies, perhaps the loveliest of insects. Of the more than forty-odd species commonly seen in the state, some thirty have been spotted on tours of the Park by the Xerces Society, an organization concerning itself with insects. The tours for years were led by the late Lambert Pohner, the unofficial Park naturalist, a kindly, nature-minded, white-bearded gentleman. Eastern tiger swallowtail, spicebuch swallowtail, spring azure, eastern tailed blue, hackberry, and painted lady have been among the species noted.

Nothing was included in the survey about microscopic soil life for the very good reason that, in general, nobody pays attention to it. Yet it is a critical factor in the smooth functioning of Central Park—not to mention the rest of our planet. The organisms—algae, bacteria, fungi, and proto-zoa—live in a strange, darkened, lilliputian world. Were a man to enter it, shrunk to the microscopic size of a bacterium and provided with a tiny light by which to see, he would glimpse an eerie scene. One inch down in the soil's region of everlasting night under normal summer conditions in the Park, a moist realm would stretch before him into a misty, expanding vista of huge caves to whose boulder sides would cling sheets of water inhabited by blue-green algae far larger than himself. Lakes filled with swimming protozoa would be there, and monsters roaming on their shores in the shape of micro- and macro-animals too diversified, horren-dous, and threatening to be briefly described. It is a fantastic scene, per-haps one of the few sci-fi possibilities remaining to be used as a cinema setting.

Along with the microscopic inhabitants are other larger ones, among them ants, beetles of various kinds, earthworms, millipedes, and wireworms, which create relatively enormous passageways in the soil, providing wide conduits for the entry of air and water and thus substantially increasing the pace at which life can be carried on below. Other more familiar creatures are in the subsurface environment, too, such as toads and shrews.

The primary job of the microscopic soil life is to break down the stuff of dead plants and animals, extracting from them in usable form compounds of carbon and other elements. Carbon is the essential ingredient of all organic, or living, matter. The supply that is available for life's continuance is limited. Were it not for its recycling, chiefly by these agents, it is estimated that within fifteen years the planetary stock of carbon would be gone. Life on the globe would then grind to a halt.

No matter what the season or environmental conditions, the microscopic soil creatures are always busy, adapting themselves to whatever conditions may prevail. They vigorously attack and decompose leaf and tree litter, and such animal matter as infertile insect eggs, dead larvae, cast skins, the excrement and corpses of macro-invertebrates, and those of such vertebrates as the shrew and the toad, not to mention the dead bodies of the microorganisms themselves. Because of this activity, the carbon dioxide content, for example, in the soil may be from ten to one hundred times higher than in the air outside, to which, of course, the gas is constantly escaping to help in the production of photosynthesis. This is the process by which all vegetation grows—the plant uses water, carbon dioxide, and sunlight to provide its food of carbohydrates (sugar). Photosynthesis allows the existence of vegetation. Vegetation supports all other life.

Healthy vegetation throughout the Park, as the horticultural folk well know—trees, shrubs, flowers, and grass—depends on the microscopic soil life and its associates doing their job. Soil compaction, which occurs when pedestrians fail to use prescribed Park paths, is the greatest threat to the Park's botanical health. Compaction destroys the healthy world below, with its tiny lakes, cliffs, caves, and weird inhabitants, and with it the health of the vegetation above—the trees, shrubs, flowers, and grass. To counteract compaction, walks are being redesigned to channel and control visitor use, especially at entrances. Areas within the Park, too, will be redone, the Great Lawn being a prominent example. With compaction under control, turf and tree health will benefit greatly.

*W*HEN IT COMES to pastimes and sports, Central Park is a veritable cornucopia. This is so whether people are participating alone or in groups, and whether one measures these goings-on against other parks in the nation or around the world. In the way of active recreation for the individual, there is bicycling, both for the beginner and the more serious biker, perhaps a member of the Century Road Association. The association—to avoid conflict with joggers—organizes early morning races on Saturdays, some of them as long as fifty miles, in which speeds of about forty miles an hour may be attained. Birding, of course, goes on assiduously, regardless of season, throughout the Park. Plant identification, its botanical equivalent, is also a year-round pursuit. Fishing is permitted in any of the Park water bodies except Conservancy Water, the model boat pond. Horseback riding, most of it in the picturesque northern part of the Park, now occurs over a four-and-a-half–mile bridle trail, eventually to return to the original six.

Jogging, one of the most noticeable activities, is especially popular on the more than a mile-and-a-half cinder track circling the reservoir. Some of the more than ten thousand runners there daily regard it as a country club where they meet friends, knowledgeable ones who discuss other tracks, the circuit around the Imperial Palace in Tokyo and such, comparing them to the reservoir course, usually considered to be the busiest running track anywhere. Runners everywhere are in great numbers in the Park. Much of what they do is orchestrated by the New York Road Runners Club, with headquarters in a townhouse off Fifth Avenue on 89th Street, which plans dozens of events throughout the year for its thousands of members. In the records, members, both men and women, are listed by occupation, in the top thirty job categories. Of these, the leading categories are lawyers, administrators, students, and educators. Thus the runner you see panting along the Park's West Drive is apt to be an LL.B. or maybe even a judge.

Continuing the list of active diversions for the individual, there is kite flying, especially on the Sheep Meadow, where a Kite Jamboree is held in the spring. As well as rowboats, a gondola may be rented on the Lake, a gift of Lucy Moses, a long-time benefactor to the Park. The gondola is propelled by a trained gondolier. The rebuilt Harlem Meer boathouse will also eventually rent rowboats, if it already isn't doing so by now. Skating, both ice and roller, goes on. The former, including figure, plain exercise skating, and ice hockey, is done on the Lasker Rink in the Meer and at Wollman Rink. Furthermore, when the cold is deep, making a supportable surface on the Park's other water bodies, there is skating on them as well.

Marked recreation lanes now border the Park drives, and it is on these, and on the closed central driveway in the south central part of the Park, that the roller skaters may be found. After a snowfall, skiers perform downhill on any knoll and speed cross-country over the flats, with occasional bouts of ski-joring, being towed on skis by a horse. And young folks descend the landscape on sleds. During warmer times of the year, swimmers splash in the Lasker Pool in the Harlem Meer.

Walking is one of the great individual activities, perhaps the greatest

For the young especially, a white Park brings high spirits.
(Sara Cedar Miller, Central Park Conservancy.)

in the Park. And it can be so satisfying. . . . It's Sunday . . . An April Sunday. . . . The sky is blue . . . the air is balmy. . . . Ah-h! But apart from strolling, one can participate in clinics and races sponsored by the New York Walkers Club, whose program, formerly known as race walking, is now called health walking. Free clinics and workouts are offered on Saturday mornings at the Park's Fifth Avenue and 90th Street entrance.

As for active group recreation, ballroom dancing in the Tavern on the Green can be enjoyed by its paying patrons. Baseball, hard and soft, is played on the Park's twenty-six diamonds, which during the season's weekends are often busy from morning till night. Basketball courts are expected to be built northeast of the Great Lawn. Boccie, an Italian variety of the game of bowls, is often played on any convenient lawn, as is a somewhat similar French pastime, boules. Cricket, the British sport, is played on the baseball diamonds when they are available. Members of the New York Croquet Club play on the turf of the Bowling Greens at 70th Street near the West Drive; there the National Croquet Championships are often held, the last time in 1985. Lawn bowling's place is there, too, of course. Clad in spotless white, the men and women of the New York Lawn Bowling Club, numbering some fifty-odd, bowl four days a week and on all holidays from May through November. In 1984 some of the national tournament matches were held there. Folk dancing takes place Saturdays and Sundays by King Jagiello's statue east of Turtle Pond at the level of 80th Street.

Football, both touch and the rougher sort, is a feature on the playing fields in autumn. Frisbee tossers, however, are active year round on, among other places, Frisbee Hill north of the Sheep Meadow. Handball players use the courts by the North Meadow Center in the middle of the Park at the level of 98th Street. Field hockey teams gravitate to the Park's open spaces. Soccer is played on the Park's playing fields. There are thirty tennis courts around the South Meadow Tennis House, which also offers rental lockers to players. Paddle tennis, a winter variety of tennis, takes place on the courts by the North Meadow Center, where in 1985 the Masters Competition of the Budweiser's Paddleball Classic was held. Also here are the racketball courts.

And to complete the active group recreations we must include courtship, even advanced forms of which seem permissible in the Park.

All kinds of passive activities are available, too. Leisurely carriage rides start from the Park's southeast corner at Fifth Avenue and 59th Street. "The last vestige of romantic Victorian New York," one driver told me.

"We and the Park itself." Chess and checkers can be played at the Chess House atop the Kinderberg southwest of the Dairy at the level of 54th Street, outside in fair weather, inside in foul. A circular vined arbor has been established around the house, standing at some distance from it, recalling the original one that used to cover the entire Kinderberg. Agreeable dining in pleasant surroundings for those who seek it can be had at the Tavern on the Green, off Central Park West at 56th Street. And painters and sketchers may, and do, sit on the banks of water bodies and

meadow sites. The same can be said of the legion of amateur and professional photographers.

Finally, picnics are a happy commonplace, sometimes involving several
blankets, catered baskets of delicacies, and a wine cooler. Quiet seated
contemplation, however, is, for many, one of the best forms of tranquil
recreation. Sunbathing is another such activity calling for no exertion. On
summer days the Park turf is crowded with its votaries.

Children have recreations tailored especially for them, although adults,

*Cherry Hill
Concourse and
Fountain.
Originally this
spot was a
parking area
for carriages;
the fountain
basin was a
water trough
for the horses.
The restoration
was completed
in 1981.* (Peter
Niemi.)

a necessary evil, usually tag along. The Carousel, a youthful favorite, is one of the oldest concessions in the Park. Since 1872 the merry-go-round has been turning by one means or another to the delight of child riders, with or without parents, its calliope blaring forth old-fashioned tunes. Today's brightly painted steeds are among the largest hand-carved wooden horses in the world. Another attraction, marionette shows, also regarded by juveniles with particular esteem, are produced all year Monday through Friday at the Heckscher Puppet House in the Heckscher playground, about the center of the Park at the level of 62nd Street, and at the reopened Swedish Cottage Marionette Theatre on the Park's west side at the level of 82nd Street. This building, originally known as the Swedish Schoolhouse, was made in Sweden and modeled after a rural school for the Swedish display at the 1876 Centennial Exhibit held that year in Philadelphia. Because the Swedes didn't want to ship the building home the following year, it was brought to Central Park and set up where it stands today.

Some twenty playgrounds are in the Park, the largest of which is the seventeen-acre Heckscher. The majority are located around the perimeter and comprise the ordinary type of the Moses era with swings and seesaws and the later, more elaborate adventure playgrounds with timber-form play equipment and concrete climbing structures, some of which also have wading pools.

Rides in pony carts over the track south of the Zoo, an entertainment that began over a century ago, are, alas, a thing of the past. At first the little carts were pulled by goats. Those who wonder about the fate of the seven faithful ponies that most recently supplied the motive power will be reassured to know they were sent to good homes in the Blue Ridge Mountains or to a Long Island petting zoo. Storytelling for children, "the longest running children's show in town," takes place every Saturday morning from June first to the end of September at the feet of the Hans Christian Andersen statue, sculpted by George F. Lober and erected in 1956.

The Children's Zoo, standing just northeast of the main zoo, may be closed when this appears. At the time of this writing, bids for its renovation had not been received. As soon as possible, however, following reconstruction, it will be functioning again—daily, as in the past. The zoo, completed in 1960, consisted of a number of little structures that housed such exhibits as the African pygmy donkey, raccoons, snakes, and Edgar the raven. At the center was an irregularly bordered pond with assorted varieties of wild and domestic waterfowl. The small buildings, quaintly angled and brightly colored, looked as if they might have been blown in not long ago from the Land of Oz. After renewal, there is no reason to suppose its charm will not remain.

For the *smallest* of children, the infants, there is the daily good weather airing in the Park.

Finally, let us not forget people watching, an activity that myriad Park visitors pursue. Not long ago, two young swordsmen, stripped to the waist and on a patch of grass south of the Dairy, ardently practiced moves and combat with broadswords in preparation for forthcoming work on television. Under some trees not far away was a bustling film company whose actors in makeup and Victorian costume were, before portable Kleig lights, running through a series of outdoor scenes cast in the last century. "Hundreds of films have been shot in the Park," a gardener standing near me said. "Sinatra, Streep, O'Toole, you name one, they've been here."

In addition, especially in mild weather, musical combos with a variety of instruments stroll the Park, enlivening the scene both audibly and visually. Self-appointed clowns, jugglers, and musicians make the Park an

The Children's Zoo, gift of Governor and Mrs. Herbert Lehman, has always been a storyland compound of quaint structures and the kinds of animals dear to children. (Parks Department Archives.)

interesting grab bag of unscheduled events. Not to mention the activity of countless fashion photographers snapping models of both sexes.

Visitors pursuing sports that require equipment can usually rent it: rowboats from the Lake boathouse and the Meer, when reopened; roller skates at the Mineral Springs Pavilion northwest of the Sheep Meadow at the level of 69th Street; horses at Claremont Stables, 175 West 89th Street; and bicycles at the Loeb Boathouse on the Lake.

Casual eateries provide acceptable snacks as well as more substantial offerings. Among them are the Ice Cream Cage and the Deli, both at Conservatory Water and furnishing, among other things, a "jogger's Continental breakfast"; the Lake's Loeb Boathouse, with seats on the waterside terrace, supplies sandwiches, fruit salad, and so forth at its fast food counter and also has a full-service restaurant; a Health Bar is at the Mineral Springs Pavilion; a food counter is found in the Tennis House on the west side at the level of 95th Street north of the reservoir; and finally, many little food carts selling hot dogs and soft drinks are scattered here and there, most prominently on weekends.

Although the Park's recreations are plentiful, totaling more than fifty, its educational and cultural offerings are even more numerous. One feature that occurs every Sunday, rain or shine, and on some Saturdays, year round is the official Park walk. Led by Park Rangers, with a focus on education, they last approximately an hour and a half and change constantly. Their diversity can be shown by descriptions of the walks from each of the four seasons. A recent spring exemplar was "Rambling Warblers: We'll teach you how to sort out the differences between Blackburian and Blackpoll warblers and other such confusing birds"; in summer, "The hilly, craggy terrain of Central Park's north end tells the story of the Revolutionary Army's retreat and the fortifications built to hold back the British invasion in the War of 1812"; in fall, "Explore the scenic vistas and rolling meadows that were designed to make Central Park resemble the English countryside"; and in winter, "What happens to plants and animals when the pond freezes over? How do they survive the cold?"

From time to time, the Rangers lead a walk along the nearly four-mile Central Park Heritage National Recreation Trail, created by the U.S. Department of the Interior in 1979, the first such trail in any urban park in the country. Starting at the southern end of the Park, the trail touches fifteen major landmarks, including, from south to north, the Dairy, Bow

Built during the War of 1812 to defend the city from British attack,
this blockhouse overlooks the plain of Harlem. It is the oldest structure
in the Park. (Herbert Mitchell Collection.)

Bridge, Conservatory Garden, and the Great Hill. The Rangers also conduct bus tours through the Park to historic spots.

A series of changing educational exhibits is provided at the Dairy. Administered by the Conservancy, the Dairy now acts as the Park's Visitor Information Center and Exhibit Hall. A permanent display there is a seven-minute video show, *Oasis in the City.* Actors portraying Olmsted and Vaux conduct a little girl through their creation, showing how it existed in the past and lives on today, demonstrating the continuity of its form and purpose. A schedule of changing exhibits is also maintained. Two from the recent past were "Angels! Angels! Angels!" with pictures from Victorian times of angel decorations and photographs of angels on statues and buildings in the city; "Skating Through Time" was another. Its illustrations depicted skaters in past and more recent decades on the Lake and Wollman Rink.

In addition, on various Saturdays and Sundays, the Dairy hosts family workshops. Up to twenty children and parents take part in what are usually hour-and-a-half sessions, starting at 1:30 P.M. In 1989, two of these were "Behind This Mask: Create a mold of your face and decorate this fanciful mask while you learn how masks have been used by many cultures" and "Flights of Fancy: Design a kite for spring and fly it high over Central Park." Reservations are needed for the workshops.

Gauges of three weather instruments hang inside on the walls of Belvedere Castle, the Park's Learning Center, to be read by any visitor. They report the data being obtained moment to moment by a weather vane, an anemometer for measuring the velocity of the wind, and a contrivance for checking the amount of sunshine. The instruments themselves are attached to the outside of the Castle. Three others—a thermometer, a hydrothermograph to record the dew point, and a telepsychrometer to read the humidity—are behind a stout metal fence to the south of the Castle, all in a rather odd-looking structure perched on the ground.

The instrument readings are sent electronically to the Rockefeller Center weather office, which, after concocting the forecast, dispatches it to the media. Radio broadcasts include the phrase, hardly unfamiliar to any listener, "The temperature in Central Park is . . ."

This same information from the Park, initiated in the mid-1860s, comprises one of the longest continually logged weather records of the country, but it started far from electronically. The observatory was in a large room at the north end of the Arsenal. Measurements began soon after the Civil War, when it was, said a writer of that time,

under the immediate direction of a gentleman who, if appearances go for anything, is, undoubtedly, the original Clerk of the Weather . . . with his queer little queue, his powdered hair, his knee britches, and worsted stockings, and low-cut silver-buckled shoes and, better still, an old-time courtesy of manners such as one rarely meets in these scurvy days! Here all day, and, doubtless all night, too, for that matter, he lives among his multitude of instruments and watches with unwearied vigilance, the whims, and vagaries of his thermometers, barometers, and rain-gauges, and takes note of all Nature's doings with his telescopes, microscopes and the whole staff of mechanical detectives.

From the data of this quaint individual, the 1867 commissioner's report noted the city's first official batch of weather information, the monthly highs and lows, barometric pressures, duration and depths of rain and snow, number of thunderstorms monthly, and, surprisingly, the monthly total of igneous and luminous meteors. The former are large fireballs and the latter thin, silvery streaks, both created by celestial particles of different sizes that catch fire upon entering our atmosphere. From the report, these apparently were monitored desultorily by the weatherman looking out the window at various times of day and night. He saw six hundred twenty seven fireballs; luminous meteors were less than a quarter of that. The meteorologist with the queer little queue and silver-buckled shoes was Dr. Daniel Draper, memorialized today by a plaque on the walls of Belvedere Castle.

The uninterrupted weather information from the Park is particularly interesting to forecasters since it has been gathered at a spot that, for New York City, amounts to being in the country. Thus the century-plus data have been relatively unaffected by urban distortions—hot and cold exhaust drafts, summer heat stored in masonry and skyscraper-directed wind eddies, all highly undesirable features of a long-time weather record. Meteorologists regard Central Park's climactic history as a jewel as do sewer contractors and other laymen with a long-range interest in the weather.

Of interest to environmentalists, a study in the Park a few years back showed the air cleanest at two o'clock in the afternoon of an April day and dirtiest at eight of a December morning when furnaces labor. But anyone entering the Park at any time benefits. For in comparison to the rest of the city, its open spaces and vegetation reduce the atmosphere's sulfur dioxide by almost half.

The Learning Center's main responsibility today, however, is not the weather but the children who are introduced to its educational programs. The center is open every day but Monday twelve months a year, except on federal holidays. The staff of three full- and three part-timers is often assisted by specialists in whatever area is being presented. Over four thousand persons attend the center's programs in a typical month. Weekends the presentations customarily are for children and their parents; weekdays are generally for elementary school classes with their teachers, several of these a day being the usual quota. Thus something more than five hundred sessions are the work of the center each year.

Both educational and cultural programs are free. In the first category, three contrasting examples are: "Feathered Focus: Use microscopes to see how feathers 'zip' and then do some 'quilling' with the Birdman (a specialist)"; "Weaving with Wool and Walnuts: Stir the dye pot, color the wool, and weave a wall hanging"; and "Minibeasts: Explore with Princess Belva [the costumed and imaginary ruler of the Castle] the underground world of small creatures in the leaves and soil and rotting logs of Central Park." In the second, "Classical Ballet: Enjoy the versatile dancing of young members of the Anglo-American Ballet Foundation"; "Chinese Folk Music: Be educated by the sounds of the chru and the pipa played by Music from China"; and a drama treat, "The Kings Men: Be royally entertained by the Kings County Shakespeare Co., Inc., presenting a *Shakespeare Sampler,"* in which, to the young audiences' delight, the performers lustily engaged in swordplay, as did the Bard's own players.

Apart from the Castle, there are other opportunities for cultural appreciation, largely but not exclusively for adults. The Dairy features free Sunday afternoon concerts in the summer furnished by such as Robin Greenstein, the guitarist and vocalist, playing a musical medley, and the Metropolitan Soloists' Octet. Saturdays there is other entertainment. Among the performers have been Daring Dr. Quackenbush, a juggler and stilt walker, and Cheryl Byron, a storyteller, whose Tales of Wonder are told to the accompaniment of musical instruments. Art, too, has a prominent place in the Park. Showings, which usually last a period of weeks, occur regularly in the Gallery on the third floor of the Arsenal. Such things as the annual exhibit of traditional and nontraditional Christmas wreaths and John Manship's oil paintings and watercolors of New York City have been featured, but there are dozens of other showings a year as well. However, the big thrust of art in the Park usually comes from the Public Art Fund, which every six months arranges for new installations on the Doris Freedman Sculpture Plaza in the Park at Fifth Avenue and 60th Street. A past choice was *Carmen,* Alexander Calder's twenty-five-foot-tall polychrome steel mobile, which replaced a sculpture by Henry Moore, *Reclining Figure: Angles.* Another sculpture by Henry Moore, *Two-Piece Reclining Figure: Points,* was displayed for about a year on a floating platform on the Pond.

Then there are Central Park "events." These have included New Year's Eve fireworks at the Heckscher ballfields; a performance of dance, music, and crafts on the East Meadow by twenty-eight Australian aborigines; the Annual Celebration of Spring on Frisbee Hill, with professional singers and dancers combining Celtic and Greek myths to celebrate the oncoming warming sun; a star-gazing session under direction of astronomers from the Hayden Planetarium; a Ranger-led moonlight tour on horseback to examine the Park's arches and bridges, which cross in many places above the bridle trail; and a Winter Carnival with ice-skating races, costume parades, and prizes.

Certain major special events incorporate both spectators and participants. The New York City Marathon is one. In recent years more than twenty thousand runners have started from Staten Island. If they are able, they end in Central Park to the welcoming cheers of thousands of family, friends, and the general public. Other established races are the Fifth Avenue Mile, from 82nd to 62nd Street down Fifth Avenue along the Park's eastern perimeter; the Hispanic Half-Marathon, 13.1 miles through the Park; and the Museum Mile up Fifth Avenue between 81st and 105th streets. More thousands watch these.

Art is also represented in special events with several exhibits a year as artists display their work along Central Park South. Other nongraphic forms of art also occur. In the summer we have the hugely popular Shakespeare-in-the-Park Festival, directed by Joe Papp, with six performances a week, Tuesday through Sunday, in the Delacorte Theatre at the south end of the Great Lawn. In July the Metropolitan Opera company gives three grand operas at the north end of the Mall. And in August the Philharmonic concerts, which follow a tradition of musical entertainment that began in the Park as early as 1859, attract audiences of more than one hundred fifty thousand to the Great Lawn, where in advance of the performance picnickers gather. On one occasion the crowd exceeded eight hundred thousand, a record for a Park event, surpassing the population of South Dakota. The equally popular Summer Stage at the Naumberg Bandshell offers music and dance and other forms of entertainment by artists from both hemispheres, a highly eclectic mix.

OVERLEAF. Two of the three sections of Conservatory Garden, all of which have fountains. At right is the formal North Garden, with paving surrounding the Untermeyer Fountain. Beside it is the Center Garden, with lawn and fountain, reached by the Vanderbilt Gate at Fifth Avenue and 105th Street, the entrance to the Garden.
(Langdon Clay.)

Another musical special event occurs in warm weather at the Conservatory Garden, a lovely, secluded, four-acre tract at Fifth Avenue and 105th Street, the only formal garden in the Park, comprising three parts—the center, largely smooth turf and flowering trees; the northern, formal French garden; and the more relaxed, English-type southern garden. The beauty shown in the flowerbeds, shrubs, and trees is a tribute to the director, Mrs. Lynden Miller, possessor of a superior horticultural talent as well as an enviable eye for floral excitement and symmetry. With her skill, her botanical problems tend to be minor ones, such as the mystery of the vanishing rue anemones, delicate wildflowers with spindly stalks and several white blossoms. After planting, these kept disappearing from the beds. Mrs. Miller found there was a similar problem at the Botanical Garden in the Bronx. The belief there was that the plant is valued in voodoo rites and is more effective if stolen.

At the garden, guided tours are held in July, August, and September, sometimes followed by a concert. At other times, couples may celebrate their weddings in these bucolic surroundings. More and more are beginning to do so, with a modest fee due the Conservancy. Through these affairs, and through increasing word-of-mouth, the beautiful Conservatory Garden, once one of the Park's best-kept secrets, is becoming better known.

Back of the garden on an eminence the convent and chapel of the Sisters of Charity of Mt. St. Vincent once stood, buildings preceding the Park. Today the Park's composting operation is there. The order left when the Park started; the convent became a tavern and the chapel a statuary gallery. Fire in 1881 destroyed the tavern and a popular restaurant took its place. In 1917, however, the entire mount was cleared of buildings. In the future it may house a much-needed Park administration headquarters.

The only other garden in the Park is the Shakespeare Garden west of Belvedere Castle at the level of 79th Street. It began life in 1912 as the Garden of the Heart, but four years later, on the three hundredth anniversary of the death of the Bard, the Shakespeare Society took over. The ground was planted with flowering species, and a marble bust of him was placed on the site. In time, from want of care, the garden deteriorated and the bust was destroyed by vandals. Not until 1975, when the Park was at its lowest ebb, did a devoted band of volunteer gardeners, led by Peggy McGarrahan, start the garden back on its Shakespearean path. "We planted rosemary, that's for remembrance; and pansies, that's for

A pre-Park structure, the Mt. St. Vincent Convent of the Sisters of Charity, as reflected in the Meer. Destroyed by fire in 1881, it was replaced by a popular restaurant. Eventually the Park's composting operation succeeded it.

thoughts," said Mrs. McGarrahan. "And also lilies, roses, fennel, and columbine." In 1987, the Rudin family gave a grant to restore the garden, and the volunteers, after twelve years, departed. Their successors, a crew of up to a dozen gardeners, work under the direction of Karen Urruttia-Orme.

Ethnic gatherings are prominent special events. They are held at the Bandshell in warm weather and include the India Festival, the Korean Day Festival, and the San Juan Fiesta. Ethnicity is also represented in parades, which either touch on some part of the Park or terminate there—Saint

Patrick's Day, Cuban Independence Day, Salute to Israel Day, Puerto Rican Day, and Columbus Day—all with thousands of marchers and spectators, illustrating the centrality of the Park to city life.

Other special events indicate the versatility of their planners: the program for Christmas carolers traveling melodiously through the Park; the Easter egg roll; the Glenfiddich Games, where braw Scots toss the caber; and Frisbee Hill's Fetch and Catch meeting, a contest for owners and frisbee-catching dogs. The cornucopia overflows.

꙰ With so many people in the Park, especially on weekends, the unavoidable health emergencies are cared for by the Central Park Medical Unit, a four-person volunteer unit, more than ten years old, with a specially designed ambulance donated by the Chase Manhattan Bank; it is the only volunteer ambulance in Manhattan that can negotiate curbs, low branches, and narrow paths. The unit is on duty weekends and at major special events (with an average of ten to twenty calls each appearance). Weekends these are mostly bike mishaps, skating falls, and other athletic injuries. But in the event of more serious emergencies, the driver knows every Park road and the location of all nearby hospitals. The unit has handled almost every possible medical emergency in its decade-plus of service. Weekdays the accident front is covered by the Rangers and a number of Arsenal employees; both groups have had paramedical training.

A burdensome chore after a sizable special event is the cleanup. This is an area where the Parks Department's high morale shows itself. The department's deputy commissioner of operations is the man on whom this responsibility falls. He plans the logistics in advance, and it's a measure of the overall efficiency that even when the Great Lawn is left ankle deep in litter, by dawn the litter has disappeared, thanks to Parkie rakers with plastic bags and the filling and refilling of a bevy of specialized vehicles—three each of super-packers and vac-trucks and two ordinary packers. The loads are taken to Sanitation Department dumps. Annually, the compacted trash from the Park equals about 330,000 cubic feet, give or take a pop bottle or two.

*S*IX OTHER AGENCIES besides the Parks Department, including a federal one, have responsibilities in Central Park. To its users, the most important by far is the New York City Police Department. The personnel of the Central Park Precinct is housed on the 86th Street Transverse Road, in a long, low Calvert Vaux building, completed in 1871 as a stable. The force consists of a captain, four lieutenants, eleven sergeants, and one hundred and nineteen police officers. Its members patrol the Park on foot, on two- and three-wheel scooters, in squad cars, and in four-wheel-drive and all-terrain vehicles. Twenty officers are normally on duty of a Saturday. On Sunday the number increases by half a dozen. And the same is true of nights, when certain officers are accompanied by dogs. During major events, help is brought in from the outside, including, when necessary, mounted personnel. (Park mounted police await the completion of an on-site stable.) Also two special squads work out of the precinct, CPOP (Complete Patrol Officer Program) with nine beats, headed by a sergeant and ten officers, and SNEU (Street Narcotics Enforcement Unit), with a sergeant and eight officers.

Captain Charles Gunther, the precinct commander, in his midforties, has been on the force for more than twenty-three years. He says, as have many of his predecessors, that the precinct has the lowest crime rate in the city, in this respect passing all the rest of New York City's seventy precincts. But he concedes it has a somewhat larger proportion of violent crimes than many. This is because the precinct's overall crime rate is so low and because many of the other precincts' crimes do not take place in Central Park. These are crimes of stealth in which dangerous confrontations or the employment of weapons do not occur—sneak thievery, auto theft, or burglary of unoccupied premises. Such nonviolent crimes are never, or rarely, reported in the papers. But in the Park, crimes, particularly violent crimes, get immediate and full media coverage, immediate and full public concern. Some areas in the city may have more than a murder a night. The media hardly take notice. Not so in Central Park.

Robbery is the Park's commonest crime. A security study of several years ago, using figures from the recent past, confirms this. Weapons, naturally, were almost always used. Tourists were noted as profitable targets. Thousands, of course, visit the Park each year. Many come from countries where crime in parks is rare. They are conspicuous by their clothing, jewelry, and cameras—all highly provocative to a thief.

The study found that ten areas, six of them in the less-frequented northern section, accounted for more than half the robberies. But the largest number occurred in the Ramble, where the winding paths and vegetation screens are unquestionably an aid to criminals. In addition, more than a fifth of the robberies were found to happen at gates, led by the one at Central Park West and 72nd Street.

The police face all sorts of situations in the Park, the ludicrous as well as the critical. An instance of the former occurred when a vegetarian continually visited the zoo during the era of Robert Moses to thrust bunches of radishes, carrots, grapes, and the like into the cages of the carnivores in a determined effort to improve their constitutions. A different sort of problem arose some years back when Charles Sanfilippo, an emotionally disturbed taxi driver with a dislike of cops, clad in homemade armor and carrying two repeating shotguns, appeared in the Park, where several thousand policemen were gathered at a memorial service to honor their brother officers killed in the line of duty. Sanfilippo opened fire. He wounded a lieutenant, a patrolman, and three civilians before police gunfire felled him.

The officers of the Central Park Precinct are assisted in their work by another unit, the Central Park Precinct Auxiliary, a force of some sixty men and women in uniform. The first uniform is furnished to auxiliary members by the city. Those who perform at least one hundred twenty hours of service over a minimum of eight months receive an allotment for uniform replacements. To become a member, a candidate must have no criminal record and take a fourteen-week course whose curriculum includes law, civil liabilities, first aid, and self-defense. The candidates must then pass three written tests and the requirements of a course in self-defense. Monday, Wednesday, and Thursday evenings, members of the auxiliary patrol the Park from 8 P.M. to midnight; Saturday and Sunday, when the Park is most used, from 10 A.M. to 6 P.M. This is done on foot, in patrol cars, and on horseback. Although Auxiliary members are permitted to make arrests when a crime is committed in their presence, they are not encouraged to do so. Their main job is to act as eyes and ears for the conventional police and to notify them over their short-wave radios when they sense trouble.

Further aid comes from members of the Park Enforcement Patrol, a citywide Park Department outfit, commonly known as Pep. Clad in the official green uniforms of the Parks Department and wearing the Smoky Bear hat, these men and women are New York City special patrolmen and have peace officer status as defined in the New York State Criminal Procedure Law. They may make arrests, issue summonses, apprehend juveniles (a young person under sixteen who commits a violation or crime), and confiscate illegal wares and contraband, such illicitly sold goods as food, alcohol, and fireworks. Their duties are to enforce the regulations that protect the public and public property, thereby helping make the Park what the administrator and her staff hope and expect it to be—increasingly secure. A Pep's authority, however, is only valid on Park property and while working. Outside the Park—or off duty—the officer cannot act as one.

The Peps come from Manhattan's pool of sixty-six Pep officers and supervisors. They cover the Park for twenty-four hours and are assigned according to specific needs, which vary by season, day, and hour. Naturally there is more work on weekends, when there are normally six to eight Peps on patrol during any one of the four daily tours of duty. On the first, from 6:30 A.M. to 2:30 P.M., the officers are in green, four-wheel-drive Parks Department cars. Apart from detection of serious crime, their mission is to be watchful for breaches of regulations such as fires in cold weather, cars improperly parked on the grass, illegal food vendors setting up shop, and owners failing to clean up after their dogs.

The second tour, by officers on foot, begins at 10 A.M. and ends eight hours later. It concentrates on preventing violations in areas generally south of 72nd Street, such as the Bandshell, Sheep Meadow, Pond, Heckscher playground and ballfields, and Sherman Plaza. On weekends, two officers on this patrol abandon foot duty and drive mopeds. According to a Pep supervisor, "The mopeds allow our officers to move through congested park pathways and drives on busy weekends without annoying the patrons as vehicles do. They make the officers more approachable than if they were in a vehicle; the officer can patrol an area several times faster than on foot; the officer can go into hard-to-reach areas that a vehicle could not enter; the officer can also keep a bad guy in sight while calling for backup or police."

The third tour starts at 4 P.M. and ends at midnight. Emphasis is on preventing littering, loud radio playing, the sale of alcohol, unleashed dogs, Pooper-Scooper violations, banning athletic teams from newly seeded ground or ones that are still too delicate to bear a session of play, and watching out for the safety of joggers and other Park patrons at dusk or as night envelops the area.

The fourth and last tour begins at midnight and goes till 8 A.M. The job then is to guard facilities such as the Arsenal and Tennis House against break-ins and to catch graffiti perpetrators. The officers ride in unmarked cars, staking them out near monuments, buildings, statues, and other likely targets. The results of the graffiti artist are a blot on the Park. Many law-abiding visitors would like to retaliate, but few have provided such appropriate punishment as did one jogger a few years back. While on the move, the jogger spotted a would-be artist armed with the usual weapon, an aerosol spray can. Pausing briefly, the runner wrested it from him, sprayed him a fetching baby blue, and departed the scene scarcely breaking stride, leaving the astonished victim with the aerosol can at his feet.

Graffiti is a continual problem. The markings normally come from spray cans of paint held in the hands of male adolescents. Some few people, usually teachers of graphics, consider graffiti a form of art; many more citizens view it as objectionable and worse. "Graffiti is an urban plague," says Commissioner Stern. "It's a private claim of dominion and an assault on the public."

Since January of 1985 the Parks Department has mounted an energetic antigraffiti campaign with the Peps. Offenders caught in Central Park are subject to the provisions of Section 78-A of the General Municipal Law, which orders financial restitution for damages inflicted. But the Parks Department allows those offenders over sixteen to perform eight hours of work as an alternative to monetary damages. Those under sixteen do four hours of work. Then they are led on a four-hour tour of the Park by a Ranger. With rehabilitation in mind, they are asked to write an essay on graffiti for the Parks Department files. Since the start of the Peps campaign in 1988, and through November of that year, twenty graffitists were nabbed in the Park; none was a repeater.

In addition, the Park has an efficient graffiti-removal team, funded by the Conservancy, often through grants from the Bankers Trust Company.

Forty thousand square feet of multicolored graffiti ornamented Park buildings, stairways, rock outcroppings, walls, playgrounds, and monuments when the campaign to erase it began shortly after the start of rehabilitation. Workers use chemicals such as heavy-duty paint strippers and abrasives such as certain minerals including sand. These are applied either by hand with a wire brush or by powerful portable washers that emit streams with pressures of from one to two thousand pounds per square inch. Today any graffiti seen in the Park is less than a week old, except that on highly delicate surfaces like carved sandstones. Methods to remove these are nearing completion under the direction of one of the Conservation Department's deputy directors. While the Park now is relatively graffiti-free, the Peps' stakeouts continue. As one of the administrator's team has said, "Keeping the Park graffiti-clean adds substantially to the public's sense of security, a goal we constantly seek."

In addition to other Pep forces, a mounted unit of four officers works part time in the Park, patrolling in daylight hours. In cooperation with the police, it focuses mainly on high-visibility areas near woodlands where drugs are sold, the elimination of which is a high-priority objective with both the Park administration and the police. The horses are boarded at Claremont stables. Plans for the projected stable in the Park itself have been on hold until space can be found, perhaps in a structure west of police headquarters.

The Rangers, uniformed like the Pep officers, are the final force aiding safety in the Park. A permanent detail of six to eight men and women, including supervisors, works there. From October through May they are on one shift seven days a week from 9 A.M. to 5 P.M.; in the busy season the rest of the year the number doubles through the addition of temporary Rangers. Then there are two shifts, the first as before and the second, also every day, from noon to 8 P.M. They can make no arrests. They enforce regulations by persuasion. If this fails, they use their walkie-talkies to summon Pep or police help. They are trained to act in medical or other emergencies.

Rangers know the Park intimately and can direct visitors who need assistance, thereby fulfilling one of Olmsted's important directions to his own police. And another of their great services is leading the many guided tours through the Park.

Despite these services—despite the fact that crime in the Park is less than in any other precinct—the Park is not utterly safe. Visitors should realize this and abide by certain simple rules. Don't leave valuables unattended. In woodsy sections like the Ramble, visitors, especially women and the elderly, should go in pairs; so, in the more isolated sections, should joggers. Park users should know that help can be obtained from any uniformed person and through the nearly fifty police call boxes, painted yellow. Calls go directly to the police precinct, which routes squad cars to the scene immediately, the location of the box being shown. Nevertheless, don't go in the Park after dark unless en route to a scheduled entertainment. Most of all, avoid dangerous-looking persons. Many police officers say that instinctive recognition of danger by an intended victim is the best form of protection. Turn away at once from any person who seems suspicious.

One federal agency—the Department of Commerce, through its National Oceanic and Atmospheric Administration—looks after the weather instruments in and around the Belvedere; the others are all city bodies. The Department of Environmental Protection maintains the Park's sewers and, by means of its Bureau of Water Supply, the reservoir and waste water collection. The reservoir is part of the nineteenth-century Croton Reservoir system, whose water comes from twelve reservoirs in Westchester and Putnam counties and is brought down by the New Croton Aqueduct. The reservoir serves only low-lying areas in Manhattan and the Bronx. Its contribution, in normal times, is about 10 percent of the water the city consumes. The rest is brought down from the much larger Catskill and Delaware reservoir systems through two huge tunnels.

Of the two reservoir gatehouses, only the southern is manned by a crew of two men per shift, three shifts a day, seven days a week, to attend to the water chlorination. In times of drought, as in 1985, the south gatehouse is used as a pumping station, and one stationary engineer then comes aboard, one per shift, three shifts a day, seven days a week. He uses two twenty-five million-gallon-a-day pumps, run by electricity, to send about forty-eight million gallons a day to the East and West sides between 59th and 96th streets, normally served by one of the big Catskill water tunnels.

Before World War II, when the reservoir fence was lower and it was easier to toss things into the water, an employee used to cruise the surface in a rowboat, using a net to fetch out extraneous objects—guns, dead seagulls, lamps, waste paper, and once a nearly complete set of the

Encyclopaedia Britannica. During World War II the fence was raised as a safety measure. Joggers may be surprised to learn that the reservoir running track is under the jurisdiction, not of the Park, but of the Department of Environmental Protection.

Two of the remaining agencies involved are the Department of Transportation, responsible for the good health of the Park's lights and lamp posts and the care of the roadways within the Park, including the transverse roads, and the Sanitation Department, which clears the traffic arteries after a snowfall.

The final agency is the Fire Department, which manages the fire alarms and responds to fires in the Park. But it also has a permanent presence in the Park. On the 79th Street transverse road there is another long, low, Calvert Vaux building of white concrete set into the rock and also completed in 1871, as was his brick police precinct house on the transverse road further north. The Fire Department building is the hub of the Manhattan fire alarm system, the Manhattan Central Office of the Bureau of

Workmen cleaning drains on a transverse road. Woody material on the bank above is a hazard for the catch basins.
(Sara Cedar Miller, Central Park Conservancy.)

Fire Communications. Manhattan's nearly two thousand fireboxes feed the alarms into here, whence they are parceled out to the proper firehouses.

The building is located where it is for a very good reason. If much of Manhattan were engulfed in flames, the Park would not be and the system would still function. Thirty-four fire alarm dispatchers divide the two daily shifts. They enter and leave by the transverse roadway. Remote—they are hardly Park dwellers at all.

The reality of the Park's rehabilitation became much more solid when, six full years after the work began, separate budgets for a series of the Park's fiscal years were produced, the work of the Parks Department's deputy commissioner of finance. Previously, operating costs were tucked into those for the Parks Department as a whole. Consequently, nobody knew the cost of running Central Park. With the new budgets, this has changed. Fiscal outlays, at least in the case of the budgets for recent years, are clear; those outlined for the future are, naturally, more theoretical.

For fiscal year 1985, for example, the cost of operating Central Park came to a little over $8.8 million. In the five main categories of upkeep, the Conservancy led in horticulture and visitor services, the city in maintenance and operations, preservation, and security. Conservancy input for its share was about one-third of the total. Other costs—office salaries, design and planning, and fund raising—were intermingled. That year the Park employed three hundred ninety eight workers.

Looking ahead at a future budget, we find the projected operating plan for the fiscal year 1995, when five hundred fifty one are expected to be employed, comes in at more than $22 million, an increase of over 250 percent from a decade earlier. Of this the Parks Department bears more than three-quarters, and the Conservancy the balance. Here the Conservancy leads only in the category of visitor services. Also, its contribution, although exceeding $5 million, is relatively diminished.

However, all is not outgo. There is some income from fees and concessions. All told, in a typical year for the Park these amount to $1.5 million. Sources are varied. The funds come from permits and other fees for sports. Tennis is a big one, during one recent year contributing over $360,000 in diverse fees from nearly thirty thousand players. Food concessions, however, are the largest earner. There are over seventy of these, from the crown jewel, the Tavern on the Green, the only establishment in the Park permitted to sell spirits, to places like the Conservatory

Water snack bars and forty or more wheeled carts, some with—and others without—assigned locations, one of which offers Chinese cuisine. The money that came from those, with the Tavern on the Green's six figures leading the way, was nearly $1 million in the above-quoted recent year.

In addition to these sources, there is a trickle of funds from balloon vendors, the Carousel, bookstalls along Fifth Avenue, newsstands at the corners, model boat lockers and rental, and rental for roller skates. And in 1985, for example, there were also seventeen contributions or donations from those who staged special events in the Park such as running races, the take amounting to just under $200,000.

The Conservancy enters the scene, as well. In 1988, at the Dairy, Belvedere Castle, and Conservatory Garden, spots managed by the organization, a total of $48,200 was collected from sales of books and postcards and fees from photographers, filmmakers, wedding parties, and the sponsors of small celebrations at Belvedere Castle and Conservatory Garden. An individual donor, actor Robert Redford, has from time to time provided a manned authentic 1910 Dunbar Wagon near 60th Street and Fifth Avenue from which is sold "Newman's Own Old Style Picture Show Popcorn." One year he donated a profit of $11,000 to the Conservancy.

Four

The Future in Sight

1990-1995

*A*RGUABLY, the Central Park Zoo is the nation's oldest. One year after the Park's opening in 1858, a bear cub was presented and accepted. For the historical record, a man named Philip Holmes was appointed the bear's keeper, the first keeper of the first animal in the nation's presumed first zoo. The gifts kept arriving. At the start, they were housed in cages in the Arsenal's basement. Then the overflow was moved outside to the building's rear. On view, among others, were eagles, foxes, prairie dogs, and bears, an adult of the last having been sent from the West by General Custer. To address the question of age, another zoo sometimes cited for the title of oldest zoo is Philadelphia's. It was founded in 1859 but not opened to the public till 1874, more than a decade after people began seeing the Central Park animals.

By the time Robert Moses had become park commissioner in 1932, the original zoo had ballooned into an assemblage of nearly two dozen decrepit, flimsy wooden buildings. Instead of strengthening or rebuilding the structures, the lax city administrations of the pre-LaGuardia era did nothing. The people then at City Hall were accommodating. They accepted as donations from residents (voters) all sorts of uncharacteristic creatures, such as canaries or poultry. Veterinary care was inadequate. The exhibits included a puma with rickets, a palsied baboon, and a tiger with senile dementia.

Moses changed all this. By 1934 he had a spanking new zoo, equally hailed at the time by the media and public. Its buildings of red brick and white limestone trim were fetchingly sited back of the Arsenal. The arrangement formed a U-shaped border around an attractive central garden in whose center was a sea lion pool studded with resting rocks for the occupant's leisure. The buildings were nine in number, and important in terms of the present zoo. From the south, going clockwise around them, they were the Birdhouse, the Smaller-Hoofed Animal House, the Larger-Hoofed Animal House, the combined

211

Horned Animal and Small Mammal House, the garage and its auxiliary offices along with the animal kitchen, the Elephant House, the old cafeteria, the Lion House, and finally the Monkey House.

However, as time rolled along, people's ideas underwent a change as to how animals should be exhibited. The Moses zoo, which received so much approval at its onset, eventually came under heavy fire. A few years back, for example, the *Defenders of Wildlife Magazine* had this to say, in part, about the zoo:

> New York City's Central Park Zoo is known, in gentler terms than it merits, as an old-style zoo. Its inhabitants while away lifetimes in solitary confinement, in cages with no room to run or jump, or even a padded bed to lie on, sometimes with only a board to sleep on.
>
> Abuses have been blatant in the last few years: a capuchin monkey scalded by a keeper with hot water; other animals left for hours hurt, bleeding, unattended.
>
> Almost without exception, those who know it condemn the Central Park Zoo, including such organizations as the Humane Society of the United States, the Society for Animal Rights, the World Federation for the Protection of Animals and such individuals as Roger Caras, the noted naturalist, and William Conway, director of the Bronx Zoo.

The old zoo was closed for several years. An objective of the new one was to correct past inhumanity. Therefore, under the most humane conditions possible, and in settings that—although manmade—would mimic the freedom and habitats of nature was the environment to be provided. The New York Zoological Society, the knowledgeable operator of the Bronx Zoo and the New York Aquarium, two of the world's best managed and widely admired wildlife exhibits, was the organization tapped for the job. Not only is the society a humane manager of menagerie animals, it is a master of the arcane art of mimicking nature. It has done both for the new zoo, which opened in August 1988 to abundant and well-deserved media and public praise. The society's director, William Conway, one of the complainants cited above, now supervises the workings of the zoo, making further complaints about animal maltreatment unlikely.

When the old zoo, which had one hundred fifty animals, was closed, other zoos quickly accepted the animals. Three problem cases were exceptions—Tina, the elephant; Caroline, an elderly gorilla; and Skandy, a polar bear. Tina was crotchety. As a herd animal who had been without a herd for twenty-five years, her temper was uncertain. Caroline was "post-menopausal," that was the rap on her. Zoos like breeding gorillas. And Skandy had killed a man who, suicidally motivated, climbed over Skandy's bars one night and into his cage. In time, all three problem cases found new homes.

Happy to relate, also, is that the new zoo is a place not only for visitor amusement but also for enlightenment and knowledge about life that inhabits our world with us. The casual spectator may get this osmotically through the vividly naturalistic settings the society has installed. But there are frankly informative arrangements as well, principally for schoolchildren in the old Monkey House and the new Intelligence Garden.

The zoo's designers had no easy task. They had to work with an inflexible area of five and a half acres along with more than half a dozen demanding criteria, among which were that the plan must be in keeping with the Park's identity as a historic landmark and, at the same time, be enjoyable as a public park as well as possessing a soothing visual impression. Also, the old zoo pattern was largely to be followed, its buildings to be used where possible, with new ones arising not to exceed the height of the old. Furthermore, as a very important requirement connected with pedestrian traffic, all major exhibits were to lie to the west of the heavily travelled north-south walkway directly behind the Arsenal, thus allowing this stream of traffic to move as smoothly as possible.

What the designers have provided is a captivating layout. It follows, but greatly improves upon, the old scheme. Five of the nine former buildings remain in altered form—the Small-Hoofed and Large-Hoofed animal houses, the previously mentioned Monkey and Bird houses, and the garage. As in the past, there is a central garden with a sea lion pool in its middle. Surrounding it, except on the north-south path back of the Arsenal, is an ingenious architectural innovation. A series of octagonal red brick columns with white limestone trim, the material used in the Moses zoo, carries a succession of wooden trellises; these, in turn, support a glass roof, stippled to be somewhat sun-repellent. The entire structure forms a covered archway from which all the major exhibits can be viewed or entered without regard to weather conditions. Eventually vines will crawl over the glass roof.

Three contrasting habitats comprise the main exhibits, featuring the arctic, temperate, and tropical zones. Visitors entering the northern arm of the archway will come upon the Polar Circle, whose first showing is in the Penguin Building. Called "The Edge of the Ice Pack," the display

An aerial view of the new zoo. The Sea Lion Pool in the Central
Garden leads the eye back to the glass-roofed colonnade, behind which
is the Temperate Territory. The Tropic Zone Building is to the left.
(Sara Cedar Miller, Central Park Conservancy.)

consists of chilled salt water which, from time to time, breaks into waves,
a ledge of ice, areas of dry land, frosty air, and the twinkling of the Southern Lights. It stands on the site of the old Lion House and contains a
snowy owl, a large white, diurnal, avian predator; a dozen puffins, chunky
sea birds from cold North Atlantic waters about a foot high with heavy,
triangular beaks; and flocks of some sixty highly aquatic Gentoo and Chin-
strap penguins, native to the Antarctic, all about a foot tall, that are speedy
torpedoes under the water. As in each case where exhibit animals sub-
merge, the new zoo provides a view of the underwater activity.

The Polar Circle continues with an outdoor exhibit, part water, part
earth and rock. This contains harbor seals, a small spotted seal native to
the coasts of the northern hemisphere. Arctic foxes are also there, small
examples of the fox family, white-coated in winter and bluish or brownish
the rest of the year. Normally they are found living on sea ice or the solid

ground adjacent. The last Polar Circle offering is likely to be the most popular, a large open-air accommodation for polar bears. Visitors can see these intriguing creatures on land or immersed in their pool. The animals swim overhead when viewed through a glass partition below the pool's surface.

The next length of the colonnade, the one parallel to the Arsenal, runs in front of the exhibit of the Temperate Territory, consisting of pieces of water and land. Its animals, native to our latitudes, are quartered behind the colonnade where once the old cafeteria stood. With that gone, the architects have provided us with pleasant glimpses of the Park to the west. The sector has paths supplied with benches. Here visitors can sit and watch muntjacs, a small Asian deer, and red pandas, a couple of feet long, natives of China, members of the raccoon family and somewhat distant cousins of the giant panda.

The water here has native water birds, fish, turtles, and sea otters. Japanese macaques, or snow monkeys, the most northerly of the world's monkeys, are on an island. Energetic and playful, they provide a day-long show. Neither winter winds nor summer heat can make them uncomfortable. Their thick fur insulates them against either weather extreme.

In nature, a tropical rain forest holds more life forms than any other environment. Situated on the site of the old Elephant House, on the last, or southern leg, of the colonnade, the Tropic Zone Building provides a graphic presentation of one. The scene is astonishingly realistic, despite the fact that all habitat fittings have been made by man. Enormous buttressed tree trunks with branches, thick vines, and orchidlike plants decorate the interior.

Along the branches perch, prowl, or slither toucans, monkeys, and pythons. Also present, aloft in the trees or below, are flying geckos, a small Southeast Asian lizard with skin flaps for gliding; double-crested basilisks, an eighteen-inch-long tropical lizard that can run on its hind legs; and small South American frogs whose skin glands provide a lethal poison when applied to the tips of darts. In the air, winging freely about, are tanagers, barbets, sunbirds, and others, including small Asian tropical parrots, the size of sparrows, that can eat their food, fruit, and nectar, hanging upside down. The water environments have caimans, a form of alligator, and piranhas, the small but very voracious South American meat-eating fish. Walkways with railings built at different levels in the setting let visitors see life both high and low in the forest. Unobtrusive glass partitions make them safe.

Altogether there are some four hundred animals numbering approximately one hundred species in the zoo. School and general audiences now meet for educational talks in the old Monkey House, which has been altered to provide classrooms and a small auditorium and renamed the Heckscher Zoo School. The old Bird House on the other side of the Arsenal has become a bookshop and store for the sale of zoo-connected items—trinkets, T-shirts, and such.

Down the walk from the Tropic Zone Building, at the entrance to the last length of the colonnade, is the Intelligence Garden, once the locale of the Horned Animal and Small Mammal House. It commemorates the name given by the Chinese emperor Wen Wang, in 1100 B.C., to a group of rare beasts that he put on show in his palace grounds to educate his subjects about nature and underscores also the zoo management's aim to spread popular knowledge about world wildlife. Here, before starting out on a tour of the zoo, school groups with teachers gather to hear helpful ecological information.

Near here as well are two more buildings in the new zoo. One is an indoor-outdoor cafeteria. Its entrance gives onto the Arsenal side of the north-south walkway diagonally across from the Intelligence Garden. The old Smaller Hoofed Animal Building is the other, located near the cafeteria. It is an administrative annex for that part of the zoo management staff for which space could not be found in the Arsenal.

When the zoo reopened without its former bars, concrete floors, and restrictive cages, a new batch of sea lions arrived. Doubtless they were gratified by their new surroundings. The pool is well equipped with resting rocks and larger than the old. At first, there were three occupants. Since then, two have been added, a mother and pup. Sea lions are herd animals. Thus the newcomers posed no problem. Speaking generally, with sea lions the more the merrier.

No large, free-ranging quadrupeds such as the antelope and deer of past years are shown. Under the policy of lifelike habitats, there is no room for them in the zoo's limited area. Much less for elephants.

Because of the careful work of the designers, not a tree from the grounds of the old zoo has been lost. Its four pieces of statuary—the Dancing Bear, the Dancing Goat, the Eight Eagles, and Tigress with Cubs—are back in place. (The Children's Zoo, as has been mentioned, may be closed for renovation when this appears and may not open for a year or two.)

The zoo is part of the City Zoos Project, a new development that forms

The Sea Lion Pool at the new zoo. (Sara Cedar Miller, Central Park
Conservancy.)

the nation's largest metropolitan system of wildlife exhibits, all managed
by the New York Zoological Society. The other members besides the
Bronx Zoo and the New York Aquarium, already under the aegis of the
society, are the Prospect Park Zoo and the Flushing Meadows Park Zoo,
each of which, like the Central Park Zoo, will be redesigned to have a
personality of its own, although their completion is some years off.

As for Central Park, the consequences of the new management's policies look easy to predict. Under the society's staff—those wizards of
animal care and presentation and habitat fabrication—the result seems
bound to be not only healthy and happier animals but happy and more
enlightened viewers.

The zoo cost over $35 million. Almost $22 million of this came from the
city's capital improvements kitty. Originally the society was to supply
$6.7 million. This was the deal at the beginning. Later, however, the
society kicked in an additional $6.7 million for enhancements, an enlarge-

ment of the sea pool, for example, and major landscape flourishes beyond what was first agreed upon.

The zoo, unlike its predecessor, is not free. Admission is one dollar for adults, fifty cents for senior citizens, twenty-five cents for children twelve to three, and no charge for those under three. Because of the fee, the zoo is enclosed and provided with gates.

Hours from November through March are ten to four-thirty every day. The rest of the year, Monday through Friday, hours are ten to five; Tuesdays till eight; and weekends and holidays, ten to five-thirty.

The new zoo, like the old, is enormously popular. A fair Sunday afternoon finds the walks packed with lively, cheerful visitors, making the rounds of the displays, trailed by skeins of excited, jubilant children.

The administrator, echoing general approval, said, "The restored zoo is just another piece of the mosaic we are putting together as we rebuild Central Park. With the new imaginative and educational exhibits provided by the New York Zoological Society, it will undoubtedly draw more people than did the old one." (The administrator's enthusiasm is a bit tempered by the zoo's separation from the Park. "I miss the normal Park visitor's ability to stroll through the zoo," she says. "But perhaps the animals' present happy freedom outweighs pedestrian freedom in that limited space.")

From Commissioner Stern: "When I was appointed parks commissioner by Mayor Koch, I said I would be a Man for All Species. The Central Park Zoo is the place where Animal and Vegetable Kingdoms most happily meet. I welcome back the gentle creatures whose ancestors taught and amused generations of children and adults, and hope their wisdom leads us to be kind to, and concerned about, our fellow inhabitants of earth."

*P*ERHAPS the most beautiful feature of the Park—and a somewhat surprising one—is its stupendous rock outcrops. Few visitors realize the characteristics and history of the ancient stony layers that support their feet or gladden their eye. The vistas of their bold, diverse shapes are as varied as forms in a multiclouded sky. While certain stones may peep shyly through the turf, others tower commandingly in audacious, scenic precipes, or rise as crags standing alone in a meadow.

Having been formed long, long ago in the Proterozoic Era, they are ancient objects whose age almost daunts understanding. Life on earth then had barely begun, and what there was of it was confined to the sea. In that distant time the place where the Park now stands was the bottom of a shallow arm of the ocean stretching into the large, unified land mass that scientists have named Pangea. This supercontinent embraced the whole of the planet's land above water. All the continents we know today rested within it. Later, as the eons rolled along, they gradually and slowly separated. To the west of the shallow inlet was Pangea's land mass; to the east lay a chain of volcanic islands. Both contributed sediment to the sea floor, the continent by the natural process of erosion, and the island chain both by erosion and by the accumulation of volcanic material. This went on year after year, the material on the sea arm's bottom ultimately reaching a thickness of many thousand feet. Its weight carried it deeper and deeper into the earth, where it consolidated into a sedimentary rock known as sandy shale.

Then terrestrial activity thrust the shale much deeper into the earth. Under the great temperature and heat prevailing there, the shale metamorphosed into a much harder substance called schist. Minerals scattered in tiny amounts throughout the former shale agglomerated into clumps. As the schist cooled, the minerals formed crystals of quartz, feldspar, mica, and garnet. As part of this major geologic process—a procedure technically known as orogeny, or mountain building—the earth on either side of the arm of the sea was pushed up to huge heights, obliterating the inlet. Thus the newly manufactured schist that now lies at the surface of Central Park became the core of a lofty mountain range, perhaps as high as the present Himalayas.

After an interval, the schist was further altered by the intrusion of inlays of molten magma from the earth's interior. This mottled the schist with magma-filled cracks ranging from an inch or two wide and a few feet in length to ones a yard or more wide and scores of feet long. The magma was almost always a granite pegmatite, a coarse-textured igneous rock consisting mostly of quartz and feldspar but bearing other minerals as well, some of them rare. As the magma cooled, these agglomerated and took the shapes of beautifully formed crystals, sometimes of very large size.

All mountain ranges, however high, erode, and so did the range above the schist in Central Park. With the lightening of the overlying load, the schist rose slowly and steadily from the earth's depths. Geologists agree that by the time of the dinosaurs, the schist was exposed at the surface of Central Park as it is today, affording rambling room for these reptiles that ruled the earth for millions of years (but only a fraction of the time since the history of the Park's sandy shale-cum-schist began).

The schist is known formally as the Manhattan foundation or Manhattan schist. It is the topmost of three layers of rock that underlie Manhattan. These are known collectively as the New York City Series. With other units in adjoining areas, they make the geology of the New York area one of the most diverse of any metropolitan region in the world. Directly below the Manhattan schist is the Inwood marble foundation, laid down earlier in the same sea arm as a whitish limestone and metamorphosed eventually into a dirty white, sugary marble far less durable than the schist. Its name derives from its frequent emergence in the Inwood section of Manhattan. In the Park, it appears only in a limited way at the extreme northern end at the level of 106th Street, a fault causing it to have slid up and over the Manhattan schist there. The final formation of the New York City Series, originally a sandstone and formed in the gulf below the marble and the schist, is known as the Fordham formation or Fordham gneiss, into which it changed upon metamorphosis. It is an attractively banded black and white stone and is as hard as schist. Its name comes from its frequent occurrence in the Fordham neighborhood of the city. Its closest approach to Central Park is at 110th Street and Second Avenue. A thin strip of it has been found there forty feet down.

Manhattan schist is not only the bedrock of the Park, it underlies much of the island. Its diamondlike hardness posed a dramatic challenge to New York's early real estate developers. Builders for decades were obliged to level the island's rock humps into flat surfaces amenable to their structures; it was no easy task. But today the problem of yesterday is a developer's blessing. The thick, tough schist forms a secure floor for our lofty modern piles, however high they may soar.

During the age of the dinosaurs, when the schist at last appeared on what is now the Park's surface, the Atlantic Ocean was "born." At first a slender opening showed itself between sides of the slowly separating single large land mass, all this being part of a process that gradually, but without letup, continued until the continents became the integral units they are today. Also, at this time, the Palisades across the Hudson River in New Jersey arose—another feature that makes our metropolitan-area geology so diversified.

The last geologic event to leave its mark on the Park was the glacier of the most recent Ice Age, an episode that began about thirty thousand years ago. The huge ice cover, estimated to have been as tall as the World Trade Center, pushed gradually southward from Canada until it covered all of the city down to northern Staten Island. As it crept along, its weight scoured the earth's surface. Embedded rocky material produced various effects on the rocks of the Park. Distinct gouges are to be found at, among other spots, the point where Sixth Avenue and 103rd Street would meet and in the North Meadow at the level of 99th Street.

After nearly twenty thousand icy years, our climate warmed. As a result, the glacial sheet slowly retreated northward. Debris held in the frozen mantle dropped to the Park's surface, leaving obvious mementos of its presence. West of the Bandshell, for example, at the upper end of the Mall is a large boulder called an erratic, the technical name for such stones released by glaciers. It is very hard, made of a material called diabase, and, during the glacier's advance, was wrenched from its seat on the Palisades, where it had been embedded for untold thousands of years.

A different example of glacial activity is to be found under the Chess and Checkers House, which sits atop the hillock of schist called the Kinderberg. The Kinderberg's northern slope, which the glacier approached, is polished and lined with both shallow and deep striations, made when the stones held in the glacier's foot slid over the slope, gouging the rock like chisels. The southern, or departure, face is more steeply worn because of what geologists call the "plucking" nature of the ice. The entire hillock is a fine example of a *roche moutonnée,* French for sheep rock, because it resembles a sheep recumbent in a meadow. The southern

slope is so smooth and highly polished that, on fair evenings as it reflects the light of the setting sun, it shines like a mirror.

A few rods east of the apartment building at 25 Central Park West is the only known glacial pothole in Central Park. It was found some half century ago by an inveterate Park stroller, who happened to be a scien-

Grooves in this massive outcrop were carved some twenty thousand years ago by sharp-edged boulders of the last glacier. Masses of ice towered hundreds of feet above the Park's site. (Sara Cedar Miller, Central Park Conservancy.)

tifically minded osteopath, Dr. Ernest Tucker. The hole, then a rather mysteriously placed depression on the flat surface of an outcrop, was partially plugged with sod. Tucker suspected that it might be just what it turned out to be, a pothole. Shortly thereafter, alerted by Dr. Tucker, a scientist from the American Museum of Natural History, armed with a Parks Department permit, a necessary document for that kind of errand, dug to the bottom of the hole. Yellow clay turned up, dating back to the time of the glacier's departure, when hairy, long-tusked mastodons shuffled across the newly emerged surface of Manhattan.

Potholes are formed near the front of a thawing glacier on exposed stone outcrops. Over the years, melting streams carrying sand, gravel, and rocks descend, usually through a crevasse, and form a whirlpool on the outcrop. The abrasives in the vortex carve out the pothole. Today the Central Park pothole is once again largely plugged with turf.

The light-colored pegmatite magma that forced itself into the schist is an interesting mineral. Customarily it carries a great number of crystals— beautifully formed, many oversized. Among them are beryl, garnet, spodumene, and tourmaline. Of the two thousand minerals that are known to occur on earth, almost a quarter are obtained from pegmatites. Of the more than one hundred seventy mineral species so far identified from Manhattan's bedrock, more than 80 percent come from pegmatites. Manhattan has an exceedingly large number of mineral varieties considering that the island has never had mining development. The explanation, of course, is that Manhattan's extensive building and subway excavation have revealed the pegmatite-bearing schist.

Among the most notable crystals that Manhattan's pegmatites have produced is a ten-pound garnet from Broadway and 35th Street, a nine-inch-long, ten-pound tourmaline from Fort Washington Avenue and 171st Street, and from Riverside Drive and 93rd Street one of the finest chryso-beryl crystals ever discovered in North America, a yellowish mineral, like the others sometimes used as a gem. Were mineral exploration allowed in the Park, a wealth of similar minerals and gems would undoubtedly be unearthed, including veins of lightly speckled gold-bearing quartz embedded in the schist. But rockhounds cannot perform their searches in the Park.

Nor can those seeking fossils. Actually, there are no fossils in the Park's bedrock, which is metamorphic; the heat and pressure of metamorphosis precludes this. But the glacial till on the surface could harbor fossils. The Park's till is the unstratified material—clay, sand, gravel, and boulders—that was dropped there over the centuries by the melting glacier. Doubtless fossils are in it because the till around the Park contains them. A mastodon's molar tooth, for example, was picked up just to the west in an excavation at Broadway and 69th Street. Its owner, a husky, hirsute, and larger relative of our elephant, lived hereabouts until ten to six thousand years ago. Fossils that are obvious discards from a collector's shelves have, of course, been found in the Park. One was a hunk of Burgess shale, identified as being from British Columbia, and laden with trilobites, those common denizens of Paleozoic seas.

Man as well as Nature has altered the geology of Central Park, mainly by boring two systems of tunnels through the schist. The first, the smaller, is a pair of tunnels for what is now the New York City Transit Authority, one of seven tunnel sections known collectively as the 63rd Street subway tunnel, designed as part of a high-speed express line to Queens. The section in the Park was begun in July 1971, and its basic construction was completed five years later. Additional work on the system lagged, but service began in Fall 1989, when trains ran to the 21st Street Station in Long Island City. The Park's tunnels enter the bedrock not far under the surface at Fifth Avenue and 63rd Street, going in a southwesterly direction. They separate at the Wollman Rink, one exiting the Park at Sixth Avenue and 59th Street, the other one block west at Seventh Avenue. The shorter leg at Sixth Avenue was once an open cut, but today the only sign of the tunnel's presence in the Park is a large ventilator grid inside the perimeter wall at Fifth Avenue and 63rd Street.

The second system is part of the largest tunnel currently under construction in the western hemisphere: a conduit, known as the Third Water Tunnel, being built for the Bureau of Water Supply of the city's Department of Environmental Protection. It starts from the Hillview Reservoir in Yonkers, proceeds south to Manhattan, and ends across the East River in Long Island City. Work has been going on for some twenty years. The huge tunnel will be from twenty to twenty-four feet in diameter. It enters the Park below 96th Street and Central Park West and crosses in a southeasterly direction to exit below the Metropolitan Museum of Art, where it is some seven hundred feet down in the schist.

About two hundred feet below the museum, a huge chamber has been carved. It has a base of forty-four by sixty-nine feet, with an arched ceiling reaching a height of sixty feet. Here will be installed the many valves, controls, and other machinery needed to govern the passage of water in the tunnel. The water rises under pressure from the upstate reservoirs almost five hundred feet to the chamber where the various mechanisms control and regulate the flow of the water in the tunnel. The engineers have found two pegmatite dikes in the path of the tunnel under the Park. Besides feldspar and quartz, the dikes contain biotite, a black or dark green mica, a silicate of aluminum; and iron, magnesium, and potassium in this deepest penetration below the Park.

ᴗ The buildings surrounding Central Park are a highly diverse lot. Over two hundred and sixty structures line the one hundred and eight blocks fronting the triangular-topped stone wall. Some are towering, others merely modest buildings of several stories. The ensemble includes the Academy of Medicine, apartment houses galore, a bank, churches, co-ops, condominiums, a consulate general, a convent, hospitals, hotels, museums, the New York Historical Society, a planetarium, private clubs, homes and schools, synagogues, and a United Nations mission.

The buildings gain in value substantially from their location, a fact realized early both by Olmsted and public officials. In the report of a committee appointed by the State Senate over a hundred and twenty years ago to investigate the public investment in Central Park, this passage is found: "Although the committee does not think it proper for municipal corporations to purchase lands on speculation, yet it cannot be concealed—that the Central Park has been, and will be, in a purely pecuniary point of view, one of the wisest and most fortunate measures ever undertaken by the City of New York. It has already more than quadrupled the value of a large extent of property in its vicinity."

Later, a report of the Board of Commissioners of Central Park, using facts supplied by Olmsted, noted the cost and benefit to the city of the Park through the end of 1873. A total of $13,902,515.60 had been spent, of which $5,028,844.10 was for land and $8,873,671.50 for improvement. However, the increase in taxes on the adjoining property exceeded the annual interest on the cost of the Park land and its development by over $4 million a year. The conclusion was that after fifteen years the city had experienced in the Park a financial windfall beyond all expectations.

However, alive as Olmsted was to the monetary benefits bestowed by his creation on the city, he was equally aware of other nonpecuniary benefits that the adjacent buildings afforded their occupants: ". . . the advantage in value [for the buildings] will be found to be largely dependent on the advantages of having a residence near a place where, without reference to the sylvan attractions found in a large park, driving, riding and walking can be conveniently pursued in association with pleasant people, and without the liability of encountering the unpleasant sights and sounds which must generally accompany those who seek rest, recreation or pleasure in the common streets."

To those whose quarters face the Park, glorious views of lakes, trees, and lawns unfold around the clock. Nor does night erase the splendid scene. The relative quiet then only adds to the charm which, although differing with the seasons, is always present, always restful. Water flowing or frozen, trees verdant or bare, grounds lush or snow-topped are all illumined soothingly in the dark hours by moon, stars, or city lights, those twinkling, ever present lamps in the night-drowned urban cosmos.

As for the monetary aspects of the buildings today, their assessment is naturally a fraction of Manhattan's figure presently approaching $40 billion. This represents all the taxable properties that crowd the island's built-up twelve miles of length. Yet the Real Estate Board of New York estimates that the combined assessments of the Park's perimeter buildings equal $600 million with a real value of $2.5 billion. These figures, of course, enable lucky owners of the property to charge high rents and, at time of sale, to market their holdings for large amounts.

In all of this, the city gains financially, just as it did in times past. Through the increased taxes, both on sales and on annual assessments, it reaps a welcome harvest. To put it all in a nutshell, a while back real estate developer William Zeckendorf said that the presence of Central Park adds more than $1 billion to the value of its surrounding real estate. Olmsted knew this intuitively more than a century ago.

$\mathcal{I}$N *1985* the Conservancy chairman, William Beinecke, stepped down.

His successor, James H. Evans, like Beinecke a Manhattan resident, had been a member of the Conservancy board since 1984 and a person actively interested in parks and nature. He was founding chairman of the National Recreation and Parks Association of Alexandria, Virginia, where he serves as a life trustee, and a member of the governing board of the New York Botanical Gardens. He said his intention was to continue the Conservancy agenda laid down by Beinecke.

Seven months after Beinecke left, there was another change in the Conservancy's upper echelon. In February 1986, Pamela Tice, the executive director, departed, taking her title with her. She became vice-president of strategic planning and development at the Cathedral of St. John the Divine.

The vacancy was filled by Myra Biblowit, who was named vice-president for development. As the post required, she was a very capable fund-raiser. Previously she had done this for the Mt. Sinai Medical Center, the imposing three-block facility on upper Fifth Avenue. At the time of her appointment, Mrs. Biblowit was thirty-seven years old, a graduate of Tufts College. She headed a staff of about twelve quartered at 10 Columbus Circle. (In 1989 she became the Conservancy's executive vice-president.)

At the time of Evans's accession, he worked with a forty-one–member board. Loyalty to the organization has been strong. Twenty-two of the first thirty-four board members were then serving, and in 1988 the number still remained close to twenty despite the passage of time and the professional attrition that goes with it.

For Evans and his Conservancy board, what now lies ahead?

For the parks commissioner and his staff?

For the administrator (who has now been named the

president of the Conservancy) and her associates, all of them, in seeing the job of rebuilding Central Park is finally brought to satisfactory completion?

When the project began in 1978, the plan for renewal called for a ten-year span and an outlay of $100 million. Now that estimate has climbed to more than $150 million with the projected finish coming around 1995. But in works of this size, estimates of time and cost often turn out to be understated. Thus, at this point, those figures are merely the best possible guesses.

However, in the roughly ten years that have passed, about 50 percent of the job has been done. By the end of fiscal year 1988, over $84 million had been expended. The city will have contributed more than $60 million, the Conservancy $21 million, and the Zoological Society more than $13 million.

The Conservancy tackles its job with ingenuity. Alert is often the word for its people, board members and staff. For example, a few years back Lewis Bernard, the Conservancy vice chairman and a managing director of Morgan Stanley, got word of a new Chase Bank credit card. Each time the holder used it, a small sum went to some charity or other. Bright light over Bernard's head. Thomas Labrecque, the Chase Bank president, is a Conservancy trustee. Bernard handed the idea over to Biblowit's staff to see if Chase would do something similar for the Conservancy. Late in 1987, the Chase Premier Visa card was issued. Each purchase on it provides the Conservancy with twenty-five cents, furnished by Chase.

The Conservancy is alert to new opportunities, too. A while back it obtained the services of an educator to develop and administer new programs for inner-city youth, particularly the minorities residing around the northern end of the Park. The educator provides classes on environmental studies, the range of the arts, and ways to utilize the Park's spaces healthfully. Classes are held both in the Belvedere and in open reaches of the Park.

A reconstruction that did not involve the Conservancy but that it applauded was the renewal of the long unserviceable Wollman Rink. This ill-starred venture took six years to fix. Since the rink's inception a generation ago, it had been the happy haunt of thousands of skaters, young and old. Then, for six years, no ice. To its users, it was a major catastrophe. To the administrator and the Parks Department, it was a heavy cross.

In 1951, in the era of the sports-minded Robert Moses, the site of the rink had been cannibalized from the five-acre Pond, reducing that water body to three acres. The rink itself was a large, flooded concrete apron below which a lacework of pipes carried a brine solution. Under the influence of electricity, this acted as a refrigerant, freezing the water on the apron above to a mirrorlike surface. Skaters could rest, warm themselves, and eat in a restaurant beside the rink. In the 1970s in the warm weather, concerts were given at which huge crowds sat on the apron.

In 1980, after nearly thirty years of service, the refrigerating system broke down, perhaps, some say, because of the weight of the summer crowds. In any event, the city allocated a little more than $9 million for a new system to be ready in two years. Only this time, freon, described as the preferred state-of-the-art refrigerant, was to be used. However, what the rink got was not a state-of-the-art refrigerant but state-of-the-art gremlins. Under the newly laid concrete, the twenty-nine miles of pipe that had been filled with freon sprang hundreds of tiny leaks, credited by some to stray electric currents in the environment, by others as galvanic action from different kinds of soil impinging on the pipes, and by still others as corrosion coming from air pockets in the concrete. Nobody, with the possible exception of the gremlins, could be absolutely sure.

Investigation after investigation was conducted, and the years rolled by. Although several million dollars above the projected $9 million were spent, the root of the problem remained a mystery. In the summer of 1985 an eminent firm of consulting engineers was hired to sift all possibilities and come up with the cause. Early in 1986 the firm reported its failure to do so. Saddened Park Department officials said that at least two skating seasons would be missed.

Comes the summer of 1986 and enter Donald Trump, who waved his hand, scoffed at the problems, and said he could have the rink ready in four months—in time for the 1986–87 skating season. Trump, whose far-reaching empire of construction projects gives him enormous power with contractors, was able to make this surprising proposal because he, unlike the city, is not hampered by the Wicks Law. This ordinance demands that city contracts be divided among various construction specialties—electricians, plumbers, steel riggers, and so on—a complex bidding process that can eat up months. Trump merely has to say to a builder, "Build!" In fifteen seconds the builder starts.

After a flurry of conferences, Mayor Koch announced that Mr. Trump had agreed for a price of $2,975,000 to have the snake-bitten Wollman Rink ready for action by December 15th. "If it costs less, we pay less," said a relieved Koch. "If it costs more, he pays more."

This time the old-fashioned brine solution was used. Trump delivered. And he more than kept his promise. The rink opened the middle of November and has been fine ever since. The renovation totaled around $15 million, Mr. Trump coming in $750,000 below his projected figure.

↶ Returning to what in the way of renewal still faces the administrator, the Parks Department, and the Conservancy, the answer is: heavy sledding. Scores of projects large and small lie ahead over the years. But in the light of accomplishments since 1978, the task is not undoable.

To pick at random those planned for the immediate future, there is the sector around the Harlem Meer, the eleven-acre lagoon in the Park's northeast corner. Its boathouse, close to the water, stood just inside the Park's terminal wall along 110th Street—or Central Park North as the new name is. The structure was a vandalized, burnt-out wreck when the original Park rehabilitation started. Erected in 1966, it once offered food and rental rowboats to residents of nearby Harlem and Spanish Harlem. Now it has been razed. Replacing it will be a concessionaire-run restaurant providing three meals daily at moderate prices, cafeteria or tablecloth style, as well as a catering service.

Eventually the Conservancy, aided by grants totaling more than $2 million from the Cissy Patterson Trust, the Dana Foundation, and the Lila Acheson Wallace Reader's Digest Fund, will furnish the area with facilities for rowboat hire, a Ranger station, a visitor center with rooms for meetings and classes and space for exhibits, as well as a plaza beside the Meer.

As for the Meer itself, it was drained. Dredging will be done. Like all Park water bodies, the Meer had accumulated sediment over the years, estimated at two and a half feet, or around forty thousand cubic yards. After removal, part of it will form an island of about an eighth of an acre some seven feet above water level, replacing one destroyed some years ago by the Lasker Rink. Trees and shrubs will grow on it, and boaters will be prevented from landing by an underwater fence. When refilled, the Meer's depth in places will exceed eight feet. The level will be controlled by new valves and the circulation improved. This will benefit the new population of fish, comprising the same species present before. Earlier these were netted and transferred to other Park havens—largemouth bass, bluegill and pumpkinseed sunfish, carp, and banded killifish. The bass in particular had been special targets of Meer anglers in the past.

The Harlem Meer's vandalized boathouse, a burned-out wreck in pre-renewal days. It will be replaced by a restaurant. A hopeful angler stands in the foreground, for fish still inhabit the water. (Sara Cedar Miller, Central Park Conservancy.)

Presumably they will be again when a fish-stocking program is reinstituted.

Once even a small part of the renewal has been achieved, the whole area is expected to perk up. Fishing and ice skating will be attractive. And in the adjoining Lasker Pool and Rink—three acres confiscated from the Meer in 1966—swimming will be possible, always a great draw.

Before renewal, traffic in this area of the Park was desultory, mostly people walking dogs or sitting on benches. A recently refurbished playground at Fifth Avenue and Central Park North enjoyed a fair trade, but one at 108th Street and Fifth Avenue had scarcely any users.

A further improvement here will be the dredging of the Pool, the westernmost unit of the northern water system. Some unwanted trees will be removed, colorful sumac specimens put back again, the north slope cleared to become meadow once more, and various vegetation introduced to the borders and water to encourage wildlife presence.

The Great Lawn under Belvedere Castle near the center of the Park is also marked for early action. It is the spot where the old Croton Reservoir, that ugly rectangular box of stone, once stood. It was woven of necessity into the Park design because it supplied water to the city residents of that day. When the need for its services ended because of improved facilities, it was drained and given to the Parks Department in 1929. During the Depression, hundreds of homeless men lived in the empty pit in jerry-built shacks of waste lumber and flattened tin cans. Moses, in 1934, turned the hole into the Great Lawn, giving the surrounding terrain part of the look it now has—the little Turtle Pond, once the Belvedere Lake, a relic of the reservoir, to the south; the large oval lawn in the center, two children's playgrounds to the north; and a bevy of landscaped walks over all.

Today, added to these, there are half a dozen ballfields with backstops on the Lawn. In addition, the Lawn also sees thousands and hundreds of thousands of people gathered on it during summer evenings for numerous kinds of special events, including concerts and rallies. The Delacorte Theatre, erected in 1960, overlooks it to the southwest, and to the west are the Shakespeare Garden and the Swedish cottage. In 1971, in the area's northwest corner, the Ross Pinetum went in, a gift of Arthur Ross, a Conservancy trustee and a frequent Park benefactor. It contains a collection of over seven hundred pines of fifteen worldwide species, some of them rare, such as the Himalayan pine; the mungo pine, native to mountainous parts of Europe; and the Swiss stone pine.

Plans call for the Great Lawn area to be enlarged and shifted two hundred feet north of its current setting; Turtle Pond to be increased in size and in irregularity; the two children's playgrounds, now little used, to be returned to turf; and east and west walkways to be placed in better positions to handle the pedestrian traffic.

Another ongoing improvement is the combined repair of the Grand Army Plaza and the Pulitzer Fountain area, a joint and highly noticeable unit at the southeast corner of the Park. In 1989 installation began on new plumbing and electrical systems for the fountain, which is topped by a marble statue of Pomona, the Roman goddess of fruit and gardens. She and the neighboring statue of General Sherman on his horse across 59th Street are to be cleaned and conserved while the spaces on both sides will

A summer-evening crowd on the Great Lawn, complete with radios,
blankets, and picnic baskets, awaits one of the popular events that are
features of the Park. (Brian Rose.)

get new pavement, lighting fixtures and benches, landscaping, and pedestrian safety zones. The Park's entrance here is its major one, architecturally speaking. The result will be an improvement on the most impressive
of the Park's four corner pieces.

The Obelisk, standing on a knoll back of the Metropolitan Museum, is
in a somewhat dilapidated condition. Nevertheless, at present there are
no plans for preservation such as have been tried in the past. The Obelisk,
a seventy-one–foot shaft of pinkish African granite, weighing two hundred
and twenty-four tons, was originally set up on its square, fifty-ton pedestal
in Heliopolis in ancient Egypt in the reign of Pharaoh Thothmes III thirty-
five hundred years ago. The Obelisk is not only the oldest manmade
object in the Park but the city's largest outdoor antiquity. Thothmes has
been called Egypt's greatest pharaoh, and the monument bears hiero-
glyphic inscriptions of his accomplishments. A couple of centuries later,
another eminent pharaoh, Ramses II (whose daughter found Moses in the
bulrushes), added some inscriptions of his own, as was common in those
days.

For a thousand years, the Obelisk stood in Heliopolis until Cambyses, a
Persian invader, toppled it. In 12 B.C. the Romans moved it some hundred
miles northward to Alexandria, where it remained on the shore of the

Mediterranean Sea for nearly two thousand years until 1879, when Ismail, the khedive of Egypt, gave it to the United States. Shortly thereafter, its long journey, lasting over a year, began.

Getting it here was no cinch. For one thing, the pedestal and much of the base had long since sunk into the ground; almost two thousand cubic yards of earth had to be removed before the pieces could be embarked. The trip over water terminated at 96th Street and the Hudson River. But that was far from the end of the voyage. Passage through the 86th Street transverse road took nineteen days. Much of the way the shaft rode on cannonballs. When the Obelisk finally stood on the knoll in Central Park, William K. Vanderbilt had paid over $100,000 to put it there.

Some weeks before this, the slightly more maneuverable pedestal was laid with doings that seem among the strangest of the whole episode. Beneath the pedestal, a veritable treasure trove of articles was buried, extraordinary in their number and diversity. A partial, but only partial, list given in a 1938 issue of *The New Yorker* magazine, follows: a set of medals engraved with the features of all the presidents up to 1880, the Congressional Directory and the official Army Register for that year, a copy of the Declaration of Independence, a summary of the Ninth Census, a replica of the propellor of Admiral Farragut's flagship, medals denoting victories in the War of 1812, a new type of anchor, a Webster's Unabridged Dictionary, and the writings of William Shakespeare. All were put down in sealed lead receptacles. Mysteriously an effort to include a complete telephone switchboard failed, perhaps because of the problem of providing a lead container big enough to hold it. But many books of the New Testament in ancient and modern languages were interred as well as a gold plate whose engraving gave the history of the Obelisk's travels.

Twenty thousand people attended the official dedication ceremonies in February 1881. The Obelisk was then called Cleopatra's Needle, a name it had brought from overseas. The phrase was simply nineteenth-century hyperbole. There is no indication Cleopatra ever set eyes on the Obelisk.

What concerned the city fathers immediately, however, was the ratty look of the sides. Bits of granite had fallen away, blurring the hierogylphs. Attempts were made to preserve the stone, one of which, in 1885, used hot paraffin. This caused eight hundred pounds of stone to fall off, an Egyptologist at the Metropolitan Museum said recently. A benefit occurred, though. The weatherproofers renamed Cleopatra's Needle the Obelisk.

Actually the spalling that had worried the city fathers had started long,

long ago, when the column, having been moved from the hot, dry interior of Egypt stood for centuries by the sea. There the moist salt winds had done their work, penetrating and loosening the surface stone. Alexandrians in the khedive's time broke off chips to sell to tourists.

Today the museum people who keep an eye on the Obelisk say the deterioration has apparently stabilized. And that, for the moment at least, gives the administrator one less worry.

For the intermediate future, the Park's southwest corner, the sector nearest Columbus Circle, has been earmarked for repair. Its reworking is due to start in 1990. Many of its components need attention, particularly the six arches, more of which are contained here than in any other part of the Park: Dalehead, Dipway, Driprock, Greyshot, Playmates, and Pinebank arches, all designed by Calvert Vaux, each different in style and materials and each charming, qualities generally inherent to this imaginative architect's work. With time, the beauty of the archways has been badly marred by vegetative invasion, siltation around the bases, and lack of maintenance on the structures themselves. Marianne Cramer, the Park's chief of design and planning, views the southwest corner as the area in the Park most seriously warped from a design point of view.

Repointing, part of major renewal work at one of the Park's
thirty-six arches and bridges, no two of which are alike.
(Sara Cedar Miller, Central Park Conservancy.)

Another task for the intermediate future is improvement of the Park's perimeter—its six-miles of wall and the objects just inside and out of it.

The stone wall, a major part of Olmsted's original barrier plan, is less than four feet high and easy on the eye yet an undeniable visual marker. Its foundation and core are schist, some of it rubble from blastings during the Park's construction. The base tier, just above the sidewalk in greywacke, a fine-grained conglomerate, and the facing of the upper part and the entire triangular capstone is, in almost all places, yellow freestone, a sandstone from the Canadian province of New Brunswick, called freestone because of its resistance to shattering when cut. The quarry that supplied it is known, is still working, and can furnish replacement pieces if desired. However, in at least one section of the wall, that from 90th to 96th Street along Fifth Avenue, the upper part is, for some unknown reason, composed of Inwood marble, a soft limestone that, without affecting its solidarity as yet, leaks during very wet weather. Capillary action over the years has drawn up water through the wall to the facing, which in places has dissolved and emits dribbles.

The wall as a whole varies in condition from good to unsatisfactory. Repair crews move immediately to check crisis cases when they are found. Work on other elements in the perimeter is generally undertaken in conjunction with correction of nearby problems. But sidewalk elms along Fifth Avenue are monitored constantly for Dutch elm disease. Eventually, among other improvements of the perimeter, the whole wall is to be repointed, and the gingkos along Central Park North and South replaced by trees that are also resistant to street conditions in the city but will afford more shade, a highly desirable consequence both to people and to the carriage horses along Central Park South.

In the future, planned for 1993, is the decision about the role of the present Reservoir in the Park. It is by far the Park's largest feature, and its future status is probably the renewal's largest decision. The Reservoir is one hundred and six acres, about one-eighth of the Park's surface. By the early 1990s, when it is estimated that the Third Water Tunnel will be finished, the Reservoir's function as a water-holding body will be over, and the Bureau of Water Supply in the city's Department of Environmental Protection will give it to the Parks Department.

Then what?

It's a big question.

Thirty years ago Moses said he'd like to turn the Reservoir into a gigantic swimming pool. Since then, at least two other ideas have been considered. The first is simply to fill in the Reservoir for additional parkland. The second, far from simple, would have part filled in and part left wet. On the disparate sections there could be ballfields, a concert lawn, a jogging course, an arboretum, and, on the watery part, a marina and a swimming beach.

At the moment, the Parks people lean, sort of, in Moses's direction. This is what the Master Plan says on that score:

The Reservoir is the Park's largest feature, its 106 acres comprising one-eighth of the site. Its future disposition is one of the knottiest problems facing renewal. (Parks Department Archives.)

Although the old Reservoir was filled in to form the Great Lawn, the present plan envisions keeping the Reservoir as a body of water and redesigning it as an attractive, natural-looking lake. The shoreline would be made more irregular and soft-edged than it is now and parts of the artificial berm that rims it at present could be lowered to create a more naturalistic littoral.

The 106 acres of water opened up to public use will offer an abundance of recreational opportunities. There could be swimming from a beach or pier, sailing or wind-surfing.

But this, like all else in the Master Plan, is not a policy set in stone.

Meanwhile, James Evans, at the head of the Conservancy, intends to tackle the problems of the immediate future along the same lines as proved so successful for his predecessor—expanding the support of business, foundations, and individuals through the activities of his fund-raising committees. And he is, of course, heartened by the existence of the Greensward Trust and the Campaign for Central Park, designed to aid in future maintenance.

*O*DD THINGS happen in Central Park.

A couple who yearned for a garden, using necessary stealth, planted a rosebush in a remote spot. After the thorny bush was smuggled in, the woman did the digging. Her husband, pretending that they were picnickers, presided over a fake spread, keeping a sharp lookout for Rangers. Once the bush was firmly embedded, the couple furtively and regularly tended it. When the press broke the news, the administrator was not surprised. "Hardly the first time," Betsy Rogers said. "Only the other day there was this weird little pear tree standing among our Fifth Avenue elm population."

Once at the zoo, a sea lion surfaced with a revolver in its teeth.

A nighttime pedestrian reports, "By an inlet on the Lake, there was this young man with a flute, playing a gentle, wispy tune. A lot of ducks on the water were listening. It was a cold, classical sight, a little hard to believe, a little hard to forget."

A nursemaid and her charge were seen sliding down a grassy knoll on a large silver platter. In another "slide" story, we have two small dogs whose owner used to take them at night to a playground. There they rocketed down the slide, enjoying it immensely. During the day, when the dogs passed the slide, they pretended they'd never seen the thing.

In the winter of 1988, to the marvel of many, an enormous frozen sculpture of the Japanese artist, Toshihiro Takenaka, rose from the bank of the Pond hard by the Plaza Hotel. Hollow columns of ice twenty feet high were made even more startling at night by a rainbow glow from multicolored lights within.

A casqued hornbill, a large bird, was reported as an escapee from the zoo. "It went by my apartment window like an express train," one witness said. After twenty-seven hours and forty minutes of freedom, the bird was captured. While at liberty, it led a small army of keepers, photographers, policemen, and personnel from the American Society for the Prevention of Cruelty to Animals down the streets and over the roofs of the East Side. One of the places it alighted was the penthouse terrace of Brooke Astor, who later visited the hornbill at the Park. Its quarters seemed to her a little cramped. As a director of the Bronx Zoo, she was able to have it moved into more spacious digs.

A master dog look-alike contest was held last year. Whether credible or not, there was a winner. In the view of the judges, the long, soft ears, soulful eyes, and other features of Mona, an adolescent cocker spaniel, most nearly reflected those of her unabashed owner, Ted Kelton.

A cab driver was puzzled when he picked up a fare at the Plaza Hotel and was told to drive through the Park at twenty-two miles per hour, no more, no less. As an additional mystery, the passenger held something out the window. Seeing the driver's puzzlement, he explained, "I'm breaking in a meerschaum pipe. Long ago I discovered that air going through the bowl is like smoking. Motoring is great for this. But the car must go at an even twenty-two miles per hour. More, the load burns too fast; less, the pipe can go out."

Finally, when people seek powerful emanations, they know where to go. Central Park, naturally. On August 16, 1987, some two thousand persons gathered before dawn inside the wall at West 83rd Street, bearing candles and bells to create worldwide concord and amity. For hours, well into the morning, they rang their bells and blew on conch shells to achieve universal harmony. At the end, they were well satisfied. "We were guided to this place," one of the leaders said. "It is a spot of very high energy." The locale was Summit Rock, the point in the Park nearest heaven.

While all such variegated, sometimes surprising, events are going on, the rehabilitation of the Park (over two hundred capital projects) moves steadily onward. Witness a few items from the official Central Park Daybook:

Iron railing restoration is beginning at Playmates Arch. Brick patching and soil work will begin in March, weather permitting. . . . Top soils will be spread by Trentini Paving at W. 85th and W. 93rd drainage and path paving projects. . . . The walls and roof of the Ballplayers House at Heckscher will be built by Herbert Construction after building permit delays. . . . Top course asphalt will be installed by Emerald Construction to complete the paving and drainage of work north of Heckscher playground. . . . Horticultural crews will then begin landscape work. . . . Concrete work by Herbert Construction is proceeding under Pulitzer Fountain. . . . New bronze caps will be fabricated and installed by C.D.M. Associates in late March for the end pillars around the base of the Obelisk.

When the end of renewal does come, whenever that may be, a number of pending policy matters will have been decided by Park officials and interested others. This is standard democratic procedure. And it is called for because some of the decisions will be vital to what the Park offers.

One is the form the Reservoir will take when, in a few years, it ceases to be needed for city water. Will it be a swimming pool, a sailboat pond, or both? Will there be a pier with fishing from it? Will the Delacorte Theatre be relocated to stand on a peninsula with picnic lawns around it bordering the water?

What else should be done to make the Park enjoyable?

The last survey of visitor use showed that 57 percent of entrants came to relax—to stroll, sit, birdwatch, picnic, sunbathe, and savor other forms of passive recreation. It was an overwhelming majority of those who come to the Park. The next largest group amounted to 9 percent, those who play sports. In light of the disparity, should some, or all, sports be transferred, over time, elsewhere, as accommodations for them are constructed?

While opera and Philharmonic performances will doubtless continue, should large mass events like political rallies and rock concerts be excluded?

These are but a few of the questions to be answered.

Yet no matter what happens, the Park will be alluring as always. Ramble paths will be as inviting as ever, playgrounds will bustle with youth, joggers will be on the loose, and resurfaced bridle paths springy to the hoof.

I went for a walk in the Park the other day in the cool, new spring. I entered in the early morning at the northwest corner by the Pool. It was Sunday. I was alone. The mists had not risen completely. The trees and lawn dripped with quiet and serenity. All around me earth was hushed. Under its spell I altered some lines of Swinburne—Here where the world is quiet, here where all trouble seems, long past, dispelled forever, on soothing wings of dreams. Repose . . . it touched me on all sides in this momentary cloudland.

I wandered east toward the Meer. In a marshy spot by the Loch, a skunk cabbage appeared. As the sun rose, the mists lifted. A breeze sprang up. By the Meer, the vandalized boathouse was being razed for the new. Some people began walking their dogs around the water. On a hill toward the south, I saw the Green memorial bench. Nobody was sitting on it.

At 105th Street the Conservatory Garden was touched with beauty. A few people were already threading the walks of the three sections. Rose bushes were leafing out. White tulips, magnolias, grape hyacinths were in abundance. So were Dutchman's breeches and wake robins. The walkways began to fill up. Some people were taking pictures. A hugging match was going on between two sisters, aged two and four. Songbirds trilled from the swaying, flowering trees. The breeze had become a wind. It rose and fell during the day periodically. I tarried long, minute after minute, drinking in the scene—the loveliness.

The tennis courts had players. But in the nippy air few wore shorts. Whitecaps ruffled the reservoir. Over it, seagulls slid down the wind. Runners were thick on the track around it, going clockwise and counterclockwise. Clippety-clop, clippety-clop went the shoes. A white-haired woman traveled at her own pace. "What a day to run!" she said as she passed me.

But runners were all over the Park. Mostly these were joggers along the drives, now closed to automobiles. The most notable I saw was right below the reservoir. A stalwart, thirtyish fellow, he occasionally broke his jog with a prance, carrying on a small tray a bottle of Martini & Rossi which never wavered. Below the reservoir I also saw a pair of horsemen on the bridle path making their way north at a trot.

The straight, stone shaft of the Obelisk, metal capped, with the mysterious glyphs, rose high behind the museum, its four corners underpinned by large metal crabs resplendent in their coats of green verdigris. A couple was reading the metal tablet at the base, giving a translation of the glyphs, boastful tales of ancient kings. Others sat on benches around the enclosure, soaking up the sun. People were there. People were everywhere.

Under the cloudless blue sky the upper terrace of Belvedere provided a sweeping panorama of the Park in all directions, that to the north being especially grand with the town's high towers there more than a mile away. In the Ramble, birders were on the prowl, binoculars held to their eyes, their necks craned upward. I asked a young couple what they'd seen. "Green heron, brown thrasher, winter wren," they replied. Rowboats were on the Lake. So were people around the Bethesda Fountain, the

The restored Belvedere Castle. From its loggia and several terraces,
one can take in sweeping vistas of the Park and city skyline.
(Brian Rose.)

architectural highpoint of the Park. Nobody stayed very long. But ingress and outgo seemed to balance. Years ago Calvert Vaux had planned elaborate sculpted figures of Day, Night, Science, Art, and so on to stand upon the pedestals of the stone screen around the Esplanade, the tiled terrace that sweeps out on all sides from the fountain. Marble finishings, wall fountains, and trompe l'oeil paintings for the walls also were included to give the look of a luxurious reception hall here where I was standing at the heart of the Park. I tried to imagine what that effect would be. I couldn't.

The premier boat on Conservatory Water, the model boat pond, was a long metal craft with sails over a yard high. It must have been remotely controlled. It tacked effortlessly this way and that without regard to the wind. But the most arresting sight was a flower-faced Asian boy of about eight, prostrate on the rim, looking intently into the water. In his hand he held a short stick with a string attached. At the end was a white strip of bacon fat. He maneuvered this near the underwater wall, trying to attract crayfish living in the cracks. When one grasped the bait, he pulled it out of the water. In the plastic pail behind him were two dark three-inch-long crayfish.

At Strawberry Fields, a handsome musician was playing a selection of John Lennon's songs, his large hat at his feet for contributions. More music was erupting at the end of the Mall. A melodious battle seemed in progress there. Two youths with amplified electric guitars were belting out 1960s-style stuff near the statue of Christopher Columbus. Sixty yards off to the east a four-piece brass band was tunefully into rhythmic jazz.

The vast, imposing Chinese elm, regal back of its iron fence, near the Fifth Avenue entrance at 72nd Street, was following its usual vernal custom. Its cloud of buds, although foretelling future life, had still, this far into the Manhattan spring, not even begun to swell, its inconspicuous autumnal blossoms only a promise deep in its metabolism. In the zoo I found the snowy owl looking glum. But dangerous. An Arctic fox was trying to hide. On the island of the macaque monkeys a great commotion was under way. Two, hurling epithets, were in hot pursuit of a third. The sea lions were showing off for the crowds. They slipped their cover of water in curveting dive after curveting dive. One of a pair of small boys watching them said to the other, "My mother says next time I run away I can stay."

Wollman, the iceless rink, held roller skaters. Child riders mostly occupied the Carousel's whirling mounts. But two cooperative fathers were on the saddles holding toddlers, bright-eyed with delight. A blue squad car moseyed down the drive, the joggers and cyclists giving way.

Families—Caucasian, black, Asiatic—wheeling baby carriages were much in evidence. Candice Bergen in white baseball cap and worn slacks went by on the drive pushing a pram. Another sort of vehicle for airing was an awning-topped pair of joined bicycles with Mother and Father atop each and baby in a forward basket. Many, many familes here in the south end.

The Sheep Meadow was dotted with users, some hurling frisbees. An agitated youth was having a hard time with his kite against the wind. Two young women evidently blessed with circulation of a remarkable kind lay on a mat in bathing suits. In the distance stood clumps of bushes crowned with purple flowers. An artist perched nearby on a large rock seemed to be sketching them. Skateboarders tootled by. Ballgames were in progress back of Heckscher playground. A girl was the swift-throwing pitcher on one team in the field. The playground meanwhile was bustling with youngsters.

Inside Scholars Gate daffodils, narcissus, and flowering magnolias lit the scene. Outside, Pomona was off her pedestal, being cleaned. A lone mallard drake cruised the Pond. To the west, a shallow cove of the Pond, under the fenced-in Bird Sanctuary, held four huge goldfish, suspended amid a dead reed bed like large red shoes. A dog walker ahead led a bouncy cocker spaniel. In the Bird Sanctuary a feral cat climbed the hill, minding its business.

I left the Park by the Artist's Gate at Sixth Avenue and 59th Street beside the statue of Simon Bolívar, the great South American liberator. Behind me thousands upon thousands continued to enjoy the world's most famous pleasure ground.

INDEX

Page numbers in *italics* refer to illustrations.